Language roduction

DATE DUE			

Language
An Introduction

WINFRED P. LEHMANN
THE UNIVERSITY OF TEXAS, AUSTIN

Random House
New York

First Edition
987654321
Copyright © 1983 by Random House, Inc.
All rights reserved under International and Pan-American Copyright Conventions.
No part of this book may be reproduced in any form or by any means,
electronic or mechanical, including photocopying,
without permission in writing from the publisher.
All inquiries should be addressed to
Random House, Inc., 201 East 50th Street, New York, N.Y. 10022.
Published in the United States by Random House, Inc.,
and simultaneously in Canada by Random House of Canada Limited, Toronto.

Library of Congress Cataloging in Publication Data

Lehmann, Winfred Philipp, 1916–
    Language: an introduction.

    Bibliography: p.
    Includes index.
    1. Language and languages. 2. Linguistics.
I. Title.
P106.L343   1982   410   82-12291
ISBN 0-394-32746-2

Text and Cover Design: Lorraine Hohman

Manufactured in the United States of America

To Elenore Lehmann

Preface

Language: An Introduction is a successor to the two earlier editions of *Descriptive Linguistics*. Since they have appeared, there has been an increasing number of handbooks in the subfields of linguistics, as the suggested readings at the end of each chapter illustrate. Moreover, the interests of linguists have been extended, especially to the consideration of texts as well as sentences, to typological structures, and to applications. If one includes chapters on these interests, the treatment of subfields like phonetics must be reduced in scope. An introduction still has to present the current concerns of the field, leaving deeper attention to specialized handbooks.

In preparing this text I am grateful to comments from students and other readers. I also express my appreciation to members of the Linguistics Research Center who assisted me in making my way into computer techniques, especially Drs. W. Scott Bennett and Sandra Eveland. And I would like to thank Arthur S. Abramson, the University of Connecticut, and Haskins Laboratories, for the spectrograms on which figures 3.9, 3.10, and 3.11 are based. As I have indicated in the past, an author of a book may be the one who profits most from its production, especially through clarification of one's own ideas. I hope that users will also profit from the presentation here, and that some of them will be led to contribute to our increasing understanding of language.

Winfred P. Lehmann
September 1982

Contents

What Is Language?

1.1 Introduction

From the age of a year or so we have communicated with others largely through language. At a younger age we express our wants through gestures or inarticulate noises. As adults we may still communicate in such ways. But we find language simpler and far more accurate than hand waving or general cries. Language provides the means for us to take our place in society, to express our wants and convey information, to learn about the people and the world around us. Language, in short, enables us to live effectively, to develop our capabilities, and to satisfy our curiosity about our surroundings. This book examines language: what it is, how we use it, and some of its impact on us and our society.

1.2 Earlier Concerns for Language and Its Use

Language has long fascinated its speakers, not only because it is their richest means for communication but also as a system with a life apart from their own. Today an understanding of it is more important than ever. Our society is more complex than were those of the past. Every day we are faced with speakers who try to persuade us of their views, to sell us products we may not need, and to inform us about events, often in imperfect ways. Moreover, we wish to use language effectively in response, to convey our own opinions and wishes, to understand the past as well as the present. We succeed better both in communicating with others and in our own expression if we are informed about our primary means of communication.

Peoples in the past have examined languages in various ways. Five hundred years before the beginning of our era the ancient Indians were at work on their language, Sanskrit, producing a grammar that has not yet been surpassed. This grammar, ascribed to Panini, treats the language of the *vedas* and other texts sacred in Hindu religion. Like any language it was changing. In the eyes of the Brahman priests, the ancient hymns would not be effective if words were mispronounced or forms were modified. Panini, a successor to earlier grammarians, produced his grammar so that the Brahmans would continue to recite and interpret the *vedas* precisely as they had been transmitted from the past.

Panini's grammar consists of an intricate series of about four thousand rules. These describe the sounds. They indicate the correct forms, noting how meanings are modified when suffixes are added and so on. Over the two-and-a-half millennia since it was produced, the grammar has helped preserve Sanskrit with little change. Since it has become known in the West, scholars have examined the basis of its excellence.

One of its outstanding features is its treatment of language as a system made up of classes and subclasses. Sounds are presented in classes according to their articulation, such as the labials *p b m*. Words are identified for classes like nouns and verbs and analyzed into roots or stems and affixes. When the grammar came to be known in Europe during the nineteenth century, it greatly influenced Western views on language. As we will see, Western scholars also describe language as a system. Grammars and dictionaries are largely concerned with indicating the interrelationships between the elements of languages interpreted as systems.

Other peoples also had insights regarding language. The Hebrews recognized that it holds societies together, for it was to break the power of "one people with a single language" that the Lord "confused" the speech of the builders of the tower of Babel. Otherwise in his view they would have been able to do anything they "have a mind to." After the confusion of language, when they could "not understand what they say to one another," they scattered "all over the face of the earth" (*Genesis* 11).

However one regards the proposed reason for the "babble of language of all the world," the perception that a people needs one language to maintain itself is accurate. Western culture long maintained its unity through use of Latin as its learned language. The increasingly centralized countries of today are taking steps to generalize one language among all their speakers. Israel is a notable example; Hebrew was long used only as a learned language, but in the last century it was revived for spoken use and adopted as the national language. China also is taking massive action, having selected the language of Beijing as its "common language"—in Chinese *Putonghua*. The new countries of Africa and Asia are taking similar steps, for they recognize that wherever a unified society exists, its members must be able to communicate readily with one another. An army speaking a large array of languages would be little more than a rabble, as would a government. Like the ancient Hebrews, modern peoples recognize that members of any group communicate most effectively by using the same language.

Still other questions about language have aroused interest in the past, such as the cause of speech defects or aphasia. An account of about 1300 B.C. by the Hittite king Mursili tells us both about the assumed cause of his speech problem and about the attempted cure. Deciding that his speech defect resulted from fright at a thunderbolt, Mursili had his priests carry out an elaborate sacrifice. The clothing and furniture he used on the fateful day were to be burned, an ox was to be sacrificed, and so on. Unfortunately we do not know if his speech was restored, because the final part of the account was lost when the tablet on which the account came down to us was broken. But it is clear that Mursili related the use of speech to psychological factors. Today as well, one of the great interests concerning language has to do with its control by the brain, with the relationship between language and mind.

A similar aim attracted Franz Bopp (1791–1867), often said to be the founder of modern linguistics, to devote his life to the study of language. Bopp was motivated by an interest in "penetrating into the secret of the human spirit and learning something of its nature and laws." Such an interest has led many subsequent linguists to various kinds of study and speculation. Today many scholars are investigating where language is stored in the brain, whether in the right as well as the left hemisphere, and in what areas of each. Other scholars speculate whether our particular language directs our perceptions. Some propose, for example, that a language with verbs inflected for tense, like English, makes its speakers more aware of time; our use of the past tense to express a past action, as in "She won the game," presumably makes us more time-conscious than would a language that expressed the action as "Her winning of the game is complete." It is well known that societies of Western Europe and the United States whose languages have such verb systems direct their lives by minutes and seconds, in contrast with peoples whose language and behavior take different patterns. But so far we can only speculate that our language brings about our intense concern with time.

Answers to these and still other questions on the uses and effects of language in a given society would provide insights into many of our views and our way of life. Success is often ascribed to control of language. A politician may fail because of inadvertent use of an expression, having blurted out, for example, that he had been brainwashed. A theologian may be rejected because he examines fundamental problems in skeptical language, dealing with a central religious tenet in a book with the title "Does God exist?"

Moreover, we live more graciously if we understand the impact of language and then speak and write accordingly. Large groups of speakers may be turned off by language they find offensive, such as *mankind* rather than *humankind, housewife* rather than *homemaker, Negro* rather than *black, janitor* rather than *custodian*. Among other reforms the Chinese today are replacing words like *ku-li*, literally 'bitter strength' and possibly a source for English *coolie*, with more dignified words; for *ku-li* they have introduced *gong-ren* 'work-man, worker.' An under-standing of the effects of language use can smooth our interrelations with others and also equip us with greater tolerance for their language shortcomings.

1.3 Language as a Symbolic System and Its Description

To achieve such understanding we need to know something of what language is. That knowledge must be based on a conception of language as a symbolic system. It is easy enough to make such a statement, but we must also ask what is meant by the characterization. What are the units of the system? How do those units function as symbols? What do we need to observe and describe language adequately and also to explain its patterns?

When we examine language as a symbolic system, we may compare it with simpler communication systems, such as traffic signals. Or as noted in a later chapter we may study the means of communication among animals such as bees, birds, porpoises, and chimpanzees. All of these use symbols of some kind to convey meaning.

In traffic signals lights of different colors provide the symbols. Red means 'stop,' yellow 'caution,' green 'go.' Other characteristics are not crucial. Some systems have red above green; some have a larger lamp for red; the exact hue of red, yellow, or green may vary. Drivers take their meanings from none of these incidentals but rather from the three colors; those of longest wavelength are interpreted to mean 'stop,' whether they are exactly 700 millimicrons in length or whether the number of millimicrons varies slightly.

To distinguish between crucial and incidental features of symbolic systems, the linguist Kenneth Pike introduced the labels **emic** and **etic.** The colors of a stoplight system are emic essentials; the size of lamps and so on are etic incidentals. Each color is a meaningful symbol, like a word. The three colors make up a set.

The entities of language that convey meaning are words or segments smaller than words. For any formal unit with meaning we use a special term: **morpheme.** Based on the Greek word *morphē* 'form,' a morpheme is the smallest meaningful unit in a language. We determine the meanings partly by their reference to the outside world, partly by their relationships to other morphemes. The meanings of 'pen' are clear in each of the two following sentences without reference to the outside world:

> *1. The pen is in her purse.*
> *2. The child is in the pen.*

The use of morphemes rather than colors or other symbols leads to a far richer system of communication. The greater richness of human language results from the far greater number of entities available as symbols. But the structure of language is also more complex.

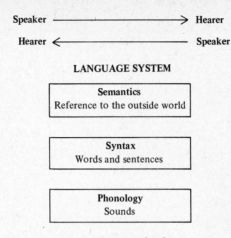

Figure 1.1 Language as a System for Communication

Unlike a system based on colors, words and morphemes are made up of elements that can be changed. To convey different meanings one does not need to substitute totally different signals, like the differing colors in traffic systems. Further words result if we change segments, such as the first, second, or third sound of *pen*, as in *den, pan, pet*. The following two sentences have quite different meanings:

> 3. *The child is in the pen.*
> 4. *The child is in the den.*

Such possibilities of substitution give language a far richer and more complex structure than those of other signaling systems.

To understand the complex structure of language we treat it in various components, as illustrated in Figure 1.1. One component deals with the sounds. It is called the **phonological** component; the term is based on *phōnē*, the Greek word for sound. Another deals with the forms that convey meaning as they are arranged in sentences. It is called the **syntactic** component, in accordance with the Greek word for arrangement and combining of entities, a word found also in 'tactics.' A third component is known as the **semantic,** after the Greek word *sēmē* for meaning; it deals with the relationship between the meaningful elements of language and the outside world.

1.4 The Phonological System

The phonological systems of languages vary in the number of elements they contain. The English system contains twenty-four consonants, Hawaiian about a third as many, Sanskrit about twice as many. Such elements are referred to as **phonemes,** units of sound. The term is important, in part because a phoneme may include sounds that differ appreciably, in part so that we do not confuse linguistic segments with letters of the alphabet. The /r/ phoneme illustrates how different sounds may be included in phonological units; many speakers of English use a somewhat different /r/ in *three* than in *red* or *deer*. And the letters we use for writing words often have little to do with their pronunciation; *wreck,* for example, is written with five letters but, like *red, rod,* and *bed,* contains only three phonemes /rek/.

The phonemes of a language are its building blocks. A phoneme does not have an inherent meaning; it simply distinguishes meaning. Neither the *b* of *bed* nor the *r* of *red* has a specific meaning, as is easily recognized by examining other words containing *b,* such as *bread, blue, bust.* The richer make-up of language as opposed to the traffic signals or the somewhat less complex system of numerals results from the availability of such building blocks to signal different meanings.

1.5 The Syntactic System

The number system may illustrate the additional complexity of language. Each number, like the colors of a traffic-light system, has a meaning. And like these the symbol cannot be substantially changed by modification of a part. We cannot substitute half a square for the top part of 0 to produce a different number as we can substitute *l* for *r* in *red.* Yet the complexity of the numeral system with only ten meaningful elements, 0 1 2 3 4 5 6 7 8 9, is so great that mathematicians have found intriguing problems in it for three millennia and more. The additional complexity of language may illustrate one of the bases for its rich structure, which enables us to use it for discussing any phenomenon in the universe.

The additional device providing richer possibilities of communication than a traffic system is meaningful arrangement of symbols. Numerals not only have meaning in themselves but also through their position in relation to other numerals. Besides the inherent values of numerals such as 1 and 5, numerals acquire additional values when standing in characteristic locations. When placed after 1, as in 15, 5 must be added to the meaning of 1 placed before it, which in this position means 'ten.' When placed before 1, as in 51, 5 is multiplied ten times to 'fifty,' and 1 is added to it. The arrangement of numerals, and of morphemes, with regard to each other is significant; in contrast, red has the same value in a traffic-light system whether it precedes or follows green, or yellow as well. To understand number as well as language systems, we must note their patterns of arrangement, that is, their syntax. The syntactic component is central in human language.

There is, however, a striking difference between the way the number system and language employ the symbols. The number system has no gaps, no unused combinations. If we accept 32, we must also accept 31, 33, 34, and so on. Similarly, acceptance of 368 requires acceptance of 468, 568, and the like.

In language, however, there are numerous gaps. We have *lit, let, lot* in English, but not *lat,[1] *lut. Changing the final element to d, we find lid, lad, led, but not *lod, *lud. These gaps permit great flexibility. If we need a new word for some new discovery—say, a new kind of bacteria produced by gene-splicing—with sufficient persuasion it could be known as lat. And language has numerous such possibilities. English permits pl- combinations as in plat, plot, but there is no *plit, *plet, *plut— and plat is not common, in spite of ten different plats in Webster's *Third International Dictionary*. Testing further possibilities like split, *splet, and so on, illustrates the numerous openings for further words.

Such exploration may suggest why the number system is restricted to the expression of quantity and the traffic-signal system to an even narrower function, while language has a design that permits expression of anything whatever. Our capabilities of expression in language become even greater when we examine possible arrangements of morphemes.

The gaps in possible elements may result from another requirement: avoidance of misunderstandings. English might well have an adequate lexicon simply by filling all the gaps among the monosyllables. As we have observed, among the ten l plus t or d combinations noted earlier, we could introduce four that are now unused. If we compare further consonants used after l and these five vowels, like the two initial consonants in this and thin, we find only one syllable: lath. Filling all such gaps could vastly increase the number of simple words in the language. But then we would invite difficulties in understanding, especially under noisy conditions. Accordingly, we maintain such gaps and use many polysyllables. Languages are redundant for a purpose. We use numbers in such restricted ways that we can afford to fill all possible gaps. Similar treatment of spoken language might well be troublesome.

The syntax of language, and of number systems, makes use of (1) meaningful elements or morphemes and (2) their arrangement. When we create an expression, such as light red, we select the desired morpheme from a possible set: light, dark, bright, etc., on the one hand, and red, yellow, green, etc., on the other. Besides their inherent meaning, such morphemes have additional meaning from their order in a sequence: red light has a different meaning from light red. One may think of language as a horizontal string with each position filled from a vertical store.

A large number of sentences may be made from a few elements, as you can see by using a few possibilities such as the following:

5.	the	car	drove	slowly
	this	boy	went	well
	that	girl	stopped	frequently
	their	driver	performed	yesterday

From these few words you can make many sentences.

Because of the large number of morphemes and words in any language and because of the many possibilities for arranging them, speakers can convey an infinite variety of meanings.

[1] An asterisk is used in linguistic works to indicate a non-attested form.

1.6 The Treatment of Meaning

For practical purposes meaning is described on the one hand in dictionaries, on the other hand in grammars. By classifying *light* as an adjective as well as a noun and by discussing differences of meaning in sequences, such as that between *red light* and *light red,* grammars deal with some of the meanings of language. The more specific meanings of words, such as *red, light, hypotenuse,* and so on, are given in dictionaries.

In their treatment of meaning, dictionaries describe relationships between linguistic elements and the world outside language. The simplest relationships to treat are those of words referring to concrete entities, for example, *dog, cat, horse.* But even these raise problems. We do indeed refer to a species of animal as a *dog;* but we also run into expressions where *dog* means 'person' as in: *You can't teach an old dog new tricks.* And if we hear someone refer to a car as a 'dog,' the relationship has shifted to an inanimate object. As these last two expressions suggest, *dog* has both a favorable and an unfavorable connotation. If someone "puts on the dog," the chances are great that that person is not "living a dog's life." The meaning of even a straightforward word like *dog* is accordingly by no means simple, nor is it simple to describe.

In order to deal with meaning, we distinguish between the referent of a word or morpheme and its reference. **Referent** is its literal meaning—of *dog,* the four-legged animal. **Reference** is the user's concept. For some, a dog is highly favored. For others, it is strongly disfavored. Such attitudes may be culturally determined; in the Middle East, the dog is despised, and when used for a person the term is highly pejorative. In Europe and North America the dog is generally valued highly, but the normal term for a female dog, *bitch,* has an unfavorable connotation, like the word for (male) dog in the Middle East.

Numerous examples could be given in support of the need to distinguish between referents and references, such as *snake.* The referent of *snake* is unambiguous, but the reference for a snake handler differs greatly from the reference for someone who has barely escaped being bitten by a poisonous snake or someone brought up in fear of snakes. By contrast, *cake* generally has a favorable connotation in its normal use, but for someone familiar with the story of Marie Antoinette, the reference involves unpleasantness if her statement is repeated: *"Let them eat cake."* The reference of words and morphemes thus varies from individual to individual as a result of their experiences in life, in reading, and in other associations.

In dealing with meaning we would like to determine how the meaning of an item is acquired and how it is stored and managed in the brain. We acquire the meanings of common words in accordance with their referent. A child comes to know what *dog* means by having the animal pointed out when the word is uttered. Such a learning process applies to the general vocabulary; it is supplemented by illustrations, today by pictures on TV. In the learning process children are often given contrasts with other animals, such as cats and horses. In this way a child learns hierarchies; dogs, cats, and horses belong to the class of *animals*.

Moreover, parallel words are taught in this way. *Dog* is associated with *puppy, cat* with *kitten, horse* with *pony*. Such associations furnish patterns of synonymy. A child learns that certain words are equivalent to others in most respects. **Synonyms** are words of the same or nearly the same meaning. In much the same way, a child learns contrasting words. *Left* is opposed to *right, no* to *yes, good* to *bad,* and so forth. **Antonyms,** or words opposite in meaning, are learned and associated with one another.

We apparently store words in such groups in some part of our brain. It has long been assumed on the basis of psychological experimentation that synonyms are stored in parallel, as are antonyms. If in playing word games we are asked to supply a list of words, they generally are from the same area of meaning; *aunt* calls up *uncle* rather than words like *pant* or *until*. When asked to furnish ten or so words, we respond with items like *lion, tiger, bear,* and *animal* rather than *lion, Easter, population,* and the like. The items we draw on accord with semantic relationships, whether that of synonyms, antonyms, or **hyponyms,** that is, inclusion under a term of more general meaning.

The determination of such relationships indicates that meanings are associated by sets; in semantic study these are known as **fields.** Investigators have dealt extensively with specific fields, such as kinship terms. These may be analyzed for distinctive features.

Our kinship system is based on three distinctive features. One is sex, as in the contrasting pairs *father/mother, brother/sister, son/daughter, uncle/aunt.* Another feature is generation; *brother, sister, cousin* are equivalent in generation to oneself or ego, which is used as base in kinship systems; *father, mother, uncle, aunt* designate the earlier generation, *son, daughter, nephew, niece* the subsequent generation. The third semantic feature is lineality; we distinguish between terms for members of our immediate family, *father, mother, brother, sister, son, daughter,* and other close relatives, *uncle, aunt, cousin, nephew, niece.*

A kinship system may have further distinctive features, such as comparative age; many systems, such as the Japanese, distinguish between 'elder brother/ sister' and 'younger brother/sister.' We also use this feature when we add qualifiers like *grand* as in *grandfather* and *granddaughter,* and *great* as in *greatgrandmother.* This dimension is not as central for us as the other three, scarcely more so than *kissing* or *first* and *second* with *cousin.* The three central dimensions characterize our essential set of kinship terms. The meanings of words in that set and in other semantic fields are determined in great part by their place in the system.

We treat other symbolic systems similarly, for example, the characters of the Chinese or the ancient Egyptian writing systems. The values of such symbols are determined by their roles and by their arrangements with regard to other elements of the system. In this way we use symbolic systems to convey meanings, whether a simple system like the stoplights, a more complex system like the ten numbers or the twenty-six letters of our alphabet, or the highly complex systems of natural languages.

1.7 Where Do the Symbols Come From?

Curiosity about the origin of symbols and of language itself is widespread. The Hebrews attributed some words to God, as *Genesis* 1 tells us: "and God called the light day, and the darkness He called night." Others were given by man, in Hebrew *Adam,* when God paraded the animals in front of him, as the second chapter of *Genesis* reports. Language in this way is associated with the earliest human beings, as it is by scholars today. Our information about these early humans is, however, slight. Accordingly, we can do little more than speculate about the origin of language. Such speculation is popular from time to time. When the possible evidence is reinterpreted with few results, however, it may be less popular. In the late nineteenth century the French Academy refused to hear further formal presentations about it. Subsequent archeological discoveries, as by the Leakeys, have revived the problem but also left it difficult because of lack of evidence on the early days of humans.

Although we can only speculate how language originated and reached its current rich state, it is also clear that we cannot introduce new elements at will. Rather than invent new terms we use available elements from our own or other languages. There was no difficulty in devising the labels *space age, space travel, spaced-out,* and the like. And *satellite* we simply extended to new contexts, using it first in parallel and then in preference to the word *sputnik* taken from Russian. Only an occasional invention, such as *Kodak,* is widely adopted.

A related question has to do with the basis of the meanings of individual words. The Greeks dealt with the question, as in the classic presentation by Plato in his dialogue *Cratylus.* Cratylus himself argued that there is some inherent relationship between words and things, pointing to words like *bluebird, blackbird, blackberry,* and so on. The opposing position was also presented, with use of words like *cranberry,* where *cran-,* unlike *blue, black,* and so on, seems to be isolated in the language, and accordingly the relationship is arbitrary. From Greek times to relatively modern times the position of Cratylus was widely held. It even led to strange procedures, such as explaining words by opposites; the Romans, for example, explained *lucus* 'woods, forest' by relating it to the word *lux, lucis* 'light' and stating that *lucus* received its name because it is not light. This explanation is still cited as a scholarly absurdity: *lucus a non lucendo.* As more and more languages came to be known, the position of Cratylus was impossible to maintain.

If indeed the make-up of words is somehow related to the things they designate, one would expect similar designations for things from language to language. Such similarities cannot even be found in onomatopoetic words. In English, dogs say *bow-bow* or *arf-arf;* in German, *wau-wau;* in French, *paf-paf;* in Japanese, *wan-wan.* Moreover, the supposed word may change in time; in Chaucer's day a cock was said to make the noise *cok cok;* his descendants today say *cock-a-doodle-do.* Accordingly, it is difficult to support the assumption that there is an inherent relation between words and things.

It cannot be denied that speculation on the origin of language and on the reasons for specific words is intriguing, but few facts are available on which to base any acceptable solutions. On the other hand many questions concerning language have been poorly explored, and these repay investigation now.

1.8 Types of Languages: VO or OV

One topic of current interest has to do with the structure of languages and the extent to which it applies. Only recently has it become clear that languages are either verb-object (VO) or object-verb (OV) languages. That is, objects stand either after verbs as in English and Spanish or before them as in Japanese and Turkish. Simple sentences illustrate the basic patterns:

6a. Spanish: *Juan vió   el   perro.*
     'John saw the dog.'
  b. Japanese: *John ga   inu o   mita*
     'John (*sub*)[2] dog (*obj*) saw.'

Verbs in this way stand at the end of clauses in OV languages, in contrast with VO languages, where they stand in the middle of clauses.

Many other constructions, such as adpositional phrases, correlate with these orders. *Adposition* is a cover term for postpositions and prepositions. VO languages have prepositions; OV languages have postpositions, as can be seen in the following examples:

7a. Spanish: *Juan vió   el   perro por   la ventana.*
     'John saw the dog   through the window.'
  b. Japanese: *John ga   inu o   mado   kara mita.*
     'John (*sub*) dog (*obj*) window from saw'

Further, in VO languages comparisons are made with the adjective and a marker before the noun compared; in OV languages these elements stand after that noun.

8a. Spanish: *El   perro es más   grande que   el gato.*
     the dog   is more big   than the cat
  b. Japanese: *Inu ga   neko yori ookii.*
     dog (*sub*) cat   from big
     'The dog is bigger than the cat.'

We will examine more such parallel patterns later. Their consistency may be understood if the three constructions—government of verbs, adpositions, and comparatives—are viewed for their underlying principle.

Each of these three constructions involves government by one element of another. This observation suggests that when we learn language and when we use

[2] (*sub*) stands for subject marker; (*obj*) for object marker.

it we employ abstract principles which may control constructions that on the surface seem quite different. The observation also helps us understand how infants can learn languages so rapidly once they have comprehended that selected sequences of sounds are used as symbols.

1.9 Further Topics for Examination

The preceding sections discuss some of the topics that earlier generations have treated in their efforts to understand language and its uses. Languages are described by means of grammars. Dictionaries are compiled to list meanings of elements. Earlier grammars differ in many ways from those now produced, but in general they regard language as a system. This system is treated in various components, such as a phonological, a syntactic, and a semantic component. Besides producing grammars and dictionaries, earlier generations concerned themselves with uses of language in society, its importance for individuals, and its origin, among other matters.

Many topics having to do with uses of language remain to be investigated. In the next chapter we will sketch some of these uses. Thereupon we will examine the structure of language and current efforts to understand it. Attempts to achieve improved perspectives on language involve the investigation of animal languages, of deficits in language use, and of the historical development of languages. Through such investigations students of language expect to gain insights into activities of the mind in perceiving and interpreting the world around them and into behavior of individuals and social groups as well as insights into language.

QUESTIONS FOR REVIEW

1. Discuss contributions of ancient Indian grammarians to our understanding of language.
2. What facet of language was of interest to the ancient Hebrews?
3. Mention some concerns of scholars today regarding language and its use.
4. What does it mean to characterize language as a symbolic system?
5. Discuss similarities between language and other symbolic systems, such as stoplights and our generally used number system. Discuss also differences between language and such systems.
6. Comparing a number like *seven* with words such as *radish, from, cattle, accelerate, give,* indicate the additional content such words have. Note which of these words can make a plural, take an object, or be inflected for tense.
7. Define *morpheme*. How is the meaning of a morpheme determined?
8. Define *phoneme*. Why is this term rather than the term *letter* used in discussions of language?

9. Discuss the role of arrangement in providing greater scope of communication in language and number systems than in a stoplight system.

10. Name components used in the treatment of language, defining each briefly.

11. Compare the explanation of the origin of language in *Genesis* with the current explanation.

12. Contrast Cratylus's view of the relationship of words and meanings with our own.

13. Discuss differences between VO and OV languages, citing constructions in which they contrast.

PROBLEMS FOR REVIEW

1. Panini's last rule has always attracted his admirers. It is simply: *a a;* that is, *a = a*. What it means is that throughout his grammar the short form of *a* has been treated as though it were pronounced *a,* but actually must be pronounced as a schwa ə, like the second vowel of *sofa*. Panini's grammar was produced at a time when all such works were memorized and transmitted orally. Discuss current grammars and their make-up by comparison. How would you react to a grammar like Panini's? What would you think of memorizing any grammar of English you know and use?

2. Immigrants to the United States in the nineteenth century wanted their children to learn English and often also wanted them to give up the language of their ancestors, whether German, Italian, Serbo-Croatian, or the like. They were supported in this attitude by the educational system. Today, in contrast, many parents want their children to be bilingual and are aided in this desire by the schools and the state. Discuss changes in the social situation that have led to the different attitude.

3. A notable example of aphasia in the past is Zacharias, the father of John the Baptist. Examine the account of his loss of speech in *Luke* 1 and compare it with Mursili's account of his aphasia. Would you describe the aphasia of either as psychological? As physiological?

4. Newspapers publish reactions to language almost daily. The day this was written a popular columnist published in her column a letter supporting her previously stated view that the title *Ms.* should be avoided. What are your views on its use? Do you think a distinction should be made in designations for married versus unmarried women? For married versus unmarried men? (At one time in the past, *Master* as opposed to *Mister* was used for boys, but it never achieved a distinctive abbreviation.)

   What do you consider the fundamental objection to *Ms.?* Unhappiness with new patterns in language? Social conservatism? Another reason? If you examine another language, such as German, French, or Spanish, you find similar distinctions in designation for married women, unmarried women, and males. To what extent do you think this division represents sexism from the past?

5. Devise a communication system to be used in a particular situation, such as roller-skating through the corridors of a library, human-powered flight across the English Channel, or hang-gliding from the university tower. You will probably need signals for *proceed; I am proceeding to the right; I am proceeding to the left;* and *caution.* You may wish to devise appropriate symbols for these simple situations and also for more complicated ones.

6. If a new technology or science is developed, new words need to be devised. In the past, many of these have been taken from Greek and Latin. More recently, such words are often taken over from imaginative writers who invent them or adapt them from other languages. Thus, Murry Gell-Mann took *quark* 'elementary particle' from James Joyce's *Finnegans Wake,* where it means something of minute value. Joyce probably adapted it from German *Quark* 'curds; trifle, rubbish.' Devise a word for any new discovery, such as a further subatomic particle, a section of the brain that may handle one bit of information, the upper or lower interior of a black hole.

7. Turkish, like Japanese, is an OV language. The following are examples of a simple sentence, an adpositional phrase, and a comparative construction.

　　1. *John köpeği gördü.*
　　　　　dog　　saw　　= 'John saw the dog.'
　　2. *John pencereden　köpeği gördü.*
　　　　　window-from dog　　saw
　　　= 'John saw the dog from the window.'
　　3. *Köpek kediden daha büyük.*
　　　　dog　　cat-from more big
　　　= 'The dog is bigger than the cat.'

Account for the use of *den* after nouns in sentences 2 and 3.

FURTHER READING

Bolinger, Dwight, and Donald A. Sears. *Aspects of Language.* 3d ed. New York: Harcourt Brace Jovanovich, 1981.

Fromkin, Victoria, and Robert Rodman. *An Introduction to Language.* 2d ed. New York: Holt, Rinehart & Winston, 1978.

Heatherington, Madelon E. *How Language Works.* Cambridge, Mass.: Winthrop, 1980.

Miller, George A. *Language and Speech.* San Francisco: Freeman, 1981.

CHAPTER TWO

How Societies Use Language

2.1 Language as Identifier of Social Groups

Speakers know that language identifies the group to which they belong as well as other groups. When Americans were fighting in the Pacific jungles, they used their language to determine opponents. If Japanese tried to pass themselves off as Americans, the GIs asked them to say *lallapalloosa*. The Japanese language has no [l]. Worse, a variant of their /r/ is something like an [l]-sound. In hearing another language with a distinct [l]-sound, the Japanese interpret it as [r] and pronounce it accordingly. When the reply in the jungles was [raraparusa], the speaker was obviously a Japanese.

In much the same way all of us identify our social group when we use language. The broadest classification, of course, is by different languages, as between English and Japanese. But there are also characteristic variants within languages, creating **dialects.**

A classical instance similar to the battle situation in the Pacific was reported by an ancient Hebrew historian. When one group of Israelites, the Gileadites, defeated another, the Ephraimites, they required each Ephraimite trying to escape across the Jordan to pronounce *Shibboleth,* the word for 'river.' In the dialect of the Ephraimites this was *Sibboleth.* Anyone pronouncing *s* rather than *sh* was killed (*Judges* 12.6).

15

The same test could be used for some Americans. In areas of Kentucky and Tennessee and elsewhere in the South, many speakers pronounce *s* rather than *sh* before *r*. Their pronunciation is *srimp, sredded wheat, srub,* and so on. Few speakers are aware of such minor differences. If you encounter such speakers, they will be surprised at learning that their pronunciation differs from the general pronunciation *shr*. And they will not adopt the general pronunciation.

Here the situation is different from that of *l* in Japanese. English speakers have no trouble distinguishing between *s* and *sh,* as in contrasts like *sip/ship, save/shave, sop/shop.* But there is no such contrast before *r*. Accordingly, the pronunciation used by a given speaker will not lead to misunderstanding or to unintelligibility; it may simply sound strange to those who notice it. Even many speakers who have spent their lives among *sr*-speakers have never noticed the variant. For those who have, it creates a subclassification, a dialect.

Dialects are generally characterized by a number of variations or by a more far-reaching variation than that between *sr* and *shr*. Such a far-reaching variation in English is the absence of *r* after vowels, as in *fear, far, fire.* Speakers who use instead of *r* a brief additional vowel are recognized as New Englanders, or southerners, or British. If they have further characteristics, such as a drawl, or an [a] pronunciation in words like *calf, path, ask, dance,* we classify them more precisely as British. But we have little trouble understanding them.

Dialects distinguish subgroups among the speakers of a language, whereas languages generally extend over a far larger group than does a dialect. German differs from English in many respects, including the lack of an initial *s;* related words with initial *s* in English, like *send,* are pronounced with initial *z* in German. English, like German, extends beyond individual countries, but by knowing dialect characteristics we may be able to identify a Canadian, an Austrian, and so on.

Speech characteristics allow us to make finer distinctions. Shakespeare illustrates this capability in the opening lines of *Hamlet*. When one guard, Bernardo, challenges another, Francisco, to identify himself in the dark night, the other, Francisco, refuses to give his name and challenges Bernardo to do so. Bernardo does not. Instead he answers: "Long live the king!" These few words are adequate for Francisco to identify the guard replacing him as Bernardo.

Even the modified speech we hear over a telephone permits us to recognize friends, to distinguish a strange voice. In addition we may be able to determine the state of emotion of speakers, whether they are happy or angry, or their age and other characteristics. Speech, as we shall see, is a complex signal produced by a variety of organs—the larynx using air from the lungs, the throat, mouth, and nose. These give it great variety of resonance and individual characteristics.

No two sets of speech organs are alike. That is to say, every speaker has distinct physical characteristics that lead to a distinct type of speech, or idiolect. The term *idiolect* is based on dialect, which in turn is taken from classical Greek; *dia-* is a preposition meaning 'apart' and *-lect* is a noun stem based on the root *leg-* 'speak,' another variant of which is found in *logos* 'word.' The prefix *idio-* means 'individual,' as in idiosyncracy. Our speech apparatus is capable of such delicate variations, as is our hearing mechanism, that we not only distinguish dialects but also idiolects.

The recognition of such a characteristic pattern for individuals has led to the development of voiceprints, which, like fingerprints, are used to identify individuals. Voiceprints, however, have not been demonstrated to be as accurate as fingerprints. That is to say, equipment has not yet been devised that can identify individuals by the sound of their voice as readily as human speakers can. Speakers have the capability of noting idiolects or individual forms of speech, dialects, and different languages.

2.2 The Natural Trend Towards Subvarieties of Language

Our uses of language correlate with the social groups to which we belong. Individuals have favorite patterns that characterize them—possibly a tendency to articulate precisely, to use particular forms like *waked* rather than *woke* or *woken* or *dived* rather than *dove,* to prefer specific words, such as *excellent* or *lovely* or *bravo,* and the like. Some of these they share with the smallest social group to which they belong, the family.

Many families use distinctive words for everyday activities, such as eating, elimination, or for locations. As children we called a remote place *Buxtehude,* taking over this name of an early composer in an idiosyncratic manner. Many more families use *Podunk* with this meaning, so many that this word for two small towns in Massachusetts and New York has been accepted in this meaning by dictionaries. Unlike *Buxtehude, Podunk* was adopted by further speakers. Favored words and patterns may in this way be shared by a larger community than the family, with fellow-members of a trade or profession.

In correlating with social groups, languages and their varieties also circumscribe them. We interact more comfortably with speakers of our own language than with foreign speakers. Dialects also have a special appeal among their users. A Southern drawl seems more friendly to other southerners, the Bavarian dialect more *gemuetlich* than its northern counterparts to Bavarians. Such groupings of speech characterize sets of speakers for outsiders and lead the speakers themselves to prefer social groups in accordance with their own patterns of speech.

If for social or political reasons such interaction is maintained among restricted or segregated groups, distinct dialects result, eventually even distinct languages. The Roman Empire in its decline illustrates the process. In France, Italy, and Spain, for example, distinct languages developed from what was once a unified language area, that of Latin. After Rome lost its centralized control, distinct languages arose in each of these territories. The increasingly different languages in turn led to increasingly coordinated political units and ultimately to the countries we know today as Italy, France, Spain, Portugal, and so on.

Such differentiation results from an inherent feature of language: It is always changing. When automobiles were introduced, their parts needed names. In England speakers called one part a *bonnet;* in America the word *hood* was adopted. Another part came to be known as a *mudguard* in England, as a *fender* in America. All such differences lead towards communication problems. If they are not reduced by continued social contacts, they ultimately bring about different languages. Fortunately, modern methods of communication and continued social contact kept British and American English from developing and maintaining many such individual usages. English remained one language, unlike Latin, which developed into the Romance languages after the collapse of the Roman Empire. The effects of change, then, can be reduced or eliminated.

Yet change is a feature of language, much as it is of all social habits. Fashions of behavior change, as do fashions of dress, sports, music, eating, and political and religious arrangements. Our grandfathers did not play football. They did not use expressions like *forward pass* or *T-formation;* the terms *block, punt,* and so on did not have the same meanings for them as they do for us. Lacking television they could not *watch the news.* All societies change, as do their linguistic habits. The geographical extent of specific changes corresponds to the extent of communication.

In this way subgroups of languages, or dialects, arise. The people of a river valley may develop restricted linguistic habits. Fishing communities use different terms from those of farming communities. Or different fishing communities may use terms with different meanings; *perch* is a slim narrow fish in the northern states, a panfish in the southern. All of such differences characterize one group as opposed to another.

History provides many examples. Peter, the disciple of Jesus, for example, came from Galilee, about seventy miles north of Jerusalem. When Peter spoke during the questioning of Jesus, a bystander recognized him by his speech differences. Even a few miles were adequate to lead to speech habits that one speaker could use to "place" another.

In much the same way we recognize New England speakers by their pronunciation of words like *bird, older,* and *idea(r)* before vowels. Using *-r* before vowels, as in *Dear Abby,* but not before consonants, as in *Dea(r) Jim,* New England speakers may introduce an *-r* after words like *idea* and *Cuba* before words beginning with vowels. Such an "intrusive *r*" identifies them clearly, and may be a source of amusement, as was President Kennedy's pronunciation of *Cuba* as *Cubar* in sequences with vowel following. If we communicate largely with speakers from a specific region, our speech may "betray" us much as did Peter's. All speakers tend to maintain characteristics that distinguish them as representatives of a given language, also of a specific dialect within that language, and of specific technical or social classes as well.

In short, if social and political conditions favor the formation of small semiindependent groups, dialects become increasingly distinct. And if the isolation continues, in time dialects differ so greatly that they can no longer be understood by speakers of other dialects. They become different languages. An area like the Roman Empire, or like India or China, may begin with one language, but in the course of time many subvarieties may develop. Specific social conditions may in this way lead to smaller and smaller areas, each with its distinct dialect or language.

2.3 The Expansion of Languages

Other social conditions may lead to expansion of the area in which a language is used. A city may gain increasing power. As it incorporates further areas, its own language will be spread; other languages and dialects will be submerged.

The language of ancient Rome is an excellent example. Around 700 B.C. it was confined to Latium, one of the many small political units in Italy. Latin, the language of this area, was spoken by fewer speakers than were Etruscan and many other languages of Italy at the time. Rome, however, greatly increased the number of Latin speakers by imposing the language on the neighbors it conquered and by about 150 B.C. on all of Italy. Through the Roman conquests, Latin was extended to the entire peninsula.

As the Roman Empire expanded, Latin was introduced into other areas: Spain, France, and other parts of Europe extending all the way to Romania. From the language of a small political group and a restricted area, Latin had become the dominant language of the Western world.

Other languages have been extended in much the same way. England began its international expansion at the time of Queen Elizabeth I (1533–1603). Through this expansion English was brought to North America and subsequently to Australia, India, and parts of Africa. At the same time, Spanish and Portuguese were introduced abroad, largely in Central and South America. Similar processes have gone on throughout human history. Chinese was extended through its present area in the second and first millennia B.C. The Bantu languages were carried throughout much of southern Africa in the first millennium A.D. Arabic began its expansion from the time of Mohammed, who died in A.D. 632. In all these expansions, other languages were submerged, many without leaving any traces.

The expansion was often carried out on a small scale. *Genesis* 12 tells us how Hebrew was introduced to Palestine, in an account well worth reading. Abraham was directed by his Lord to migrate from the area of northern Syria to his new home. His group was small, a few hundred. The account rings with authenticity because of the animals mentioned. Abraham had camels and donkeys; the horse was only introduced to the Middle East by the Indo-Europeans during their expansion. Abraham maintained himself, repulsed the armies of four kings, and Hebrew was established in the new land.

Expansion of given languages is still going on. Today it is usually associated with countries that extend their influence or come to be centralized. In India, Hindi is being spread; in Indonesia, a form of Malay now called Indonesian; in the Soviet Union, Russian. Such expansion is now more rapid because countries use schools and modern forms of communication, like radio, to teach their citizens the chosen language.

Moreover, modern countries sense a need to communicate directly and rapidly with all of their citizens. They use various means to have their people adopt one language so that social arrangements will be simpler to carry out. Selected languages then continue to expand, and eventually many of the nonfavored languages go out of use.

2.4 Language Engineering

As languages are extended in this way they must meet certain requirements. One is a writing system suitable for ready mastery. Another is a common phonology and syntax. Their vocabulary must also be adequate to meet contemporary needs, such as those of science and technology. Many languages do not meet these requirements, even until recently some Western languages. To remedy such shortcomings, nations may establish formal or informal agencies, a committee, a society, or an academy. The work of these agencies is often referred to as language engineering.

Turkish is an example. Until the establishment of the modern republic by Atatürk in 1923, Turkish used the Arabic writing system. The vocabulary for science and technology was virtually missing. Among his many reforms, Atatürk introduced the Latin alphabet and a well-designed orthography. This now is in general use. Moreover, he established a "linguistic society" that was to bring the vocabulary of Turkish up to date for the concepts of modern scientific fields. Words for subjects from linguistics to physics were to be devised. The organization is still at work.

Such attention to the language is closely related to social attitudes. Atatürk was the highly popular father of his country, as the name suggests—*ata* 'father.' He adopted the name "Father of the Turks" in 1933. Among his achievements was the guidance into the modern world of a nation that had been on the losing side of World War I and was stripped of non-Turkish-speaking areas, chiefly Arabic. Among other ideals, the new nation set out to renew its Turkish roots. Besides rejecting the Arabic writing system, it sought to rid the language of Arabic-based vocabulary. The task is comparable to an attempt to rid English of all Latin and Greek elements. The fervor for the new ideas, however, was so great that these steps were followed. Turkish is now written in the Latin alphabet. Many native Turkish words have replaced Arabic words. The reforms are maintained today, having succeeded in spite of struggles with conservatives who favored the former language patterns.

In many countries such struggles over language policy give rise to some of the most important political problems. Norway is an example. Its parliament commonly passes legislation to bring its two languages, Riksmål/Bokmål and Landsmål/Nynorsk, closer together. One such bit of legislation required Norwegians to shift from the old pattern of numerals found in "four-and-twenty blackbirds" to the order we use in English today, "twenty-four." Eventually the two languages of Norway are in this way to be merged.

Since Norway gained its independence in 1814, much of the effort to establish a distinct, national language was applied in the nineteenth century. Other European countries took steps to achieve a general language. Germany, for example, established a standard—the stage pronunciation (*Buehnenaussprache*)—only at the close of the nineteenth century. The numerous German states that existed before unification in 1861 fostered use of different dialects, even within the two major languages: Low German in the north and High German in the south. Only the traveling stage groups had a "national" pronunciation, something of a compromise between High and Low German. This pronunciation was fixed in 1898, taught in the schools, and used on public occasions. Virtually all Germans continued to speak a dialect in the home and with neighbors, but they also mastered the national language. This in time prevailed; today the extent of Low German is greatly reduced.

Third World countries, most of which achieved independence after World War II, are now going through the same process of installing national languages. India is seeking to have Hindi fill the role, encountering numerous difficulties in the process. Hindi is the language of the north-central area. Other related languages, such as Bengali, the language of the Calcutta area and Bangladesh, are also spoken by numerous speakers, Bengali by more than a hundred million. The nonrelated Dravidian languages are spoken throughout the south. Many of the speakers in these parts object strongly to adopting Hindi, and the attempt has great political repercussions. The Dravidians of the south would prefer to use English as the official language, as the language of the universities and general publication. Its widespread current use for these purposes is a heritage of almost two centuries of British rule. English, then, carries reminders of British imperialism, and for that reason is distasteful to some Indians. The outcome of the language struggles in India, as well as in the many newly founded nations of Africa and elsewhere, is very difficult to forecast.

China also faces the problem of developing a truly national language. For several millennia the country communicated through a common writing system, but sections had their own languages. In addition to non-Chinese languages, such as Thai, Mongolian, Korean, and many others, Chinese itself—also known as Han—consists of seven distinct languages, each with numerous dialects. While those who mastered the writing system could communicate beyond the boundaries of their specific language, mastery of it required great effort. It consists of as many as 30,000 characters, at least 2,000 of which must be mastered for the simple requirements of daily use. Only a small proportion of the population had the leisure to gain such mastery. As a result, China was controlled by a limited elite, and at least 95 percent of the population was illiterate.

A modern society is handicapped by the presence of illiterates. Workers and farmers as well as government officials must be able to read in order to keep abreast of contemporary practices. Yet to overcome illiteracy China faces two massive problems: It must have a simple writing system, and it must have one language. The problems are interrelated. If the new writing system were introduced today for Putonghua, the most widely used language, speakers of Cantonese, Hakka, and the other Chinese/Han languages could not read the newspapers nor the common textbooks, nor understand written government edicts and the like. The problems can only be met by extensive long-range planning.

Such planning is carried out by the Committee on Chinese Language Reform. This committee is simplifying the characters of the writing system, taking steps to spread the use of the new alphabetic system—*pinyin*—and to teach throughout the country the government-sponsored "common language"—*Putonghua,* a form of

Mandarin Chinese spoken around Beijing. The effort is without doubt the most massive application of language engineering ever carried out.

The reaction to such efforts depends on social considerations. The English orthographic system also presents problems. Maintained without substantial change since the introduction of printing in 1476, it was "phonetic" for Middle English. The vowel symbols at that time had values corresponding to those of the Continental languages and also to Latin: The vowel of *beet* was pronounced like that of German *Beet* (i.e., English *bate*) rather than like that of German *biet* 'offer'; the vowel of *life* was that of modern *leaf,* and so on. Subsequent changes of the long vowels, by which Middle English [e:] became [i:], Middle English [i:] became [ay], brought with them a departure from the Continental values, though the short vowels still approximate these, as in *pit, pet, pat,* British English *pot, put.* The lack of fit between spelling and pronunciation may be most obvious in words like *through, though, cough, hiccough, bough, hough.*

Efforts have been made to reform the English spelling system, without success; reasons will be explored in Chapter 11, Section 11.8. The maintenance of an archaic spelling system for English illustrates one of the attitudes that speakers have for their language. They resist tampering with it, regarding it as one of their most characteristic and intimate inheritances.

2.5 Does Language Have an Effect on Thought and on Our Perception of the World Around Us?

The intimate relationship between speakers and their speech has led some scholars to suggest that language determines the view we have of the world around us. Different languages segment natural phenomena differently. We name seven colors in the rainbow: violet, indigo, blue, green, yellow, orange, and red in this order or the reverse. Speakers of other languages may see only four, as did Turkish before our system was introduced, or even as few as two, roughly the lighter shades versus the darker. There is nothing in nature to demonstrate how we should chop up the spectrum of the rainbow, which is made up of a scale of various wavelengths. But when we have learned a given language, we distinguish the shades it designates, both in the rainbow and elsewhere. Many students of language assume from such a situation and other similar situations that language determines much of the shapes and patterns we see in the world around us, that it directs our concepts and actions.

One such scholar was Benjamin Lee Whorf (1897–1941). Whorf was a fire prevention engineer in the Hartford Fire Insurance Company. As one of his jobs he scrutinized claims. Among other matters that came to his attention was the contrast in behavior around gasoline drums when labeled empty or full. People were highly cautious when near full drums. But if they learned that the drums were empty, they became careless with cigarettes, even though empty drums contain explosive vapor and are perhaps the more dangerous. The *empty* label was interpreted as 'inert' when it meant 'devoid of liquid.' Whorf concluded that the word governed their behavior and that one's "world is to a large extent unconsciously built up on the language habits of the group."[1]

Changes in the choice of language, then, might modify behavior. Today gasoline trucks are generally labeled "flammable" rather than "inflammable." The *in-* prefix was often taken as equivalent to that of words like *inanimate* and *inaccurate,* where *in-* means 'not.' It is actually the *in-* of words like *intense* and *inflect,* where it strengthens the meaning. The word *inflammable,* then, means 'highly flammable.' The faulty interpretation of language, however, determined the attitudes of many speakers, who thereupon adjusted their behavior in relation to the language. Prudent truck owners have taken notice and changed the warning to "flammable."

Such observations led Whorf to a concern with deeper patterns of language, such as the use of tenses in the languages of Europe. Tense is the linguistic expression of time. English and other European languages generally require their speakers to identify the time of an event, whether present: *It's raining;* past: *It rained;* or future: *It will rain.* By contrast, many languages, such as the Hopi language of New Mexico, as Whorf analyzed it, lack expression for tense. Nor do such languages objectify time. In Hopi one cannot count days, minutes, years as though they were objects like stones or bottles. Everyday expressions like *I'll wait two days* or *Three years went by* are impossible in Hopi.

Comparing such languages Whorf proposed that our use of tense, "our objectified view of time is favorable to historicity and to everything connected with the keeping of records."[2] That is to say, because of the patterns for referring to time in English and other West European languages, their speakers maintain records and emphasize bookkeeping, accounting, and the like. Further, we are interested in calendars, clocks, and time graphs as well as in history and archeology.

The Whorfian view has been maintained by others, such as Wilhelm von Humboldt (1776–1835) and Edward Sapir (1884–1939). Known as the Sapir-Whorf hypothesis, it is also referred to as *linguistic relativity.* In accordance with it one's conception of the world is relative to the language one learns.

While the relativity hypothesis has attracted considerable attention, it has never been experimentally demonstrated to be valid. A large-scale attempt to test the outlook of Hopi-speaking children versus English-speaking children turned out to be inconclusive. It remains a task of future scholars to determine whether the hypothesis is valid and also whether one should assume a weak or strong position with regard to it. Clearly we are deeply tied to our native language. But whether it regulates our perceptions or our view of the world is still an open question.

2.6 What Happens When Speakers of Different Languages Want to Communicate with One Another?

In spite of the restrictions our language imposes on us, occasions have always arisen when speakers of different languages wish to communicate with one another.

[1] Benjamin Lee Whorf, *Language, Thought and Reality,* pp. 135–137.
[2] *Ibid.,* p. 153.

Among such occasions Western traders sought to do business with peoples of the Pacific, including the Chinese. Since neither group knew the other's language, a stripped-down and composite version developed. Such languages are known as **pidgins.**

One etymology of *pidgin* illustrates the processes at work. This etymology sees the origin of *pidgin* in *business,* so that Pidgin English is actually Business English. Chinese has no /b/. Hearing the pronunciation /biznis/, the Chinese substitute /p/ for [b]. The /i/ was adopted without change. For /z/ the sound [ž] as in *measure* was used. Since consonant clusters are difficult, a vowel and /n/ were added, and the last portion of the word was dropped. Westerners, hearing something like /pižin/ in return interpreted it as pidgin. The word is now used for all such languages, whether they are based on English, French, or any other language.

Pidgins may come to be widely used, as in New Guinea. Here an English-based pidgin became the avenue for communication among speakers of many different languages. It is now recognized officially and widely used in an area with seven hundred or so different languages. A few sentences may illustrate further some of the characteristics of pidgins.

> Call-im name belong you? = 'What is your name?'
> You savvy talk-im pidgin? = 'Do you know how to talk pidgin?'

The morphology and syntax are simple but include some features of the native language. Notable among these is the suffix *-im,* which signals a following object. Moreover, function words are used rather than inflections, such as *belong,* which indicates possessives.

The vocabulary is taken from any language, such as *savvy* from Spanish. The two sentences correspond to something like the following: 'Say your name!' 'You know (how) to talk pidgin?' Pidgins eliminate formal complexities, both in phonology and syntax, resulting in essentially uninflected languages.

Pidgins are second languages used to carry on communication beyond one's first language group. They may, however, come to be the first language of children whose parents communicate only in the pidgin. In such situations the language is referred to as a **creole.** A creole based on French has developed in Haiti; one based on English in Jamaica. Some scholars also use the term "creole" for languages that have taken over many elements from other languages. English with its many French and Latin borrowings would then be a creole even though it has never been a pidgin.

Such simplified languages are not only attested in remote areas of the world. A pidginlike German has developed in communication with the imported 'guest-workers'—*Gastarbeiterdeutsch 'guest-worker German.'* In it inflections are sharply reduced, and the syntax is simple. Scholars are studying it in an attempt to understand the processes involved in creation of a pidgin in a highly industrial modern society.

Those processes seem to be somewhat like the ones involved in baby talk. In these forms of language, adult speakers assume that a simplified form of language is more readily understandable by newcomers and by young children. If the simplified form is adopted and maintained, a new pidgin has developed.

2.7 How Do Children Learn Language?

By contrast with natives who accept a pidgin, children may be addressed with simplified speech known as baby talk, but they do not end up speaking it or a pidgin. Scholars have studied their language behavior with considerable interest, partly to determine how they learn their language, partly for the more general aim of determining how the brain handles language.

It is now held that children pass through various stages of language learning. At first, infants babble, even if they are deaf. Hearing infants react sharply to human speech. In such reaction they gradually shape their babbling sounds towards the pattern of the language spoken around them.

At about twelve months they come to understand that specific sound sequences have meaning. These are simple at first, words like *mama, papa*. Encouraged by adults they master more such sequences, treating them as full sentences. This stage is known as **holophrastic,** that is, the expression of an entire concept in one word. This word may of course be composed of elements comparable to two or more words of adults.

From about twenty-four months they build sentences of two or more distinct words, in the so-called **joining stage.** One of these words is a noun or is nounlike, the other a verb or is verblike. Sentences like *doll pretty, want ball,* and *puppy sleep* exemplify this stage. Such words are spoken individually, without articles, auxiliaries, and other function words, much like the language used in telegrams. Children are often said to pass through a telegraphic stage, during which they use only content words.

Thereupon they acquire connectives—function words and markers for agreement, as in *the doll is pretty.* This period of acquisition is known as the **connective stage.** Mastery of all the devices for tying sentences together extends over a long period, well into the final stage.

In this stage they acquire recursive grammars, that is, they deal with language through rules rather than as individual, memorized items of two or more words. The rules are often overextended. The plural *-s* may be added to words like *sheep, man, mouse* as well as to *heap, can, mess;* the past tense marker *-d* may be added to words like *come, go, run* as well as to *hum, glow, sun.* The errors indicate that the child has come to understand how language works. The erroneous forms are generally eliminated as children acquire greater control of the language.

Such mastery by stages has been taken as evidence that human beings are born with an innate capability for acquiring language. This theory is maintained especially by Noam Chomsky and adherents of generative transformational grammar. It is in sharp contrast with views of behaviorist psychology, by which language acquisition results largely in imitation of the speech that infants hear. Among arguments against the behaviorist position is the observation that infants do not typically hear perfectly grammatical or even complete sentences, and yet they master the rules for producing grammatical strings. Resolution of the problem has encouraged a great deal of research into language acquisition.

Jean Piaget, who worked intensively on cognitive development of children, represents something of a middle position. By his theory language acquisition is one part of a broader context in the development of sensorimotor intelligence. The course of this development involves "formation of the symbolic function," of which language is one manifestation. The contrasting theories were the topic of a notable debate in 1975 near Paris, in which adherents of Chomsky and Piaget also participated.[3] Piaget and Chomsky share many views as opposed to the behaviorist position. But in the debate they did not come to any agreement on the problem of whether human beings have a special capacity for language as opposed to other manipulation of symbols. These and other problems are now being intensively investigated, as we note further in Chapter 9, especially Sections 9.2 and 9.4.

2.8 Toying with Language

In the process of learning language, children often play with it, as do adults. A common form of play is Pig Latin, in which words are remodeled in some fashion. In one well-known kind of Pig Latin the initial sound is placed after the word, with its own vowel, as in *ig-pay atin-lay*. Besides rearrangement, as in the example here, Pig Latin may involve repetition and substitution.

These devices are also found in nursery rhymes and in imitative language. Clocks seem to advance by ticks and tocks. A nursery rhyme substitutes *h* and *d* for *t* with repetition and rearrangement of these "sounds."

> Hickory, dickory, dock,
>   The mouse ran up the clock,
>   The clock struck one,
>   The mouse ran down,
> Hickory, dickory, dock.

Nursery rhymes also rely heavily on musical patterning of language, as do simple verse forms, such as limericks. The nineteenth-century popular poet Edward Lear produced many of these, generally with reference to places that seemed exotic in the England of his day; among these he knew India better than others, as the following example with its mispronunciation of an American name may illustrate.

> There was a young man in Iowa
> Who exclaimed, "Where on earth shall I stow her!"

[3] See Massimo Piatelli-Palmarini, ed., *Language and Learning. The Debate between Jean Piaget and Noam Chomsky.*

Of his sister he spoke,
Who was felled by an Oak
Which abound in the plains of Iowa.

Toying with language is by no means confined to verse and is often a part of daily conversation. Some speakers take pleasure in being strikingly creative in their use of language. One example is the use of puns. These appeal to children, as in *Alice in Wonderland*. When Alice was discussing education with the Mock Turtle, he said: "I only took the regular course." "What was that?" inquired Alice. "Reeling and Writhing, of course to begin with," the Mock Turtle replied: "and then the different branches of Arithmetic—Ambition, Distraction, Uglification, and Derision."

Modern advertising uses these devices. A group of motels invites tourists with a pun on "turn in," appealing to drivers and also the weary. A moving company uses rhymes to call attention to itself: "U-HAUL . . . has it all." A telephone company sets out to expand its business, using a metaphor to suggest that patrons "reach out and touch someone." In advertising, such playful expressions are designed to have audiences remember the service or product.

Among our interests in examining these devices are the insights they provide on the mastery of language by speakers. Pig Latin indicates the speaker's ability to manipulate phonemes, as they separate initial elements. The examples of advertising language indicate awareness of syntactic and semantic patterns. The expression *turn in* can be either transitive [*turn your car in this way*] or intransitive [*turn in for the night*]. The expressions *reach out* and *touch someone* have literal and figurative meanings. We can find many such examples in our own culture, but such toying with language has also been documented in many other cultures.

Among the most remarkable examples are "secret languages" devised by children who for some reason set out to isolate themselves from adults. Such languages usually never develop to any extent and are abandoned. But one, Spaka, has recently been described. Maintained by two adult sisters, it "started out by adding [əm] at the end of every English syllable."[4] Then [əm] came to be a marker for subjects and predicates, and other characteristics were introduced. Such play languages resemble pidgins in having as a basis a natural language. And like pidgins, they provide evidence on control of language by speakers, both of the segments that are preserved without change and those that are modified.

Play may also be reflected in segments of language. Reduplication is widely found in imitative expressions, such as *pitter-patter*. Chinese and Japanese contain many examples; *Ping-Pong* is borrowed from one of these meaning 'sound of rain on the roof.' In many languages, reduplication is used as a grammatical device, often to express repetition and intensification; the word *memory* preserves such a reduplicated Latin formation. More than Latin, classical Greek and Sanskrit used reduplication to signal the perfect tense, that is, completed action. While such

[4] Randy L. Diehl and Katherine F. Kolodzey, "Spaka: A Private Language," *Language* 56 (1981), 406–423.

effects of language play are found in grammar, their most prominent results are in rhetoric and literature.

Public speakers commonly use repetition to signal emphasis. Rhyme in literature is often used to signal the end of metric lines. The limits of Old Irish poems were marked by using the same word at the end as at the beginning.

But the most common uses of playful devices in literature have to do with meaning. Hebrew poetry is based on repetition of the meaning in clauses, as in Psalm 136.1:

> O give thanks unto the Lord; for he is good:
>> for his mercy endureth forever.

The two clauses beginning with 'for' are parallel in meaning.

Repetition may involve puns, as in a notable episode of Homer's *Odyssey*. In relating his feats of blinding the one-eyed monster Polyphemus, Odysseus uses one of the most famous puns in literature, giving himself a name which literally means 'No-one.' A variant means 'cunning.' The pun assures his escape. After Polyphemus is blinded by Odysseus, he calls to his friends to help him take revenge. When they learn that 'no-one' is his enemy, they do nothing to help him but advise that he pray to Zeus. In this way Odysseus sails away unharmed, happy about his "cunning." Toying with language is thus not restricted to children's rhymes, but is found in the highest forms of literature.

Much of the appeal of literature comes from imaginative use of language. The superb masters of language, like Homer and Shakespeare, have the capability of conveying information while manipulating language artistically. While poets have special gifts for creative uses of language, all speakers share this ability and therefore appreciate the special talents of the few who possess it in abundance.

2.9 Technical Uses of Language

Although we use language imaginatively in games, for our amusement, and for literature, we also restrict its possible patterns in technical use. For technical purposes we try to delimit our syntactic patterns and carefully control our vocabulary so that words have a clear, definite meaning. In imaginative literature, on the other hand, we enjoy skillful ambiguity. Shakespeare's work contains many examples. Punning on *grave* in its use as adjective to mean 'serious' and its use as noun, Shakespeare has Mercutio say in *Romeo and Juliet,* Act 3, Scene 1, lines 101–102: *ask for me tomorrow, and you shall find me a grave man.* If a company report similarly described its president as *grave,* it would scarcely be well received, whether by the stockholders or the president.

Technical and scientific language aims at precision. Its users seek a wide audience, also international readers who may be puzzled by complex or ambiguous expressions. Such language is designed in such a way that it can readily be translated. The need to translate large quantities of technical material became obvious as scientific publication grew in this century. Shortly after computers were developed in the forties, scientists proposed that they be applied for translation. In 1952, Leon Dostert, who was Eisenhower's translator for French and then became director of the Institute of Languages and Linguistics at Georgetown University, arranged a demonstration in which a short passage of Russian was translated by computer into English. Through this demonstration, machine translation attracted broad attention. Its development has been slow, however, largely because both the early computers and our knowledge of language were inadequate. Yet great advances have been made. They are evident in the small computers now produced to furnish foreign-language phrases to travelers, or to teach children, as in the "Speak-and-Spell" learning device. They are also evident in increasing uses of computers for communication, as in banks that use spoken signals to give information to customers.

An understanding of all such uses depends on a detailed knowledge of language. We need to know the characteristics of its sounds and how they relate to one another. We need to know its forms, their order in sentences, and how they convey meaning. Such knowledge is essential for understanding how best to teach language, whether to the deaf, to nonnative speakers, to children, to students, and for many other applications. It is essential for understanding changes in language, as between the English of Alfred the Great (d. 901), Chaucer (d. 1400), or even Shakespeare (d. 1616), and our own. A basic knowledge of the structure of language also assists us in dealing with language problems, whether for reforming English spelling, for confronting propaganda, or for remedying objectionable usage such as sexist language.

It is also important to know the attitudes of speakers to matters such as dialects, foreign languages, bilingualism, foreign accents, attempts at modifying languages, and so on. Attitudes to language vary almost as much as attitudes to music, and both include a large number of varieties. Some speakers prefer dialects just as many music lovers prefer country music. Others insist on classical music, just as many speakers put a high premium on literary style and on a form of language often referred to as correct.

Societies also avoid certain forms in certain circumstances. Until recently obituaries never listed cancer as the cause of death. Our society even attempts to avoid the words 'death' or 'die,' using substitutes such as 'pass on.' Such practices are known as **taboos.** The attitudes towards taboo words are very complex. Though such words may be avoided in certain circumstances, many of them have etymologies going back five millennia. Accordingly they have been handed down for many generations, even though they are supposedly suppressed.

Speakers have become highly aware of racist and sexist language. Within a generation such awareness has brought about changes, such as the use of black rather than Negro, the abbreviation Ms., and avoidance of the generic 'he.' Attitudes to "male-female" communication also involve patterns of speech, movement accompanying speaking, and so on.[5] The recent awareness of discrim-

[5] See Mary Ritchie Key, *Male/Female Language* and *Nonverbal Communication*.

ination expressed in these ways provides many examples of the interplay between language and cultural conventions as exemplified in publications, in TV productions, and in daily communication. The modifications produced by this new awareness also illustrate the control speakers can exert on language.

We are also highly versatile in our use of language. No one speaks to a child in the same way as to an adult. When we answer the telephone we carefully control our voices, often shifting from the mood we happen to be in to one reflecting equanimity or even cheer. We also are sensitive to the attitudes of others concerning our speech. In some countries, such as India, attempts to impose a given language have resulted in riots, leading to loss of lives. None of us is happy when someone abruptly corrects our pronunciation. We are similarly unhappy when we try to be amusing but are misinterpreted. Attitudes to language, then, are very significant, both in our use of language and in observation of its place in society.

The following chapters treat the structure of language, first its sounds, then the devices to convey meanings, in words, sentences, and discourse. These chapters also examine grammars developed to account for the phenomena of language. Later chapters discuss in greater detail some uses of language by individuals and social groups throughout history and in our various contacts with others, all of which are illuminated by knowledge of the basic structure of language.

QUESTIONS FOR REVIEW

1. Cite some examples of language characteristics that identify dialects.
2. Distinguish between the following: language, dialect, idiolect.
3. Discuss the processes by which languages develop dialects.
4. Discuss how dialects develop into independent languages.
5. Sketch the expansion of Latin. Of English.
6. What is meant by language engineering? Use Turkish or Hindi or Chinese or any other language to supply examples.
7. Where might the procedures of language engineering be applied to English?
8. What is meant by linguistic relativity? Which linguist is commonly associated with it? How did he use Hopi and English to support his analysis?
9. What is a pidgin? Distinguish between pidgins and creoles, giving examples of each.
10. Discuss similarities and differences between pidgins and baby talk.
11. Describe stages in the acquisition of language by children.
12. Cite various kinds of language play, giving examples.
13. Discuss characteristics of technical language, contrasting it with literary language. Which is easier to translate by computer?
14. What are some of the requirements for language applications, such as teaching the deaf, teaching nonnative speakers, dealing with language problems?

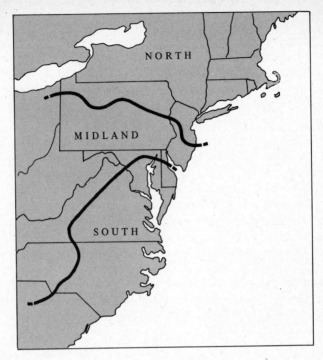

Figure 2.1 Major Dialect Areas of the Eastern United States

TOPICS FOR REVIEW

1. Dialect alignments have been disturbed by massive shifts in population, such as those in World Wars I and II. Nonetheless it is interesting to examine speakers for specific dialect characteristics. The large dialect groupings in this country reflect early settlement patterns (see Figure 2.1). The **northern dialect,** bounded by a line extending westward in northern Pennsylvania, reflects the speech of New England settlers. The **southern dialect** extends through northern Virginia to the Appalachians and then south, corresponding roughly to plantation culture. The **midland dialect** starts from the central area in the east, and then fans out, reflecting the migration patterns to the central and western states.

   Pronunciation of the middle consonant in *greasy* characterizes northern speakers, distinguishing their dialect from midland and southern. If [s] as in *cease,* the speaker is northern; if [z], as in *seize,* the speaker is midland or southern.

   Having made this determination, one can distinguish southern speech from midland and northern by checking the use of *you-all,* which is southern.

   Other characteristic features of the three dialects are as follows:

   1. Northern: *pail* (vs. *bucket*); *brook* (vs. *creek*); *angleworm* (vs. *earthworm,* etc.); *eavestrough* (vs. *gutters* on roof).

2. Midland: *blinds* (vs. *window shades*); *skillet* (vs. *frying pan*); *green beans* (vs. *string beans*); quarter *till* nine (vs. *to*).

3. Southern: *snap beans* (vs. *string beans*); *fritters; low* (vs. *moo*); *harp* or *mouth harp* (vs. *harmonica*).

By determining your own usage and that of others, you can learn something of linguistic heritages, whether the items in question were learned in the family, from acquaintances, or in school.

2. Another dialect area to explore is that of the low back vowels, as in *rot, wrought, wrote*. In the midland dialect these have the vowel of *wrought* in such words as *fog, frog, hog, dog, log, on, wash, wasp*. Northern and many southern speakers have the vowel of *rot* in at least some of these words. Northern speakers may also distinguish *horse/hoarse; forty/fourteen; morning/mourning* as they do *wrote* and *wrought*. In the northwest corner of this country and adjoining sections of Canada, speakers may pronounce *shone* with the vowel of *wrought*. Although these patterns exist in general, the social conditions of today lead to mixed dialects. It is highly interesting, then, to check your own forms of speech and to try to reconstruct how and where you acquired these— from your family, from friends, from teachers, or from some other source you may have accepted as a model. It is also interesting to explore the speech of your friends.

3. The "development of English in the United States" as H. L. Mencken phrased it in his book, *The American Language*,[6] provides many topics of interest. Among them is the fate of non-English dialects in America. Mencken has an appendix on these, which provides the starting point for those who wish to carry out further investigations. In keeping with the aims of this book, it is suggested that you pursue such a topic only if you have personal knowledge of speakers with one such language in their background—Greek, Polish, Portuguese, Swedish, or another. You could then produce a welcome contribution by examining the current use of that language in comparison with English.

You could concentrate on one of the following topics. Is the non-English language used only for restricted purposes, as in prayer, in discussions that are intended to be private, primarily by older speakers, by men or by women or by both, and so on? If used more widely, what is the age of the predominant speakers? Has it influenced the English speech of its users? To what extent has English influenced it? How do its speakers regard it? As an imperfect, often characterized as low, form of the language? As a bond with ancestors? With the homeland?

If you write a paper on this topic, you should note that the fourth edition of Mencken's book came out some time ago, in 1936, before any recent immigrants settled here. The two supplements came out somewhat later, in 1945 and 1948, but they focus on matters other than foreign language. The subsequent one-volume edition, by Raven MacDavid, may also be consulted.

---

[6] H. L. Mencken, *The American Language* (New York: Knopf, 1936).

4. The following topics on uses of language in society may also be selected for papers or for gaining insights into the variety of language.

  a. Topics dealing with variety in language
1. Why the English of my friend from Boston sounds funny. (For Boston you may substitute Atlanta, London, Delhi, Canberra, etc.)
2. How the language used in telephone conversations differs from normal language. Or how my friend Jay uses different ways of speaking on the telephone than in face-to-face conversation. (You may substitute *in selling insurance, in sportscasting,* or in some other situation.)
3. The editorial writers of the *Daily Chronicle* cannot write clear English. (For *editorial writers* you may substitute *textbook writers, scientists,* or other occupational group.)
4. Newspaper headlines and the confusion they cause.
5. Misleading advertising. (For example, "Nothing is cheaper than Jeffrey's tonic." Does *nothing* refer to another tonic or medicine, or does it mean absence of anything?)
6. How to say nothing and succeed in politics. (For *politics* you may substitute *administration, advertising, journalism, the legal profession, literary criticism, science,* or other occupation.)

  b. Topics dealing with attitudes to language
1. Words that turn me on and why
2. Words that turn me off and why
3. People who observe language taboos are dumb
4. Reasons for expanding your vocabulary and getting ahead in the world
5. Soul talk

  c. Topics dealing with mastery of language
1. Why I hate (or like) learning a foreign language
2. One of the most important characteristics of an educated citizen is an ability to communicate effectively
3. Why French (or some other language) is a funny language
4. Why English is a funny language. (Substitute your native language if you first learned to speak a language other than English.)
5. Foreign language study is unnecessary in the modern world. Or everyone should try to learn one artificial auxiliary language such as Esperanto.
6. No one in the modern world can be considered educated unless he or she has studied one or more foreign languages

  d. Language games
1. Pig Latin
2. Jokes depending on manipulation of language rather than situation
3. Riddles
4. Ritual insults (if you are personally acquainted with their use)

FURTHER READING

Clark, Virginia P., Paul A. Eschholz, Alfred F. Rosa, eds. *Language: Introductory Readings*. 2d ed. New York: St. Martin's Press, 1977.

Dale, Philip S. *Language Development: Structure and Function*. 2d ed. New York: Holt, Rinehart & Winston, 1976.

Dillard, J. L. *American Talk*. New York: Random House, 1976.

Jespersen, Otto. *Mankind, Nation and Individual: From a Linguistic Point of View*. London: Allen & Unwin, 1946.

Key, Mary Ritchie. *Male/Female Language*. Metuchen, N.J.: Scarecrow Press, 1975.

———. *Nonverbal Communication*. Metuchen, N.J.: Scarecrow, 1977.

Kirshenblatt-Gimblet, Barbara, ed. *Speech Play*. Philadelphia: University of Pennsylvania Press, 1976.

Nilsen, Don L. F., and Alleen Pace Nilsen. *Language Play: An Introduction to Linguistics*. Rowley, Mass.: Newbury House, 1978.

Piattelli-Palmarini, Massimo, ed. *Language and Learning. The Debate between Jean Piaget and Noam Chomsky*. Cambridge: Harvard University Press, 1980.

Sapir, Edward. *Language: An Introduction to the Study of Speech*. New York: Harcourt, Brace, 1921.

Sherzer, Joel. "Play Languages: Implications for (Socio-) Linguistics." In *Speech Play*, edited by Barbara Kirshenblatt-Gimblet, pp. 19–36.

Whorf, Benjamin Lee. *Language, Thought, and Reality. Selected Writings of Benjamin Lee Whorf*. Edited by John B. Carroll. New York: John Wiley, 1956.

CHAPTER THREE

The Sounds of Language

3.1 Characteristics of Sounds and Their Production

Language, according to a widely used definition, is a system of sounds for conveying meanings. In our literate society, written language may seem to be more important than speech. But even in the world today many people are still nonliterate. In the past only small numbers have been able to read and write. And some languages are still unwritten. Speech rather than the written language is accordingly primary. To understand language we must therefore know something about speech sounds. The study of them is now referred to as the speech sciences. These investigate the production of sounds, their characteristics, and our perception of them.

It is easy to demonstrate that writing systems represent speech imprecisely, especially a writing system like that of English, which was fixed five hundred years ago. In a sentence like the following, we cannot determine from the spelling whether the verb is in the present or past tense.

1. They set the table.

Moreover, unless we know the elements of the word *goshawk,* we may pronounce the first syllable as we do that of *goshawful;* when we relate it to *goose* and *hawk,* however, we pronounce it correctly. Children often have problems with spelling, as do foreigners. We ourselves have great difficulties with British place-names, which often have a transparent spelling but a considerably different pronunciation; for example, *St. John's College* is pronounced [sínjənz], *Cholmondely,* [čɔ́mli]. American place-names may also be treacherous, for example, *Connecticut, Milwaukee, Bexar* [pronounced like *bear*]. These and many other examples indicate that our spelling system is conventional rather than phonetic; it provides less indication of pronunciation than does the spelling system of many other languages, for example, Spanish. To understand our language we must go to the spoken rather than the written form.

Besides studying speech sounds to understand our own language, we benefit from a knowledge of speech sounds when we learn a foreign language. We generally find that its sounds differ in some respects from our own. To determine the differences, it is useful to know how the sounds of each language are produced. For example, the *r* in Spanish *radio* is made with a tap of the tongue tip in contrast with the gentle friction of the American *r* in *radio*. Our *t* and *d* are pronounced farther back in the mouth than the Spanish *t* and *d*. Such dissimilarities between comparable sounds in differing languages are the rule rather than the exception. Unless we know how we manipulate our vocal organs, we may fail to recognize these subtle differences and also fail to learn how to pronounce the language properly.

The general characteristics of speech sounds have long been known. In the nineteenth century this knowledge was greatly expanded, partly through concern with teaching the deaf. The family of Alexander Graham Bell, inventor of the telephone, was deeply involved in such teaching. Bell's own invention of the telephone in 1876 stemmed from his understanding of the sounds of language.

To represent these graphically, Bell's father published in 1867 an intricate system of writing known as Visible Speech; by indicating how the speech organs are used in articulating sounds, Visible Speech was designed to let the deaf see how to speak accurately. This system came to the attention of the celebrated English scholar Henry Sweet (1845–1922), who proceeded to become one of the masters of phonetics. His mastery was memorialized by George Bernard Shaw in *Pygmalion,* later *My Fair Lady,* where Professor Higgins is based on Sweet. As the play indicates, Sweet was remarkable in controlling the sounds of speech and in teaching them. Such mastery is based on knowing how speech sounds are produced and what their characteristics are.

The vowels, as in *Pete, top, cool,* are musical sounds. They are produced by our vocal organs, which we manipulate much as we would a wind instrument such as the clarinet, saxophone, or oboe. Of these the oboe with its double reed is most nearly parallel to the complex make-up of the vocal organs. Like the vibrating oboe reed, the vocal folds produce the fundamental tone. This tone is modified as it passes through the throat and mouth, which function like the resonating cavity of a wind instrument. By modifying this cavity through actions especially of the tongue and lips, we produce the vowels and consonants. An understanding of the vocal organs as they are used in speaking clarifies the phonological basis of language.

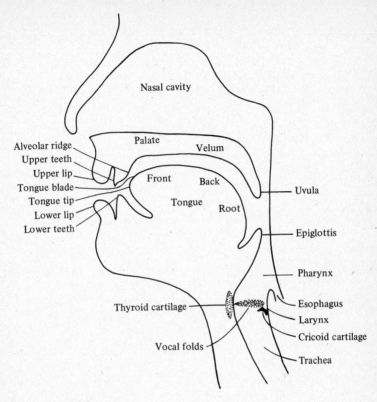

Figure 3.1 The Vocal Organs

The vocal organs are depicted in Figure 3.1. In describing their action we concentrate on (1) the vocal folds and (2) the mouth or oral cavity, for which the movements of the tongue and the lips are of central importance. A third organ, the nasal cavity, is central in the production of specific consonants and vowels, e.g. [m n ŋ ĩ ã ũ]. A fourth set of organs, the lungs, is important as the source of the air used in speaking.

The sounds produced by these organs consist of variations in air pressure. Like any sounds, they are defined by their frequency, their intensity, and their duration.

Sound frequency is a measurement of the number of vibrations per second; these are denoted as cycles. They are measured in Hertz (Hz); 100 Hertz equals 100 cycles per second. A bass speaker may produce a fundamental tone at 110 Hz. The ear interprets this as pitch; 110 Hz corresponds to A in the second octave below middle C. Instruments are generally tuned with the A above middle C at a frequency of 440 Hz.

When they pass through the vocal tract, fundamental tones are modified by its resonance frequencies. These resonances are known as **formants.** If a bass speaker pronounces the vowel of *Pete,* there will be a first formant of about 300 Hz and a second of about 2,100 Hz, as well as higher formants.

Vowels, then, are musical chords made up of three (and more) tones, the fundamental tone accompanied by two formants. Other vowels have their characteristic formants; that of *top* at about 700 and 1,100 Hz; that of *cool* at about 300 and 900 Hz. The frequencies of the formants are superposed on that of the fundamental tone. In this form they can be transmitted as electrical waves, for example, over telephone wires. They can also be superposed on radio waves, which themselves represent vibrations in kilohertz, or thousands of Hz. Transmitted as vibrations of the air the combined frequencies are perceived by our ears and interpreted as the vowels in question.

The intensity of sounds is determined by the amount of energy involved in their production. The duration corresponds to their length of production.

Speech sounds can be interpreted by their method of production, that is, their articulation. They can also be interpreted by the sound resulting from such articulation, that is, their acoustic effect. Accordingly we may describe sounds by means of articulatory phonetics or acoustic phonetics.

To represent sounds we use an alphabet based on the values of the Latin alphabet, signaling its phonetic use through square brackets [ ]. The Latin alphabet represents only a selection of the sounds of human speech. Moreover, two of its letters, *c* and *k* indicated the [k] sound in Latin, so that one of them is superfluous; we have continued this situation in English, using *k* to represent [k] before *i* and *e* as in *king* and *keen, c* before *a* and *o*, as in *caw* and *corn*. Other letters are used inconsistently; the letter *c* itself is a notorious example, having different values as in *cede, code, chief, machine*. In an attempt to achieve a general system of notation, an international phonetic alphabet (IPA) was drawn up at the beginning of this century. Today the IPA is widely used to indicate the presentation of speech, but not without some variations. The IPA chart is presented inside the front cover and on p. 40. Charts of the consonant and vowel symbols used for English and their values are given on pages 47 and 48.

3.2 The Speech Organs and Their Uses

3.2.1 The Lungs

The vocal organs below the larynx consist of the lungs with their outlets and the bronchial tubes, which merge in the trachea. In their speech function the lungs serve as containers of air. They are themselves inert but are alternately filled with air or emptied as the chest cavity is expanded by the action of the diaphragm, or they are permitted to contract when the diaphragm relaxes. When we speak, we use the air that is exhaled during the periods of relaxation. This airstream is modified as it passes through the larynx and other vocal organs.

3.2.2 The Larynx

The larynx is an organ at the top of the trachea, formed of cartilage and muscles; two muscular membranes make up the vocal folds (see Figure 3.2).

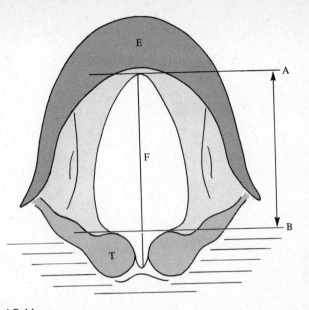

Figure 3.2 Vocal Folds

A schematic drawing of the vocal folds. *E* is the epiglottis; *F*, the vocal folds, and *T*, the tubercles formed by the corniculate and arytenoid cartilages. Line *A* is drawn tangent to the most anterior extent of the vocal folds and *B* tangent to the tubercles. (From a paper by Harry Hollien, ''Three Major Vocal Registers.'')

The vocal folds may be brought together tightly, opened slightly, or moved relatively far apart. When brought tightly together, they produce a glottal stop, [ʔ], as in *mʔm* 'no' as opposed to *mhm* 'yes.'

The space between the vocal folds is called the **glottis.** In breathing and for sounds like [f s p t k] the glottis is open; air then passes through it without friction or without producing voice. The sounds produced when the glottis is open are said to be voiceless.

When the vocal folds are brought together, so that air passing between them causes them to vibrate, the glottis is said to be closed, and the resulting sounds are voiced. Sounds like [v z b d g] are voiced, as are the resonants—for example, [m n ŋ w y l r] and the vowels.

The contrast between voiced and voiceless sounds is highly important for speech. As you will note in Figure 3.3, all the stops and fricatives may have voiceless and voiced pairs. As in Figure 3.3, the symbols for voiceless obstruents are generally listed before those for the voiced obstruents. Because of the importance of this contrast you should learn to recognize the difference. For this purpose, sequences like [sszzsszzsszz] or [ffvvffvvffvv] are helpful. If you feel your Adam's apple when pronouncing such sequences, you will note the vibration whenever you produce a [z] or a [v]. You can also put your hands over your ears, and when you pronounce the voiced sounds the accompanying vibration will be highly noticeable. All voiced sounds are accompanied by such vibration.

THE INTERNATIONAL PHONETIC ALPHABET
(Revised to 1951)

		Bi-labial	Labio-dental	Dental and Alveolar	Retro-flex	Palato-alveolar	Alveolo-palatal	Palatal	Velar	Uvular	Pharyn-gal	Glottal
CONSONANTS	Plosive	p b		t d	ʈ ɖ			c ɟ	k g	q ɢ		ʔ
	Nasal	m	ɱ	n	ɳ			ɲ	ŋ	N		
	Lateral Fricative			ɬ ɮ								
	Lateral Non-fricative			l	ɭ			ʎ				
	Rolled			r						ʀ		
	Flapped			ɾ	ɽ					ʀ		
	Fricative	Φ β	f v	θ ð s z ɹ	ʂ ʐ	ʃ ʒ	ɕ ʑ	ç j	x ɣ	χ ʁ	ħ ʕ	h ɦ
	Frictionless Continu-ants and Semi-vowels	w ɥ	ʋ	ɹ				j (ɥ)	(w)	ʁ		

							Front	Central	Back
VOWELS	Close	(y ʉ u)					i y	ɨ ʉ	ɯ u
	Half-close	(ø o)					e ø		ɤ o
	Half-open	(œ ɔ)					ɛ œ ə	ʌ ɔ	
							æ	ɐ	
	Open	(ɒ)					a	ɑ ɒ	

(Secondary articulations are shown by symbols in brackets.)

OTHER SOUNDS.—Palatalized consonants: ţ, ḑ, etc.; palatalized ʃ, ʒ: ʆ, ʓ. Velarized or pharyngalized consonants: ɫ, ɑ̶, ᵶ, etc. Ejective consonants (with simultaneous glottal stop): p', t', etc. Implosive voiced consonants: ɓ, ɗ, etc. ʀ fricative trill. σ, ʠ (labialized θ, ð, or s, z). ʠ, ʒ (labialized ʃ, ʒ). ʇ, ʗ, ʘ (clicks, Zulu c, q, x). ɪ (a sound between r and l). ŋ Japanese syllabic nasal. ʩ (combination of x and ʃ). ʍ (voiceless w). ɩ, ɣ, ɷ (lowered varieties of i, y, u). з (a variety of ə). ɵ (a vowel between ø and o).

Affricates are normally represented by groups of two consonants (ts, tʃ, dʒ, etc.), but, when necessary, ligatures are used (ʦ, ʧ, ʤ, etc.), or the marks ‿ or ⁀ (t͡s or t‿s, etc.). ⁀ ‿ also denote synchronic articulation (m͡ŋ = simultaneous m and ŋ). c, ɟ may occasionally be used in place of tʃ, dʒ, and ʆ, ʓ for ts, dz. Aspirated plosives: ph, th, etc. r-colored vowels: eɹ, aɹ, ɔɹ, etc., or eʴ, aʴ, ɔʴ, etc., or eₑ, aₑ, ρ, etc.; r-colored ə : əɹ or əʴ or ɹ or ə̗ or ɚ.

LENGTH, STRESS, PITCH.— ː (full length). ˙ (half length). ˈ (stress, placed at beginning of the stressed syllable). ˌ (secondary stress). ˉ (high level pitch); ˍ (low level); ˊ (high rising); ˏ (low rising); ˋ (high falling); ˎ (low falling); ^ (rise-fall); ˇ (fall-rise).

MODIFIERS.— ˜ nasality. ˳ breath (l̥ = breathed l). ˬ voice (s̬ = z). ʻ slight aspiration following p, t, etc. ˷ labialization (n̫ = labialized n). ˌ dental articulation (t̪ = dental t). ˙ palatalization (ż = ʑ). ˌ specially close vowel (ẹ = a very close e). ˌ specially open vowel (ę = a rather open e). ˔ tongue raised (e̝ or ẹ = e). ˕ tongue lowered (e̞ or ę = e). ˖ tongue advanced (u̟ or ʮ = an advanced u, t̟ = t̪). - or ̵ tongue retracted (i̵ or i̠ = ɨ, t̠ = alveolar t). ˒ lips more rounded. ˓ lips more spread. Central vowels: ï (= ɨ), ü (= ʉ), ë (= ə̈), ö (= ɵ), ë, ɔ̈. ˌ (e.g. n̩) syllabic consonant. ˘ consonantal vowel. ʃˢ variety of ʃ resembling s, etc.

COURTESY OF ASSOCIATION PHONÉTIQUE INTERNATIONALE

The vocal folds also provide the fundamental tone of the speaker. This tone is determined by the same characteristics as any tone produced by a wind instrument: the length, consistency, and tautness of the basic vibrating mechanism, in speech the vocal folds. Vocal folds of males are about twenty-three millimeters long; those of females, about seventeen millimeters long. Normally males produce a fundamental tone in the range of 109 to 163 Hz, females in the range 218 to 326 Hz. But the vocal folds permit a range from 42 to 2,048 Hz, as may be noted from the range of opera singers.

The fundamental tone is varied in speech, as in the intonation patterns of English sentences. Spoken by a male a typical English sentence, *How are you this morning?* may begin on a fundamental tone of 100 Hz, rise to 128 Hz, and then drop to 80 Hz.

3.2.3 The Organs Above the Larynx

The air modified for speech may be affected by three cavities after it passes through the larynx. These are the pharynx (or throat), the nose, and the mouth.

The pharynx is a tube-shaped channel leading to the nasal and oral cavities. Examples of sounds produced by it are the pharyngeal consonants of Semitic languages. It also acts as a resonating organ.

The nasal cavity consists of passages of bone, lined with mucous membrane. Since it is immovable, it is used only as a resonating body. Access to it is governed by the uvula, the fleshy appendage of the roof of the mouth. When the uvula is raised, access to the nose is closed off, forming what we speak of as a velic closure. When the uvula is lowered, air may pass through the nose, and nasal consonants or vowels will be produced. Examples of nasal consonants are [m n ŋ]. They correspond to [b d g] but in addition are produced with the velum or soft palate open.

When the uvula is lowered in the production of vowels, air escapes through both the nose and the mouth. Some languages, for example, Winnebago, have a full set of nasal vowels. Others, like French, have only a few, for example [ɛ̃] as in *plein* 'full' as opposed to nonnasalized [ɛ] in *paix* 'peace.' In still other languages, for example, English, no vowels are distinguished by nasalization.

The mouth is the cavity in which most of the consonants and the vowels are characteristically formed. Consonants and vowels differ from one another essentially because of the shape of the cavity by means of which they are articulated. The shape is determined by various degrees of narrowing or by closure at some point. Therefore, in describing any speech sound, besides noting the use of the vocal folds, we must state the place of articulation and the manner of articulation and for some the velic action.

3.2.4 Place of Articulation

The mouth is labeled for place of articulation in accordance with its structure. These labels are complemented by those for the tongue. Bounded in the rear by the throat, on the sides by the inner walls of the cheeks, and in the front by the lips, the shape of the mouth cavity is varied by the action of the tongue.

The tongue is a highly flexible organ, consisting of numerous muscles, almost any part of which can be moved. Parts of the tongue are labeled by the organs opposite them. The part opposite the walls of the throat is known as the **root;** that opposite the velum as the **back;** that opposite the palate as the **front;** and that opposite the teeth as the **blade.** The tip of the tongue is known as the **apex.** The tip may also be raised and pointed toward the back of the mouth; we speak then of *retroflex* articulation.

Possibly because of the difficulty of defining the articulatory involvement of such a flexible organ, the place of articulation is generally identified by the fixed organs opposite which the tongue is used for articulation. We have already noted that the back of the roof of the mouth ends in the **uvula,** a fleshy organ that can be trilled, as in one articulation of the French uvular [R]. Approximately 1.5 inches (approximately 4 centimeters) of the roof of the mouth from the uvula toward the lips do not cover an underlying bone; this section of the roof of the mouth is known as the **velum.** The 1.5 inches in front of the velum, with a bone as its base, are known as the **palate.** The part of the roof of the mouth that contains the roots of the teeth is known as the **alveolar ridge.** We speak then of **uvular, velar, palatal,** and **alveolar** articulation. If an intermediate position is used, we apply compound labels, as in **alveopalatal.**

You may determine the extent of the alveolar ridge by putting your finger into your mouth and noting the ridge made by the roots of the front teeth. By moving your finger farther into your mouth, you can locate the extent of the hard, bony roof, or palate, as well as the back, fleshy part or velum. A small mirror will assist you in identifying these and other characteristic vocal organs.

When the tongue is brought against the teeth, we speak of **dental** articulation; when the outgoing air is forced between the tongue and the teeth, we speak of **interdental** articulation.

The sounds articulated with the lips may be characterized by a narrowing or closure between the lips and the teeth (usually by bringing the lower lip to the upper teeth) or between the lips themselves. We speak then of **labiodental** and **bilabial** articulation. The lips may also be rounded, or spread, especially in the production of vowels. English [u] as in *moo* is accompanied by rounding; English [i] as in *me* is accompanied by spread lip position.

3.2.5 Manner of Articulation

At any of the places identified, the manner of articulation may vary. Sounds produced with a complete closure are called **stops.** Bilabial stops are produced with closure of both lips, as in English [p b] of *pan, ban.* Closure may also be made between the tip of the tongue and the alveolar ridge, as in English [t d] of *tan, Dan;* between the front of the tongue and the palate, as in English [k g] of *keel, gear;* or between the back of the tongue and the velum as in English [k g] of *cool, gore* (see Figure 3.4).

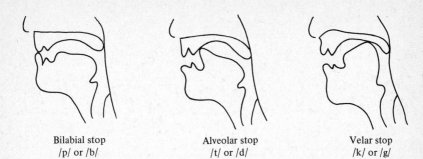

| Bilabial stop | Alveolar stop | Velar stop |
| /p/ or /b/ | /t/ or /d/ | /k/ or /g/ |

Figure 3.4 Articulation of Stops

Stops are generally made on the outgoing stream of air. Some languages, however, have sounds involving the incoming airstream at the lips and accordingly are implosive. Such sounds are known as **clicks.** They are found in languages of southern Africa, such as Xhosa. Some clicks are used by English speakers as signals, such as the dental *tsk, tsk* for expressing disapproval.

If the organs are only approximately 90 percent closed, friction is produced, and the resulting sounds are called **fricatives.** Two subclasses may be distinguished by the kind of opening. If it is relatively wide, we speak of a **slit fricative,** such as the labiodental [f v] in English *fear, veer;* interdental [θ ð] in *thin, then;* palatal [ç ǰ] in German *ich* 'I,' and in dialect German *siegen* 'win'; and the velar [x γ] in Scottish *loch,* German *ach* 'alas,' and in dialect German *Wagen* 'wagon.' If the opening is small, permitting the onrush of air through a trough, we speak of **groove fricatives.** The opening may be made over the tip of the tongue, with onrushing air producing a hissing noise against the teeth, [s z] as in English *sip, zip.* A groove fricative may be made at the front of the tongue, with the hissing noise produced against the palate, [š ž], as in English *rush, rouge.*

One further set of consonants consists of a stop with homorganic fricative, that is, stops and fricatives produced with the same articulatory organs. These are called **affricates.** Affricates may be produced at any of the places of articulation: at the lips, [pf], as in German *Pfad* 'path'; at the alveolar area, [ts], as in German *Zeit* 'time'; at the palatal area, [tš] or [č], as in English *church,* and voiced [dž] or [ǰ], as in English *judge;* and at the velar area, [kx], as in Swiss German [kxu] 'cow.'

Because stops and fricatives are characterized by articulation involving an obstruction, they may be referred to by the general label **obstruent.** Consonants other than the obstruents are characterized by sonant qualities rather than by obstruent articulation. In producing the sonants, or **resonants,** the articulatory passages have relatively wide openings. We can classify the resonants into four groups: nasals, laterals, trills and flaps, and semivowels or glides. In contrast with *obstruent* as a term for sounds characterized by obstruction, the term **approximant** is used for all ''open'' sounds, both resonants and vowels.

The **nasals** are articulated with oral obstruction at some point; since the uvula is lowered, resonance is produced in the nasal cavity. Nasals are generally voiced, and so they correspond to oral stops accompanied by nasal resonance: bilabial [m] to [b]; dental or alveolar [n] to [d]; velar [ŋ] to [g]. They may however be voiceless, for example, in rapid English utterances like *rush 'em;* they are then transcribed with the usual diacritic for voicelessness, a small circle below the letter, [rəšm̥]. Icelandic has voiceless nasals, as in *hnifur* 'knife.'

The **laterals** are produced with oral obstruction at some point, but an opening is made to the side of the obstruction. The obstruction is generally formed with the tip of the tongue, and the air is permitted to pass to the right or left of it or to both sides. Lateral resonance varies in accordance with the shape that the tongue takes. If the front of the tongue is raised, a *clear l* results, as in English *leer;* if the back is raised, a *dark l* results, as in English *rule*. A dark, or back, [l] may be marked with a cross, wavy line, as in Polish [ł]. While generally voiced, laterals may be voiceless, as in Icelandic *hle* [l̥e:] 'lee' and Welsh *ll,* as in *Llewelyn*. The French /l/ may also have a voiceless variant, as in *peuple*.

The English treatment of Welsh voiceless [l̥] illustrates how foreign sounds are often interpreted in accordance with one's native sound system. When initial, [l̥] struck English ears as beginning with a voiceless fricative. Thus the name *Llewelyn* was heard as *Fluellen*. This form of the name is used for one of the soldiers in Shakespeare's play *King Henry V*. Similarly, the name *Floyd* is based on the spoken form of *Lloyd*. In this way the names of places as well as people are often modified, so that the foreign sounds are replaced by one or more native sounds.

In producing resonants, the oral passage may be closed rapidly by a vibrating organ: the uvula or the apex of the tongue. If there is a single closure, we speak of a **flap;** if repeated closures, a **trill.** For a uvular trill or flap [ʀ] is used, as for French *ratte* [ʀat]; for an alveolar or dental trill, [r]. To distinguish a flap from a trill, the symbol [ɾ] is used for flaps. Often, as in some varieties of English, *r* sounds are not trilled, or even flapped, but the tongue is raised to produce slight friction. The *r* sound may also be voiceless, as in Icelandic *hrafn* [r̥avn] 'raven.' The French *r* may have a voiceless variant, as in *quatre* 'four.'

The resonants produced by the largest degree of opening are the **semivowels,** also called **glides.** They are articulated with relatively complete closure but also with an opening movement of the organs concerned. For example, [y], as in English *yet,* begins with the tongue close to the palate, in the position for [i], and continues with the tongue moved downward rapidly. The articulation of [w] is generally compound, involving the velar area and the lips, and begins with the tongue close to the velum, in the position for [u], with rounded lips, continuing with the tongue moved downward rapidly and the lips spreading. Semivowels may be voiceless, as in the pronunciation of *what* and *when* in some forms of English.

3.2.6 The Vowels and Diphthongs

If the articulation of the consonants is characterized by closure, that of the vowels is characterized by a relatively open position of the vocal tract. Yet despite the classification of vocal sounds into two large groups, there is no absolute distinction

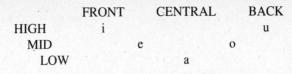

Figure 3.5   The Latin Vowels

between consonants and vowels, as the semivowels may indicate. Semivowels of English begin with relatively complete closure, as consonants, and end with a larger opening, as vowels.

In the articulation of vowels the glottal tone is modified by resonating chambers formed primarily in the mouth but also in the pharynx and nose. It is largely the use of the tongue and the lips that determines the individual vowels. The position of the tongue, whether raised in the front, the central, or the back part of the mouth, is basic to a discussion of the vowels. From the position of the tongue's highest point, we speak of front, central, and back vowels (see Figure 3.5).

The shape of the vowel cavities is also determined by the degree of opening. If the tongue is as far as possible from the roof of the mouth, we speak of a low, or open, vowel. If it is as close as possible to the roof of the mouth, without setting up friction or producing a stop, we speak of a high, or close, vowel. If it is between close and open position, we speak of mid vowels. Other intermediate positions may be specified, as on the IPA chart (Figure 3.3), as half-open and half-close.

Latin, Spanish, Japanese, and many other languages have a simple vowel system consisting of five members. These are often portrayed with the figure of a triangle, so that one speaks of a vowel triangle. IPA took the values of the symbols from Latin. These values are also observed in the languages of the European continent. They are accordingly referred to as Continental, to contrast them with the values found in English spelling. We will discuss the English values below.

An example of these is found in the Latin expression: *argumentum ad hominem* 'an argument directed at the individual' (rather than at the facts). Spanish examples may be illustrated with place-names, such as *Acapulco, Mexico,* as may Japanese: *Sendai, Honshuu.*

The lips may be spread, pursed or rounded, or neutral. Since the rounded position has the greatest articulatory effect, we speak of rounded or unrounded vowels. Back vowels are typically rounded, for example, English [u] in *cool;* front vowels are typically unrounded, for example, English [i] in *keel;* and central and low vowels tend to have neutral lip positions, for example, English [ə] in *dull* and [a] in *doll.* Yet front, central, or back vowels may be either rounded or unrounded. Japanese *u,* for example, is relatively unrounded, as in *kuru* 'come.' Two dots over a vowel symbol may be used to indicate front rounded vowels, as in German *München* 'Munich' and *Mönch* 'monk,' or special symbols may be used, as in IPA notation.

For the articulation of vowels the vocal organs are maintained relatively steady. But vocalic segments may also be characterized by motion from one position to another. When they are, the beginning and end points of the motion are specified, and we speak of diphthongs. Although various conventions are used, in recent texts the closer portion of the diphthong has been indicated by a consonantal symbol: [y] if the diphthong moves to a front position, as in *I* [ay], *boy* [bɔy]; [w] if the diphthong moves to a back position, as in *cow* [kaw].

Discussions of vowels and diphthongs often refer to them as distinct sets. But vowels may vary in pronunciation from pure to diphthongal. The vowels of French, Italian, and Spanish are relatively pure. Those of English are relatively diphthongal, especially [e] as in *may,* [o] as in *mow,* and for many speakers even others such as [i] as in *me* and [u] as in *moo*. Because of their diphthongal articulation some transcription systems indicate these vowels with two symbols: *ey ow iy uw.* The diphthongal articulation also leads native speakers of English to pronounce the vowels of foreign languages with an accent. Conversely, native speakers of Spanish and other languages with pure vowels are often recognizable because of their carryover of these into English. German has pairs of long and short vowels. The long vowels are relatively pure. They are generally distinguished from the corresponding short vowels by a colon, as in [bi:t] *biet* 'offer' versus [bit] *bitt* 'ask.' The terms *long* and *short* vowels are often used for other languages as well, even for English; but the English vowels are distinguished primarily for quality, not quantity.

Additional variations of vowels are by nasality, discussed in Sections 3.2.3 and 3.2.5, and voicelessness. Japanese has voiceless variants of vowels, especially between two voiceless consonants or after a voiceless consonant at the end of a word; in these environments [i] and [u] are often unvoiced, as in the numerals for 'one' and 'two': [hi̥totsu̥ futatsu̥].

3.2.7 The IPA Chart of Consonants and Vowels

The consonants and vowels are summarized in Figure 3.3, the 1951 revision of the International Phonetic Alphabet. When voiceless and voiced consonant pairs are given for a place and manner of articulation, the symbol for the voiceless consonant is always listed first. The symbols for unrounded vowels precede those for rounded vowels.

3.3 The Consonants and Vowels of English

Like all languages, English includes only a selection of the many possible sounds. All forms of standard English have twenty-four consonants, illustrated in Figure 3.6. There are about half this number of vowels; the precise set differs from area to area. The variety of English illustrated in Figure 3.7 has eleven vowels and three diphthongs.

Differences are also found in transcriptions, especially of the vowels. The differences result from the application of varying principles. These are evident in

	LABIAL	DENTAL	PALATAL	VELAR
STOPS vl.	/pap/ pop	/tap/ top	/čap/ chop	/kap/ cop
vd.	/bir/ beer	/dir/ dear	/ĵir/ jeer	/gir/ gear
FRICATIVES vl.	/fɪn/ fin	/θɪn/ thin /sɪn/ sin	/šɪn/ shin	/hɪm/ him
vd.	/vɪm/ vim	/ðɪs/ this /zɪp/ zip	/bež/ beige	
NASALS	/dɪm/ dim	/dɪn/ din		/dɪŋ/ ding
GLIDES	/wɪt/ wit	/rɪp/ rip	/lɪp/ lip	/yɪp/ yip

Figure 3.6   The English Consonants

/mi/ me   /mu/ moo
  /mɪs/ miss   /tʊk/ took
    /me/ may   /tək/ tuck   /mo/ mow
    /mɛs/ mess   /tɔk/ talk
      /mæs/ mass   /ma/ ma
/may/ my   /kaw/ cow   /kɔy/ coy

Figure 3.7   The English Vowels

the conventions used in dictionaries to indicate pronunciation; these conventions also lead to differences from the IPA. Systems of transcriptions vary because dictionaries aim to include symbols for all dialects of a language.

Among reasons for following the practice of the IPA is its application for other languages, not simply English. On the other hand, many of the IPA symbols are not found on typewriter keyboards. Partly for this reason some treatments of English pronunciation have used transcriptions which for the most part could readily be typed as well as written by hand. This practice owes in some part to Leonard Bloomfield, who adapted the symbols as he thought fit. Among aims influencing his and his successors' transcriptions was that of using symbols to reflect differences in pronunciation among languages. For example, the last vowel in the Spanish pronunciation of *Santa Fe* is pure, with no y-offglide as in its English counterpart. Bloomfield accordingly transcribed *bay* as /bej/, *egg* as /eg/.[1] This practice has become less common in recent texts, and we therefore follow the IPA system here.

Figure 3.6 lists the twenty-four consonants of English with characteristic examples. The transcriptions are given within slant lines, to indicate phonemic transcription. It is important to master the symbols; you can gain such mastery by daily transcribing short texts, as from a comic strip like *Peanuts*.

Figure 3.7 illustrates a vowel system with eleven vowels and three diphthongs. They are arranged in accordance with their articulation, as illustrated in Figure 3.8.

[1] Leonard Bloomfield, *Language*, p. 91.

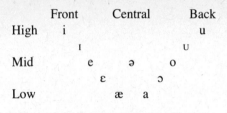

Figure 3.8   Position of English Vowels

The precise beginning and ending of the diphthongs vary. Some speakers begin the diphthong of *cow* with the vowel of *mass,* not *ma;* some speakers begin the diphthong of *coy* with the vowel of *mow* not *talk.* If you are one of those speakers you may adapt your transcription accordingly.

Learning a transcription for English is especially important because, as we noted above, our system of orthography was fixed when printing was introduced into England and has been retained with little change during the subsequent five centuries. Such a conventional spelling system may mislead us when we need an accurate understanding of the sounds, as in teaching children to read, in reading and writing poetry, in learning foreign languages, and in studying the history of languages. Practice in transcribing, as noted above, will lead to knowledge of the sound system of English and provide insights into methods for solving problems that arise in learning and teaching languages.

3.4 Intensity, Pitch, and Timing

The phonetic entities discussed so far are made primarily by the vocal organs above the larynx. The first consonant of a rapid pronunciation of [nansɛns] is articulated by the tongue's producing a closure at the alveolar ridge, with the velum open, permitting nasality. The first vowel is made by the tongue's providing a relatively large opening in the mouth and so on, with the other sounds symbolized.

But a sequence of several sounds in English is also accompanied by differences in intensity and pitch and by variations in timing. Such differences are determined by the muscles controlling the outflow of air, for example, by the muscles regulating the vocal folds.

3.4.1 Stress Accent

The significant use of intensity in speech is referred to as stress or stress accent. When we compare the two words *incense* 'aromatic substance' and *incense* 'to make angry,' we note a strong stress on the first syllable of the first, on the last syllable of the second. The difference between the otherwise similar sequences consists in the differing force with which the two syllables are pronounced. Strong stress is marked with an acute accent [ˊ]. Weak stress may be marked with [ˇ], but is generally unmarked.

Such differences may be noted most clearly in English nouns and verbs that differ only in the place of accent, such as *permit*. If pronounced alone, the noun is stressed [pə́rmɪt]; the verb [pərmít].

To illustrate the effect of stress on consonants and vowels, we may note the differing [p] sounds in *permit*. When the strong stress falls on the first syllable, as in the noun, the [p] is aspirated [pʰə́rmɪt]. When the strong stress falls on the second syllable, the [p] has less aspiration. And whichever syllable has the strong stress is also longer, as we noted above. Because stress, pitch, and timing have an influence over the consonantal and vocalic segments of speech, they are called **suprasegmentals,** in contrast with consonants and vowels, or segmentals.

The interplay of stress and other suprasegmentals has led to differing analyses of the role of stress in English. Many scholars assume a third stress for English in addition to the strong, or primary, and the weak, or lack of stress. They base this analysis on the contrasts between the two sequences like *a permit* [ə pə́rmìt] and *a poor mitt* [ə púr mìt] (as in answer to *What kind of a mitt caused Schroeder to drop the ball?*) Such a stress may be called middle and marked [`] in contrast with weak [˘] and primary [´] stresses. As here, it falls on less prominent elements, and on the second elements of compounds, for example, *workbook* [wə́rkbùk] as contrasted with *worker* [wə́rkər].

In other languages, stress may play a totally different role. In Japanese, for example, it is nonsignificant; word pairs may be distinguished by differences in pitch patterns, for example, *haná* 'flower' versus *hana* 'nose.' In Latin, stress is determined by the quantity of syllables and their position with regard to the end of the word. Most monosyllables are stressed, for example, *pếs* 'foot.' If the second-last syllable is long, it is stressed, for example, *amā́vi* 'I loved.' But if the second-last syllable is not long, the third-last syllable is stressed regardless of its quantity, for example, *discípulus* 'disciple.' Accordingly the position of stress in Latin is predictable in general terms from the quantity of vowels in the last syllables of words.

3.4.2 Pitch Accent

As utterances vary in stress, they may also vary in pitch. For example, the sequence *She wrote Harriet* may have the relatively highest pitch on any of three syllables, depending on how the sequence is used in response to various questions. In answer to *Who wrote Harriet?* the pitch pattern for *She wrote Harriet* may be represented:

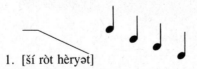

1. [ší ròt hèryət]

In answer to *Whom did she write to?* the pattern is:

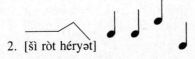

2. [šì ròt héryət]

In answer to *Why doesn't she do something about inviting Harriet?* the answer might be:

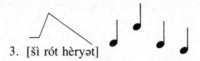

3. [ʃì rót hèryət]

When we examine these pitch sequences, we may note some essential contrasts in the use of pitch in English. The most prominent syllable is associated with the relatively highest pitch. Speech material earlier in the sentence is produced with a relatively lower pitch. At the very end of such sentences the pitch becomes quite low. Numerous methods are used to mark the contrasts. Many discussions use curved lines to suggest variations in melody. Others use musical notes, like those above. Both are troublesome to produce, especially when typing or printing texts. Accordingly numerals superposed before the syllable with pitch are often found: [1] for the low pitch level at the end of the sentence, placed before any terminal marker; [2] for the normal pitch level; [3] for the pitch on the most prominent syllable.

Using numerals, the three contrasting statements given above would be written:

1. [[3]ʃí ròt hèryət[1]]
2. [[2]ʃì ròt [3]héryət[1]]
3. [[2]ʃì [3]rót hèryət[1]]

As illustrated here, pitch generally remains relatively constant in English before the most prominent vowel and trails off gradually to the end of such simple sentences. By using three numerals then—for example, [2] [3] [1]—for the pitch sequence in the preceding sentence, we can label the sequence as effectively as if we drew lines or used musical notation—and at far lower cost in printing.

It is characteristic of English utterances pronounced with assurance that they follow a [2] [3] [1] pattern, or as in the first variant above, a [3] [1] if the first syllable is most prominent, whether they are declarative sentences, such as *He did it* /[2]hi [3]díd ıt[1]/ or questions introduced by *wh-* words *Who did it?* /[2]hu [3]díd ıt[1]/. The exact pitches will vary considerably with the fundamental tone of the speaker. A male, speaking in a bass voice, will produce his pitch [3] at a far lower absolute pitch than will a female speaking in a soprano voice. But each one's pitch [3] will be higher than his or her pitch [2], which in turn will be higher than pitch [1]. The contour of the recording of a bass speaker's sentence *I'll come along* reflects these three pitch points with initial pitch at 100 Hz, highest pitch at 128 Hz, and the lowest trailing off at 80 Hz. Comparable variation would be found in the sentences of speakers having a higher speaking voice.

Other languages use pitch in other ways, such as differing configurations on individual syllables. Such a pitch is often labeled **tone,** and the languages that use pitch this way are labeled **tone languages.** In Putonghua, for example, syllables may be pronounced with level tone (indicated with ^{1}), with rising tone (^{2}), with compound falling-rising tone (^{3}), or with falling tone (^{4}). The numeral 'one' for example has tone ^{1}, *i*^{1}; 'man' has tone ^{2}, *ren*^{2}; 'five' has tone ^{3}, *wu*^{3}; and 'two' has tone ^{4}, *er*^{4}. Some syllables with identical segmentals differ only in tone, for example, *mai*^{3} 'buy' and *mai*^{4} 'sell.' In addition to its use of pitch in this way Putonghua also uses pitch in sentence intonation patterns.

3.4.3 Timing; Juncture

Juncture is a term used for the variations in timing and quality associated with the ends of clauses or lesser breaks. Breaks in the sequence of sounds distinguish such sequences as *catch up/catchup, ketchup; say Ling!/sailing; add my ring/ admiring*. These may not be present in rapid speech. But in careful speech they separate words from one another. In transcription they are represented by + or more commonly by a break between segments.

For English, three terminal junctures have been proposed. One is characterized by a rapid drop of pitch, with fading of the speech material. It is used in crisp, businesslike pronunciation, as in assertions and questions with *wh-* words: *He's coming. Who's coming? She took the car. Hurry up!* It may also be used in greetings like *Good-bye*. When it is, however, the connotation of finality virtually makes the greeting mean 'Good-bye and good riddance' or 'It's about time you left.' Transcriptions indicate it with #, an arrow pointing downward ↓, or with a period.

Another terminal juncture is characterized by a slight upturn of the voice. It indicates politeness, a gentle, occasionally wistful, mood, and is used when we wish to sound ingratiating: *Why, that's Billie. Come in. Sure, honey, you can take the car*. Generally, greetings are pronounced with this juncture, unless relationships are ruptured and external appearances nevertheless require some kind of utterance. Transcriptions indicate it with two vertical lines ||, an arrow pointing upward, ↑, or even with a question mark.

The third terminal juncture is neither fading nor slightly rising, but level. It suggests continuation and is typically used at the ends of clauses that are followed by others in the sentence, for example, *Come in . . . and take a seat*. When such clauses are used, the pitch pattern is often /^{2} ^{3} ^{2}/ as in /^{2}kəm ^{3}ín^2| ənd . . ./. It is indicated with one vertical line |, an arrow pointing to the right →, or with a comma.

In keeping with the first indications for each of these, they are often referred to as double-cross, double-bar, and single-bar juncture. We may illustrate three characteristic English patterns by means of the example, *Who's that lady?*

/^{2}hùz ðæt ^{3}lédi^1#/ (a factual question)
/^{2}hùz ðæt ^{3}lédi^1||/ (a friendly question)
/^{2}hùz ðæt ^{3}lédi^2|/ (an incomplete question, probably concluded with a clause
  like *that you were telling me about*)

Pitch patterns associated with terminal junctures are known as **intonation patterns.** Here are some examples for *It's a yellowhead:*

$^{2\ 3\ 1}$ #   /^{2}ìtsə ^{3}yélǝhèd^1#/   (indicating assurance)

$^{2\ 3\ 3}$ || /^{2}ìtsə ^{3}yélǝhèd^3||/   (indicating doubt)

$^{2\ 3\ 2}$ | /^{2}ìtsə ^{3}yélǝhèd^2|/   (indicating incompleteness)

Such intonation patterns are essentially unchanged when the clause is extended, for example:

> *It's a genuine yellowhead.*
> *Maximilian is a genuine yellowhead.*
> *Maximilian certainly looks like a genuine yellowhead.*

Any sequence covered by such an intonation pattern may be called a phonological clause. These generally correspond to syntactic clauses, but they may not. For example, in deliberate speech one might say ^{2}*Màxi^{3}mílian^2| ^{2}is a ^{3}génuine^2| ^{3}yéllowhèad^1#.*

There are numerous intonation patterns in English, as also in any other language. Two further common ones may be exemplified. In counting, for example, one may avoid variations in pitch, as in the following:

$$/^1wǝ́n^1 \rightarrow {}^1tú^1 \rightarrow {}^1\theta rí^1 \rightarrow {}^1fór^1 \rightarrow {}^1fáyv^1\#/$$

or in the livelier:

$$/^2wǝ́n^2 \rightarrow {}^2tú^2 \rightarrow {}^2\theta rí^2 \rightarrow {}^2fór^2 \rightarrow {}^2fáyv^1\#/$$

And when counting rapidly, the numerals simply make up a clause:

$$/^2wǝ̀n\ tǝ\theta rì\ fòr\ {}^3fáyv^1\#/$$

Every language has such patterns accompanying segmental sequences. We have discussed these from an articulatory point of view. In the next section we will examine acoustic characteristics of speech.

3.5 Acoustic Characteristics of Vowels and Consonants

English and other languages have been described primarily in terms of articulation of speech sounds, as noted above. The reason students of language have relied so heavily on this approach is in part because the analysis of the actual sounds produced in speaking requires acoustic equipment. Such equipment was relatively cumbersome until the 1940s, when the sound spectrograph was devised. The sound spectrograph analyzes the acoustic characteristics of the stream of sound, providing accurate displays of the actual speech. It is also used for analysis of other sounds, such as bird song. This discussion will be limited to a brief presentation of findings resulting from spectrographic analyses of human speech and some of their implications for the study of language.

As we noted in Section 3.1, the sounds of speech have three dimensions: frequency, intensity, and duration. A spectrograph analyzes sounds for these dimensions and depicts the results on a film. At frequencies where acoustic energy is expressed, the film is blackened. On the film, frequency is indicated by marking on the vertical dimension. A vowel as in *beet* with formants at 300 and 2,300 Hz would be represented by two dark bands, in addition to that for the fundamental, as illustrated in Figures 3.9, 3.10, and 3.11. The intensity of the energy at each of these levels is marked by the darkness of the spectrogram. The duration of the energy is indicated on the horizontal dimension.

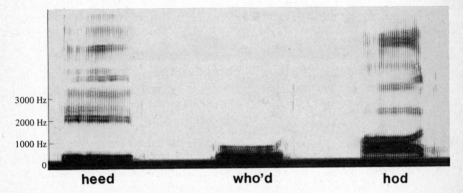

Figure 3.9 Spectrogram of the Vowels *heed, who'd, hod*

This spectrogram represents the vowels in *heed, who'd, hod*. Note the two lower formants, centering about 275 and 2300 for *heed;* 300 and 850 for *who'd;* 700 and 1100 for *hod.* Note also higher-level formants.

Formant Frequencies of Vowels

in

	PETE	COOLED	THE TOP
Third formant	3,200	2,250	2,450
Second formant	2,300	800	1,100
First formant	300	300	700

LOCUS OF SECOND FORMANT TRANSITIONS FOR p, k, t

For p: 700   (entails rise of second formant in *Pete*)
For k: 3,000   (entails fall of second formant in *cooled*)
For t: 1,800   (entails fall of second formant in *top,* but rise in *teeth*)

Spectrograms make it possible to determine precisely the characteristic formants of any speech. The reproductions given here illustrate three vowels of the English vowel system: [i a u]. As is evident from these, the front vowels have two formants relatively far apart, as given for *beet* in the previous paragraph. The first formant of [u] is also low, but its second formant is much lower than is that of [i]. The first formant of [a] is higher, and its formants are relatively close to each other. If we were to examine the formants of the other vowels, we would find a progressive rise in the lower formant of front vowels as well as back, and a progressive reduction in the second formant for both sets.

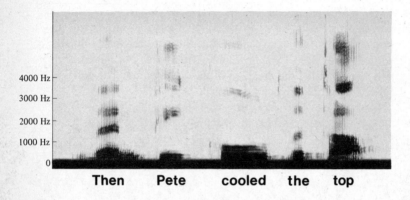

Figure 3.10 Spectrogram of the Sentence *Then Pete cooled the top*

This spectrogram represents an entire sentence. Note the formants of the vowels in *Pete* centering on 300, 2300, 3200; *cooled,* centering on 300, 800, 2250; and *top,* centering on 700, 1100, 2450. You can also see the rise in the second formant of [i] in *Pete* after [p], and the drop in the second formants in *cooled* and *top* after [k] and [t].

Such distribution of energy is interpreted by our auditory apparatus as vowels. After it has been determined, similar distribution of energy can be produced in other ways, for example, electronically. That is to say, speech can be synthesized. The process has been greatly improved; today computer-directed speech seems almost as natural as human speech. Some composers have included parts for human voices in their computerized compositions. Further improvement will upgrade the sound produced by the computerized devices used for commercial purposes, as in the Speak-and-Spell learning device. Such applications provide additional impetus for investigating in great detail the sounds of speech.

Through the investigations already carried out, certain elements of speech have been more precisely determined, such as the speech signals that we interpret as stops. Stops are produced by complete closure; this means that "speech sounds" like [p t k b d g] have no sound. Nevertheless speakers somehow "hear" them. Even before spectrographic analysis was perfected, investigations determined that stops are detected in adjoining vowels; if a tape recording of a word like *Pete* is made and the tape corresponding to the articulation of [p] is cut off, the word is still recognized as *Pete*. Spectrographic analysis clarifies the basis for the interpretation. In vowels pronounced after [p], the initial part of the second formant rises.

After a [t], as in [top], the second formant drops initially. After a [k], the drop is somewhat sharper (see Figure 3.11). In learning to interpret speech, human beings have come to interpret such configurations as stops.

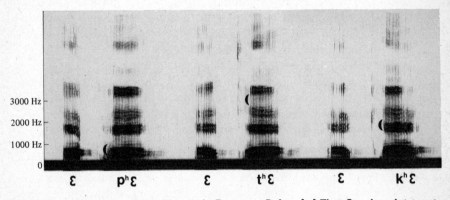

Figure 3.11 Illustration of the Change in Formants Before [ε-] That Speakers Interpret Successively as the Consonants εpʰε, εtʰε, εkʰε

This spectrogram illustrates the locus of second formant transition for *p, t, k,* as indicated by the discs. The locus for *p,* around 700, entails a rise in the second formant in (pʰ)ε; the locus for *t,* around 3000, shows a fall in the third formant of (tʰ)ε; the locus for *k,* around 1800.

Such findings are highly important for the understanding of language and its interpretation. The physical characterizations of any stop, for example, are not constant. Rather, they are conveyed in a kind of code, as the initial segment of neighboring sounds. Humans have the capability of interpreting such codes; animals apparently do not. The difference may relate to physiological differences. For the interpretation of codes, which may well be unique to human language, the left hemisphere of the human brain is especially adapted. Increased information about the acoustic characteristics of language has in this way led to important discoveries concerning the capabilities of the human brain as well as to clarification of the bases of speech.

3.6 Distinctive Features

The increasing information about articulatory and acoustic properties of speech sounds led scholars to determine their distinctive characteristics. One such characteristic is VOICE. It is the feature distinguishing the final consonants of the following: *sop/sob, sot/sod, sock/sog, safe/save, hiss/his,* and so on. These ten speech sounds are characterized either as having VOICE, denoted as + VOICE, or as lacking it, − VOICE. If instead of assuming contrasting sounds like p/b, t/ d, and so on, we indicate the central characteristic of these contrasts, we can reduce the number of basic entities in speech. The entities determined in this way are known as distinctive features (DFs).

In the study of DFs, phonologists set out to determine those basic to all languages. The number proposed varies from about twelve to twenty, depending on the theoretical position of the investigator. We will not note all of these, for we are primarily concerned with the principles involved in feature analysis. The distinctive features given here apply to English.

The feature VOICE relates to the functioning of the vocal folds. Another feature relating to a primary organ of articulation is NASAL. Through this feature, English [m] as +NASAL is distinguished from [b], which is −NASAL; similarly for the other nasals and voiced stops, [n] and [d], [ŋ] and [g].

Further features relate to place of articulation. If sounds are produced in the front part of the mouth, they are labeled +ANTERIOR, i.e. [p b f v t d θ ð s z] as opposed to [č ǰ k g š ž], which are −ANTERIOR. Sounds may be produced with the tongue raised in front, as for [č ǰ š ž]. This feature is known as CORONAL, that is, articulation with crown shape of the tongue. [p b f v] are then +ANTERIOR, −CORONAL, [t d θ ð s z] are +ANTERIOR, − CORONAL, [č ǰ š ž] are −ANTERIOR, + CORONAL, [k g] are −ANTE-RIOR, −CORONAL.

Features relating to manner of articulation distinguish stops, fricatives, and resonants. The feature distinguishing vowels and resonants from stops and fricatives is SONORANT. The feature distinguishing stops from fricatives is STOP. Among the resonants [l] is distinguished from [r] by the distinctive feature LATERAL.

To distinguish the vowels, the features refer to the body of the tongue. If the back is characteristically involved, as for [u o], the vowel is labeled +BACK, as opposed to [i e], which are −BACK. In addition two features identify the height of the tongue: HIGH and LOW. Of a three-vowel series like [i e æ], [i] is labeled +HIGH, −LOW; [e] is labeled −HIGH −LOW; [æ] is labeled −HIGH, +LOW. The features discussed may serve to illustrate analysis of a phonological system for its distinctive features.

A distinctive feature analysis is carried out not only to arrive at a smaller number of basic entities in a language; through such features one can also depict simply many alternations of sounds in a language, such as those of the English past tense marker. After sounds labeled −SONORANT, −VOICE, such as [p f k s], as with *tap, laugh, pack, pass,* this is [t]; after sounds labeled −SONORANT, +VOICE, such as [b v g z], as in *rob, rave, rig, raze,* this is [d]. The alternation between voiceless and voiced forms of the past tense marker can then be readily stated in terms of distinctive features. Moreover, only one distinctive feature is involved, both in the last element of the verb stem and in the past tense marker. Such patterning of grammatical markers is common in language.

The modification of just one feature of sets of sounds is also characteristic of language change. As we note in greater detail in Chapter 10, Section 10.2, an earlier [d] changed to [t] in Germanic, the subbranch of the Indo-European languages to which English belongs. The change did not take place in Latin, so that *duo* 'two' maintains the earlier form of the initial consonant in *two.* The Germanic change simply involved modification of one distinctive feature. In this way the treatment of speech sounds by features illuminates processes involved in grammatical markers of languages and also in sound change. Moreover, it illustrates how speakers classify similar sounds, whether in grammatical categories like the English past tense or in language change.

Feature analysis led to a further important finding about language: the functioning of paired phonemes. When two or more phonemes differ in only one feature, the one with + is often more restricted in distribution. German [t/d] provides the classic illustration. In final position only [t] is found. The noun for 'treaty' *Bund* has the form [bund] when followed by [ə], so that it has the alternating forms [bunt bund], while *bunt* 'variegated' has only [bunt]. German [t], then, is less restricted in distribution than is [d]. The more highly restricted member of such sets is known as the **marked** and less highly restricted as the **unmarked** member.

This kind of relationship has been observed throughout language. The English present tense, for example, is used more widely than the past, for it can refer to future time as well as present, as in *We leave tomorrow* and *We leave right now* compared with *They left yesterday*. Marking also applies semantically; literary words are often marked in contrast with words used in everyday speech. Besides clarifying relationships at the phonological level, the study of distinctive features has contributed an important insight into the way language is structured.

3.7 How Speakers Interpret the Sounds of Speech

Knowledge of the diversity of the sounds used in speech indicates that speakers do not identify meanings from absolute physical characteristics. On the one hand, the vocal apparatus of men, women, and children is such that they produce different sounds for any simple utterance such as *Better luck next time!* Yet when we hear any English speakers producing this sequence, we identify it as the same utterance, whether the speaker is male or female, young or old. Even the sounds of an individual speaker differ from utterance to utterance and environment to environment. English speakers produce different *t* sounds in *time, next, battle, stop,* and so on. Yet we identify the different *t* sounds as the same. Increasing investigation of languages in the previous century led to the conclusion that speakers interpret languages not by sounds but by sound classes. As we noted in Chapter 1, Section 1.4, the sound classes were labeled **phonemes,** a term that has been maintained in language study.

The assumption of phonemes as the sound units of language received support as linguists dealt increasingly with non-European languages. Dramatic examples were found in the study of American Indian languages, as the distinguished anthropologist Franz Boas indicated. In his words, Pawnee "contains a sound which may be heard more or less distinctly sometimes as an *l*, sometimes as *r*, sometimes as *n*, and again as *d*."[2] Boas added that for the Pawnee speaker it is without any doubt "the same sound." Today "phoneme" is used for such classes of "same sounds." Their variants are known as **allophones.** Examination of these

---

[2] Franz Boas, *Introduction to The Handbook of American Indian Languages* (Washington, D.C.: Georgetown University Press, n.d.), p. 11.

variants indicates that all are +VOICE and +ANTERIOR; in the Pawnee system the other features, such as NASAL, were not primary. Pawnee speakers disregard such features as redundant. English speakers on the other hand perceived Pawnee [l] and [r], [n] and [d] as distinct because speakers initially interpret the phonemic system of other languages in terms of their own. The English-speaking investigators heard different sounds; the Pawnees did not because of the way their phonological system is structured.

The term *phoneme* was introduced by a Polish linguist, Baudouin de Courtenay, and his student, Mikolaj Kruszewski, as they encountered similar problems in dealing with languages of the Soviet Union. Today the term is in general use.

Linguists differ in their use of the term *phoneme*. The differences result from the scope of material taken into consideration and from the theoretical views of the linguists concerned.

The earliest definitions were based on analysis of the sound component alone. Such definitions were proposed by linguists who investigated previously unknown and unwritten languages. In such investigation linguists first need adequate means for writing the language. Typically they collect a list of several hundred words. Then they determine which of these differ in only one respect, as do *pat/bat, pan/ pin, pick/pig.* Such contrasting sets are known as minimal pairs. In these three sets of minimal pairs we find eight phonemes: /p æ t b n ɪ k g/. Since these are identified solely from examination of the phonological component without consideration of word classes, such phonemes are labeled **autonomous.**

There were also differences among the linguists who proposed autonomous phonemes. Leonard Bloomfield regarded phonemes as the "smallest units which make a difference in meaning."[3] His definition is in keeping with his mechanistic approach to the study of language. Edward Sapir viewed phonemes as conceptual units, in accordance with a mentalistic approach.[4] Whichever approach they pursued, contemporaries and followers of Bloomfield and Sapir analyzed languages in terms of autonomous phonemes. Their treatment of the sound component of language is now known as **classical** or **autonomous** phonemics.

A late work of Bloomfield's and much of the recent study of the sounds of language have identified phonemes by their position in the system of language, not by phonological structure alone. The fundamental handbook developing this view is *The Sound Pattern of English* by Noam Chomsky and Morris Halle. This treatment of phonology is known as **systematic.** Chomsky and Halle point to variations like that in *pronounce/pronunciation*, where the stem varies between [nawns] and [nəns], in *divide/division,* where the stem varies in vowels between [ay] and [ɪ], and so on. In their view, speakers have an underlying conceptual representation, from which differing surface forms arise, as we have noted for Pawnee. In systematic phonemics, however, the representation is determined by regarding not the phonological component alone, but also the syntactic component

---

[3] Bloomfield, *Language,* p. 138.
[4] "The Psychological Reality of Phonemes," *Selected Writings of Edward Sapir in Language, Culture and Personality,* ed. by David G. Mandelbaum (Berkeley: University of California Press, 1963), pp. 46–60.

and sets of lexical items. The word *pronunciation* is clearly based on the stem also found in *pronounce*. Many words in English show such alternations: *renounce/renunciation, organize/organization, revise/revision, reduce/reduction*, and so on. The units posited underlying such sounds are known as **systematic phonemes.**

Systematic phonemes are highly abstract. Relations to them by the sounds themselves, such as [ay]/[ɪ] as in *revise/revision*, [u]/[ə], as in *reduce/reduction*, and so on are given in rules representing the processes involved. Systematic phonological study is concerned with such rules.

In rules for systematic phonemes the abstract element is placed on the left of an arrow that points to the surface element. If we propose *d* as the underlying form of the past tense marker in English, the following rule would indicate the form in such words as *pass*.

$$d \rightarrow t$$

This rule states that *d* is changed to *t*.

The rule could also be indicated in terms of the feature affected:

$$d \rightarrow \text{-VOICE}$$

This rule states that *d* becomes unvoiced.

And since the element involved is the past tense marker, rather than a sound like [d], the rule might be indicated as follows:

$$\text{PAST} \rightarrow \text{-VOICE}$$

This rule indicates that the past tense marker becomes unvoiced. That is to say, a syntactic marker is given as input to a phonological rule.

In this way systematic phonemics treats the entire language as a closely interrelated system rather than treating the phonological segment as somehow autonomous, parallel with other strata.

The rule in its forms above is obviously incomplete, because some past tense markers in English are voiced, as in *gaze/gazed*. To complete the rule, the environment in which it applies must be provided. This is done by means of a slant line followed by a representation of the specific environment—for the verbs above, after a voiceless consonant. The position of the past marker is indicated by /__. The rule then would be as follows:

$$\text{PAST} \rightarrow \text{-VOICE/-VOICE\_\_}$$

This rule indicates that the past tense marker is voiceless after a voiceless phoneme.

Phonological rules yielding the actual utterances and no unacceptable utterances are referred to as **generative.** A generative grammar contains such rules for all segments of language.

3.8 The Bases of Phonology

Students of phonology attempt to learn by means of the procedures sketched above how human beings recognize the elements of language. As phonetic investigations have demonstrated, no two sounds are alike. A mechanical analysis will not sort these into classes in the same way that speakers of a language do. But human speakers achieved such recognition long ago. As evidence for it we may point to the alphabet.

The earliest writing systems we know used pictures for words or concepts, as we will see in Chapter 10, Section 10.7. But a system of signs for words, that is, a logographic system, is cumbersome, for ideally it should include a symbol for every different word or concept. A complete set of symbols in such a writing system would add up to about 30,000 characters, approximately the number developed by the Chinese. Such a large set is obviously impossible for the average speaker to master. While the Egyptian system did not contain as many, it began to be reduced in the third millennium B.C. At some time during the first millennium B.C., the Greeks hit on the alphabet. It subsequently has come into general use and is the model for any writing system developed for nonliterate peoples today.

The alphabetic writing system assumes some kind of abstract or ideal sound, which everyone who knows a language recognizes and tries to approximate. Such sounds must be determined by relationships with other sounds, as are the elements in the vowel triangle. If we speak Spanish or another language with a five-vowel system, presumably we determine the grid of a given speaker. If we hear a female speaker, who speaks at a higher fundamental than does a male speaker, we apparently determine her vowel triangle by comparing her individual sounds—and the same for a male speaker. It is sometimes proposed that this is why conversations begin with essentially meaningless utterances—in our culture utterances such as *Hello, Hi, How are you,* then continue with comments on the weather or the like. In other societies, such as that of Egypt where the weather is too constant for any but the dullest comment, the further conversation concerns relatives, their state of health, whereabouts, and so on. Whether or not we use such a practice for tuning in on someone else's set of sounds, we somehow comprehend the great variety of speech we hear.

Machines do not have this ability, not yet at any rate. If they did, many activities would be simpler for us. If, for example, we could reach a party by speaking the number rather than dialing, telephoning would be much easier for us and for the telephone company. Scientists have been working on equipment to distinguish the ten words, *one* to *zero,* that are used to reach a party. But not even the most advanced computerized equipment has been 100 percent successful in dialing correctly by voice, even for one speaker. Similarly, our lives would be greatly simplified if we could call our banks and arrange in this way for bills to be paid rather than writing checks or dealing with a teller on the phone; banks do not allow this because they cannot identify their patrons by their voices. These problems are being studied, and also others, such as arranging for machines to comprehend and translate speech. These are tasks for the future, but tasks that human beings long ago mastered.

In efforts to understand how humans achieve such mastery, phonologists have advanced various theories concerning our recognition of phonemes. Initially many regarded phonemes as classes with a specific characteristic feature. Thus, every English /a/ would have some feature that would distinguish it from /i e æ u/ and other sounds. Others considered this view inadequate, because of such matters as the great variety of sounds in one phoneme like English /t/. Thereupon phonemes were assumed to be classes based on characteristic features and on distribution. Speakers somehow master the characteristic of English that we pronounce the middle /t/ of *Trenton* by closing the velum; we do not use this shortcut for the /p/ of /sə́mpən/ 'something' nor for the /k/ of /də́ŋkən/ 'dunking.' A velic stop in English is then interpreted as a /t/ because speakers have learned that its distribution permits this variant as well as an alveolar stop. By this view a phoneme is defined as a class of sounds, phonetically similar and distributed in complementary arrangements in a given language. Many grammars and handbooks on language follow this definition. It is the point of view held in **autonomous phonemics.**

Yet often we recognize words without hearing all the sounds, as happens on a noisy street. If under such circumstances someone says "This is Trenton," we may not even perceive all the sounds in *Trenton,* let alone hear whether the medial /t/ is made by velic or by tongue closure. To explain this situation, some phonologists propose that our perception is made in accordance with an abstract representation of the sequences of language in our brain. This is the view of **systematic phonemics,** for which phonology is far more abstract than for autonomous phonemics.

Yet not all systematic phonologists hold the same views regarding abstractness. For some, the representation in our brain is relatively "natural," so that phonemes are somewhat like the articulated sounds. Others favor considerable abstractness; Chomsky and Halle proposed as the systematic phoneme in words like *divine/ divinity* an *i* as in *seen,* that is to say, an element like the comparable element in Middle English. Theoretical assumptions, then, lead to widely varying positions.

Future investigations may provide an accurate understanding of the way in which our brain controls language. Studies in the past, however, have already clarified many of the problems regarding the phonological component of language.

3.9 Sounds and Phonemes as the Building Blocks of Language

For understanding language it is important to remember that sounds and phonemes have no inherent meaning. We cannot ascribe any meaning, for example, to the [a] of *top, bottom, John, Marge,* and so on, nor to any of the consonants. They are simply the building blocks out of which the meaning-carrying segments are constructed.

Language in this way differs from other symbolic systems, such as the numeral system. In this system the entity 2 always means 'two,' whether standing alone, after other numerals as in 32, or before others as in 283. Moreover, as we have noted above, it is the entire signal that means 'two.' Similarly, gestures are signals conveying meaning as a whole. When we wave to indicate good-bye, we cannot segment any single part of the gesture as signifying 'good,' another as 'bye.' Gestures, like numerals, convey meaning as unsegmentable entities.

The sounds of bird song also are units with such total meanings, some of warning, others of happiness, and so on. And all animal cries may be similar in not having structures, in one of which the sounds are central, in others of which the forms carry meaning. It is this multilayered structure that gives language the capability of expressing so many meanings and of being modified to express even more. The numeral system, on the other hand, can only refer to quantity and order, merely one of the many areas covered by language expressions. Nor do bird song, animal cries, gestures, and other signaling devices permit the huge number of meaning-bearing signals nor the flexibility of human language.

Meaning is carried by words, by sentences, and by texts. In any sentence, such as *Then Pete cooled the top,* we find words like *cool, top* and smaller segments like *-ed* that have meaning. Moreover, the sentence as a whole has meaning; in its form it implies that the speaker is convinced of the accuracy of the statement, is not asking a question, and so on. In addition, meaning is carried by the text in which such a sentence is found; unless we know the text for this sentence, we have only a vague idea what *top* refers to and who Pete might be. Finally, speakers determine meanings from the situations in which sentences and texts are used; unless we know the situation in which this sentence was produced, we have no idea what *top* refers to, whether the top of a hot car, of a boiling mass, or the like. The next chapters will examine how we make use of the stretches of sound known as words, sentences, and texts in communication and how we interpret them in their various contexts.

QUESTIONS FOR REVIEW

1. Compare the vocal tract used in producing speech with a wind instrument like the oboe.

2. Identify the important vocal organs.

3. Identify the basic characteristics of sounds, including vocal sounds. In what way do vowel sounds compare to musical chords?

4. Define *formant,* stating characteristic formants for specific vowels.

5. What is the IPA?

6. Discuss the various roles of the vocal folds in speech, defining also *glottis*.

7. Indicate how the nasal cavity is used in speech, identifying sounds characterized by nasal resonance.

8. Identify the *velum*, the *palate*, and the *alveolar ridge*.

9. Distinguish dental from interdental sounds.

10. Distinguish stops from fricatives and from affricates.

11. Distinguish obstruents from resonants and from approximants. Identify four kinds of resonants.

12. Distinguish clear *l* from dark *l*.

13. How did the English name *Floyd* arise from Welsh *Lloyd?*

14. Describe the articulation of the glides *w* and *y*.

15. Distinguish among high, low, and mid vowels, giving examples.

16. Distinguish among front, central, and back vowels, giving examples.

17. Distinguish between vowels and diphthongs.

18. What is meant by the *vowel triangle?* What does it represent?

19. Why is a phonetic transcription a better representation of the sounds we produce in speaking than our regular spelling system?

20. State some uses of transcription.

21. Describe briefly the role of intensity in speech. The role of pitch.

22. Distinguish between segmentals and suprasegmentals.

23. Identify the three important terminal junctures for English.

24. Distinguish among the English intonation patterns: [231], [233], [232].

25. How does the sound spectrograph portray speech sounds?

26. How do we ''hear'' voiceless stop sounds?

27. What are distinctive features (DFs)?

28. Give pairs of sounds distinguished by the DF VOICE.

29. Give pairs of sounds distinguished by the DF NASAL. By the DF ANTERIOR. By the DF BACK.

30. How does the use of distinctive features provide greater understanding of phenomena in language, such as the variation between [d] and [t] in the past tense of English verbs?

31. What is meant by marking? Which is the marked member of a set contrasting in the use of a distinctive feature?

32. Cite evidence for the view that speakers interpret their language in terms of sound classes or phonemes rather than of sounds.

33. How are autonomous phonemes determined?

34. How are systematic phonemes determined?

35. In what way does alphabetic writing provide evidence that speakers interpret their language as consisting of phonemes?

36. Why are machines unable to interpret sequences of speech accurately?

37. How do speakers interpret speech, according to the theory of classical phonemics? Of systematic phonemics?
38. How do phonological segments contribute to the conveying of meaning in language?
39. What are the carriers of meaning in language?

PROBLEMS FOR REVIEW

1. As we have noted in this chapter, it is important to practice transcription. Practice transcription with the sets of words given here.

1. foot	11. mine	21. eight	31. wolf	41. eve	51. pout
2. half	12. sky	22. law	32. rude	42. sit	52. rote
3. but	13. vein	23. whose	33. then	43. owl	53. all
4. make	14. thing	24. talk	34. knot	44. awe	54. dough
5. feet	15. tight	25. loose	35. old	45. pique	55. noise
6. pay	16. bait	26. lose	36. leech	46. walk	56. put
7. shad	17. boot	27. cheap	37. sight	47. boil	57. fun
8. yet	18. thin	28. cot	38. who	48. cat	58. cue
9. rout	19. sign	29. son	39. shock	49. hymn	59. leave
10. day	20. wait	30. shook	40. chin	50. go	60. died

2. The following words consist of two syllables, one of which is stressed, the other not. Transcribe the words, indicating the strongly stressed syllables by placing an acute accent [´] over the vowels in them.

1. debtor	11. ginger	21. today	31. manner	41. awful
2. battle	12. apply	22. lawyer	32. hanger	42. heavy
3. heiress	13. joyful	23. owlish	33. biscuit	43. suited
4. butler	14. heaven	24. attract	34. across	44. sighted
5. undone	15. needle	25. reset	35. issue	45. boiling
6. consent	16. creature	26. prefer	36. gentle	46. cement
7. obtuse	17. salmon	27. mention	37. measure	47. defend
8. drama	18. persuade	28. awake	38. water	48. gallop
9. people	19. volume	29. demur	39. anguish	49. abstain
10. suggest	20. beauty	30. suppose	40. liar	50. subtract

3. The following pairs contrast in stress, one of each pair containing a strong and a weak stress, the other containing a strong and middle. Transcribe these items, indicating the middle stress with a grave accent mark [`].

1. blackbird	blacker	6. forecast	forlorn
2. dollhouse	dollar	7. grassland	grassless
3. folklore	solar	8. longhorn	longing
4. die-hard	diet	9. Near East	nearest
5. deep end	depend	10. passkey	passage

4. The following sets deal with special problems in English. Transcribe them. Completing this exercise will help you to master these problems.

1. feud	food	6. vision	fission	11. long	longer	length
2. pure	poor	7. azure	Asher	12. was	wash	watch
3. hue	who	8. measure	mesher	13. singer	finger	ginger
4. tutor	tooter	9. leisure	legion	14. dog	mock	hog haunt
5. booty	beauty	10. beige	badge	15. soot	spoon roof	root

5. The following sentences each contain words with the same vowel to simplify transcription of intonation patterns. Transcribe each sentence, including stress marks and indication of pitch contours with their junctures.

1. Rick hit his chin.	6. They stayed eight days.
2. Ben sells shells.	7. Whose group moved?
3. Shocks stop clocks.	8. Joe's boat won't float.
4. Saul called Paul.	9. How loud now?
5. Wolf pulled.	10. Lloyd's voice joined Roy's.

6. In transcribing longer sequences, it is useful to select simple verse, if only to observe rhythms and possible rhyme. Limericks like the following by Edward Lear are good selections.

> There was a Young Lady of Russia,
> Who screamed so that no one could hush her;
>   Her screams were extreme,
>   No one heard such a scream,
> As was screamed by that lady of Russia.   5
>
> There was an old person of Dean,
> Who dined on one pea and one bean
>   For he said: "More than that
>   Would make me too fat."
> That cautious old person of Dean.   10

7. A further example of Franz Boas's on difficulties that speakers of English face in analysis of American Indian languages is taken from Lower Chinook. It contains, in the words of Boas, "a sound which is readily perceived as a *b, h,*

m, or *w.*'' What features do these three Lower Chinook allophones have in common? Why would English speakers interpret them as separate phonemes rather than as allophones of one phoneme?

8. The British joke about the four partially deaf men on the train from Carlisle to Bristol. This is a part of their conversation:

What station is this?
Wembley.
No, it's Thursday.
So am I. Let's get off and have a pint.

Cite other jokes which rely on phonetic confusion.

FURTHER READING

Borden, Gloria J., and Katherine S. Harris. *Speech Science Primer. Physiology, Acoustics, and Perception of Speech.* Baltimore: Williams & Wilkins, 1980.

Bronstein, Arthur J. *The Pronunciation of American English.* New York: Appleton-Century-Crofts, 1960.

Daniloff, Raymond, Gordon Schnuckers, and Lawrence Feth. *The Physiology of Speech and Hearing.* Englewood Cliffs, N.J.: Prentice-Hall, 1980.

Denes, Peter B., and Elliot N. Pinson. *The Speech Chain.* Garden City, N.Y.: Anchor Press, 1973.

Heffner, Roe-Merrill S. *General Phonetics.* Madison: University of Wisconsin Press, 1949.

Jakobson, Roman. *Child Language, Aphasia and Phonological Universals.* Trans. by A. R. Keiler. The Hague: Mouton, 1968.

Ladefoged, Peter. *A Course in Phonetics.* New York: Harcourt Brace Jovanovich, 1975.

MacKay, Ian R. A. *Introducing Practical Phonetics.* Boston: Little, Brown, 1978.

Schane, Sanford A. *Generative Phonology.* Englewood Cliffs, N.J.: Prentice-Hall, 1973.

Sommerstein, Alan H. *Modern Phonology.* Baltimore: University Park Press, 1977.

CHAPTER FOUR

Analytic Grammars

4.1 Traditional and Structural Approaches to Language

Grammars have been produced for millennia, from various points of view and for various purposes. In Chapter 1 we noted that Panini constructed a grammar of Sanskrit a half millennium before our era, concentrating especially on its forms. His grammar analyzes simple words, determining roots and inflectional elements. It also analyzes compound words, distinguishing formations such as those of *bluebird* 'a blue bird,' *Bluebeard* 'a man having a blue beard,' *fourteen* 'four plus ten.' With Panini's grammar we can determine precisely the forms of Sanskrit. It greatly influenced Western grammatical theory when it came to be known in the nineteenth century.

The Greeks also developed grammars concerned largely with the analysis and classification of forms. These grammars classify forms by parts of speech—nouns, verbs, and so on. They also analyze sentences for logical relationships, such as subjects and predicates. The parts of speech found in subject and predicate position are in turn identified. In a sentence like *He reads rapidly,* *he* is identified on the one hand as a pronoun, on the other hand as the subject of *reads rapidly*. Such grammars lead to a twofold analysis, once for morphological classes, once for syntactic function.

Latin grammars followed the model of Greek grammars. They were widely studied throughout the Middle Ages, when Latin was the language of learning throughout Europe. As grammars were produced for the modern languages, including English, the pattern of Latin grammar served as model. Words and also clauses were classified by parts of speech. Some traditional grammars defined subordinate clauses as those "used as a part of speech,"[1] as in sentence 1b:

1a. *I expect success.*
  b. *I expect that I shall succeed.* [noun clause]

Since such grammars were produced in accordance with a long tradition, they are known as **traditional grammars.** Traditional grammars have been maintained in our educational system for English and other languages. To use the widely available grammars, dictionaries, and handbooks on writing, it is necessary to know the bases for them. In this chapter we examine these bases and also shortcomings that have led to new approaches.

Some of the shortcomings have to do with the analysis of complex sentences. Traditional grammars have no problems with sentences like the following:

2. *A child won the prize.*

Sentences like the following, however, are less simply analyzed:

3. *It was a child who won the prize.*
4. *What the child won was a prize.*
5. *There was a child who won a prize.*

Traditional grammars introduced special terms for words like *it, what, there* as used in these sentences. Yet these seem ad hoc, designed rather to solve embarrassment encountered in treating the variants of simple sentences like sentence 2 illustrated with sentences 3, 4, and 5 than to get at the heart of language.

A different kind of problem led to a departure from traditional grammar, especially among American linguists in the first half of this century. Traditional grammar did not lend itself well to the treatment of many non-European languages. Some languages, like Japanese, do not have a separate part of speech corresponding to pronouns. Moreover, verbs and adjectives may fall into one class, as in Japanese. Other languages, such as Chinese and Vietnamese, have no inflections, making it difficult to determine parts of speech in the traditional manner. Still others, like Eskimo, combine constituents so that a sentence is equivalent to a word. To treat these languages suitably, linguists set out to develop a grammatical approach that would analyze any language in terms of its own structure. This approach is now known as **structural linguistics.**

Structural linguists analyze language in accordance with external form. A word like *child* is labeled a noun because it has inflections for the possessive and the

---

[1] George Lyman Kittredge and Frank Edgar Farley, *An Advanced English Grammar*, 1973, pp. 157–159.

plural: *child, child's, children, children's.* By contrast *I* with the three additional forms *me, my, mine* is a pronoun because it has forms characteristic of this morphological class. Japanese does not recognize this distinction; words like *kodomo* 'child' and *watakushi* 'I' cannot be distinguished by inflection. Structural grammars, then, put Japanese "nouns" and "pronouns" into one morphological class.

Structural linguists view languages as consisting of various layers or strata. Each layer is treated separately. The first layer is the phonological; analysis of the sound system of language as a separate stratum is carried out by means of "autonomous phonemics," as discussed in Chapter 3, Section 3.8. Thereupon the forms are analyzed in a morphological stratum. Subsequently sentences are treated in a syntactic stratum, in which nominals (so-called to distinguish them from the morphological class of nouns), verbals, and so on are identified. Relationships between these layers are described. An example is the representation for the morphological affix indicating the genitive; labeled {Z} at the morphological level, this corresponds to three variants at the phonological level /əz s z/. The precise distribution of these and other such phonological variants was determined. The study of relationships between layers was known by compound terms, such as morphophonemics.

Structural grammars aimed to be highly rigorous. The elements of any one language, whether at the phonological, morphological, or other levels, were solely identified by their form. Definitions based in part on meaning were rejected. Unlike the practice of traditional grammar, nouns were not to be identified as "names of persons, places, or things," but rather as elements identified by inflections. This approach was held to be greatly superior to that of traditional grammar, by which words like *fire, unicorn, abstraction* did not fit the traditional definition, for none of these is the name of a person, place, or thing.

Structural grammars were especially successful in treating exotic languages at the phonological and morphological levels. In contrast with earlier grammars for exotic languages, these were not presented as languages similar in some respects to Latin, different in others. Instead, the elements were identified by their role in the various layers. Japanese provides ready examples, such as the pattern for negative sentences.

> 6. *Watakushi wa   okane ga   nai.*
>   I (*topic*) money (*sub*) is-not
>   'I have no money.'

Here the particle *ga* marks the subject at the syntactic level, which in English is treated as object. (To clarify the difference for students, paraphrases like the following may be given: 'As for me, there is no money.') In this way a structural grammar of Japanese describes the language by its characteristics, with no regard for those of other languages.

While structural grammars were successful in their phonological and morphological analyses, they treated complex syntactic strings poorly. For example, relationships such as those among sentences 2, 3, 4, and 5 were not well handled. Capable treatment of such sentence variants was produced only by a further grammatical approach, transformational grammar, which is examined in Chapter 5. Yet structural grammars made many contributions to our understanding and description of language, especially in dealing with morphology. Because of these contributions, and because many grammars and other handbooks apply their findings, the approach of structural grammar, as well as that of traditional grammar, cannot be disregarded. The morphological classifications as well as the terminology of these grammars are used generally in linguistic study.

Moreover, in spite of differences between traditional and structural grammars, they are alike in maintaining an analytic approach to language. Both approaches aim to determine the constituents of words and sentences, concentrating as we have noted on forms. In this chapter we concern ourselves with these two types of grammar in their treatment of language, especially for its morphological characteristics.

4.2 Words and Morphemes

When we examine statements about language, we may come to believe that words are the fundamental carriers of meaning in language. Dictionaries inform us of meanings largely by listing words. But they also define smaller units, such as -ment in enjoyment, the past tense marker -ed, the noun plural marker -s, and so on. And when we examine many words we find that they are made up of two or more smaller units. Words like carport, carload, carsick clearly consist of two such units, as do government, movement, automobile, and so on. When we compare such words with others, we find that they consist of elements with a specific meaning. The first element of automobile means 'self,' so that the entire word means 'self-moving'; similarly, autograph means 'writing by one's own hand, a person's signature,' autocratic means 'ruling by oneself, ruling alone.' The fundamental carriers of meaning are such elements with meaning, called **morphemes,** as we noted in Chapter 1, Section 1.3.

It is instructive to observe how speakers deal with morphemes. Some time ago the morpheme auto was taken from the compound term automobile and treated as an independent word. And when Alexander Calder along with other artists developed moving sculpture, the element mobile was made into an independent word. The new words may be quite independent of their historical origin, as we may note from the newly coined word gasohol. This is a compound made from gas(oline) and (alc)ohol. In origin, alcohol cannot be divided into these segments. It is one of the words taken over from Arabic in medieval Spain at a time when the Arabs were superior in learning. In Arabic, alcohol consists of the article al followed by the noun kohl 'antimony'; alcohol originally meant 'the antimony.' Powdered antimony is the blue cosmetic used by Arabic women on their eyelids. The word shifted in application to the liquid because it too is smooth and silky. Other words of the same construction are algebra (from al plus gebr) 'the uniting (of parts of equations),' *alchemy* (from *al* plus *kimiya*) 'the black art,' as in *chemistry* without the article, and the famous castle in Granada, *Alhambra* (from *al-hamra*) 'the red (castle).' The inventors of the word *gasohol* obviously did not know the origin of *alcohol;* nonetheless they treated it as a compound of elements, somewhat like *automobile* and *gasoline* (from *gas* plus an adjectival form of the Latin word for 'oil' *oleum*). Such examples illustrate that speakers analyze words into smaller elements with meaning.

In dealing with any language a grammar determines its morphemes and how they are arranged. The morpheme structure typical for English roots is a syllable like *car, load, gas.* This structure is found generally in Indo-European languages; English *sit* corresponds to the Latin stem *sed-, bear* to Latin *fer-, kin* to Latin *gen-* as in *genus,* each root having a basic meaning. Arabic root morphemes, on the other hand, like those of Hebrew and the other Semitic languages, typically consist of three consonants, such as H M R 'redden, dye red' as in *Alhambra* or S F R 'travel' as in *safari,* or K T B 'write.' When words are made from these roots, vowels are added between or after consonants. Arabic *katab* means 'he wrote'; *kitaab* on the other hand means 'something written, book'; *kaatib* means 'having written.' Triconsonantal roots in this way carry the content meanings in Arabic and the other Semitic languages, while interposed vowels indicate particular grammatical or lexical forms. These examples of characteristic English and Arabic morphemes illustrate the systematic relationships between morphology and meaning.

We can think of sequences of language, words, sentences, and texts, as strings of elements arranged according to certain rules. When we speak, we select appropriate elements from a set and arrange them appropriately, for example:

7. *She bought gasohol for her car.*

When we produce such a sentence, we perform two processes: (1) we select the desired element for each position in the sentence and (2) we arrange these elements in accordance with the rules of that language. These two processes are referred to as **selection** and **arrangement.**

In producing an English statement, we generally have an initial subject, followed by the predicate. The subject most often consists of a noun or a pronoun. To produce the sentence above, we select from six possible pronouns: *I, you, he, she, we, they* as well as other subclasses of pronouns. We could also select a subject from the class of nouns; the possibilities are then far greater, for example, *Helen, my neighbor, the taxi driver,* and so on. The process of selection applies also to the other word classes, or parts of speech, and to subclasses. The nouns of sentence 7, for example, are concrete and inanimate. Grammars identify such subclasses as well as the larger classes.

As words and morphemes are arranged in sequences such as sentences, segments of them may be modified. When a sentence like 8 is spoken rapidly, the final [v] of *have* is devoiced to [f].

8. *I have to buy gas.*

In 9, the final [z] of *has* is devoiced to [s].

9. *She has to buy gas.*

This process is known as **modification.** It is widespread in English; compare the devoicing of *d* in *used to, supposed to,* and so on. An equivalent term from Sanskrit grammar is sandhi (literally 'together-put = combine'). Modification, or sandhi, refers to the processes affecting morphemes when they are arranged together in sequences.

The study of words and morphemes with regard to the three processes—selection, arrangement, and modification—is known as morphology. Here we examine selection first, especially the selection classes referred to as parts of speech.

4.3 Parts of Speech

In many languages words fall into specific parts of speech, such as nouns, pronouns, adjectives, verbs, adverbs, prepositions, conjunctions, and interjections. The first four of these are often inflected; the last four generally are not. Yet languages differ widely in respect to the parts of speech that are inflected. In Japanese, only verbs are inflected, in a common class with adjectives. Other languages have no inflections, for example, Chinese and Vietnamese. In still other languages, such as Eskimo, roots and suffixes make up complex words that are comparable to sentences. Grammars of such languages then treat morphemes rather than words. The selection classes of morphemes in such languages are generally comparable to those of languages in which parts of speech like nouns and verbs can be distinguished. Accordingly we examine some parts of speech and their patterning, taking examples from English and Latin.

4.3.1 Parts of Speech as Selection Classes

Traditional grammars, as we noted above, defined parts of speech by semantic criteria, a practice still widely maintained. A noun is defined as "the name of a person, place, or thing," a verb as "a word which can assert something (usually an action) concerning a person, place, or thing."[2] When such definitions are examined more closely, they run into difficulties. Kittredge and Farley state in a footnote that in its brief form this definition of 'verb' applies only to verbs in declarative sentences. Even traditional grammars, then, found problems in defining parts of speech as meaning classes.

Because of such problems, structural linguists came to define word classes by form and changes in form, as we noted in Section 4.1. Nouns in English, then, are defined as elements that are inflected for the plural and for the possessive, for example, *woman, woman's, women, women's.* Verbs are defined as words inflected

---

[2] *Ibid.,* pp. 4–5.

for the third singular present, the past tense, the past participle, and the present participle, for example, *give, gives, gave, given, giving.* This basis for definition also has its shortcomings, for example, *scissors* has no singular, *must* has no inflection. Subsequent grammars use morphological and syntactic criteria combined with functional criteria. Parts of speech are then identified by their selection to fill certain positions in sentences as well as by their inflections and general meaning. Because multiple criteria are applied, the parts of speech proposed for one language may not be appropriate for another.

When inflections are found in a language, parts of speech are most securely identified by them. Since Latin had characteristic inflections, it could readily be treated in accordance with the procedures of traditional grammar. These procedures as well as grammatical terminology may be illustrated with examples from Latin.

4.3.2 Sets of Inflections

When nouns, pronouns, and adjectives are inflected for similar categories, the inflections are called **declensions.** Latin has five noun declensions. The Latin first declension is made up of nouns like *rosa* 'rose,' which end in *a* in the nominative singular. Most first declension nouns belong to the feminine gender, though some, like *agricola* 'farmer' do not. The Latin second declension is made up of nouns ending in *us* or *um* in the nominative singular, for example, *hortus* 'garden' and *oppidum* 'city.' The nouns ending in *us* are of masculine gender, those in *um* of neuter; these categories are discussed in Section 4.7.1. The third, fourth, and fifth declensions follow other patterns.

Examples of Latin declension for these three nouns are given in the singular. As the forms indicate, Latin nouns have six cases, in contrast with the two for English nouns. English had further inflections in the Old English period, as *geard,* the Old English cognate of Latin *hortus,* illustrates.

The Old English spelling *ge* indicates a pronunciation like its modern form *yard.* Since Old English times there has been a further loss of inflection to the two forms of modern English. Modern English has come to use syntactic arrangement or prepositions rather than endings to express the meanings formerly conveyed by case endings. In a sentence like *She gave her daughter a book, daughter* would be in the dative case in Latin, *book* in the accusative. Latin would also use the dative case for *daughter* in the version *She gave a book to her daughter.* If the sentence included a prepositional phrase with 'from,' Latin would express this in the ablative case.

10. *Latin and Old English declensions*

Nominative	rosa	hortus	oppidum	geard
Accusative	rosam	hortum	oppidum	(geard)
Genitive	rosae	hortî	oppidî	geardes
Dative	rosae	hortō	oppidō	gearde
Ablative	rosā	hortō	oppidō	
Vocative	rosa			

Each of the Latin forms may be divided into a base (*ros-*, *hort-*, *oppid-*) and endings. The endings indicate three categories, for example, *-am* indicates that its form is in the accusative case, singular number, and feminine gender. The Latin endings are therefore compound elements, as is often true of inflected languages.

Verb inflections are known as **conjugations.** Verbs are characteristically conjugated for tense, the linguistic expression of time; for mood, the linguistic expression of manner (such as possibility, expressed by the subjunctive in Latin); and for other categories like person and number. The Latin verb has many inflected forms. Verbal inflection in English, on the other hand, has gradually been reduced. Old English verbs still had three distinct forms in the singular but only one in the plural. Today we use pronouns instead of endings for all persons except the third singular in the present, as the translations below indicate.

11. *Present tense indicative active of the verb 'love'*

	Latin	Old English	
1st person singular	amō	lufie	'I love'
2nd person singular	amās	lufast	'thou lovest/you love'
3d person singular	amat	lufað	'he/she loves'
1st person plural	amāmus	lufiað	'we love'
2nd person plural	amātis	lufiað	'you love'
3d person plural	amant	lufiað	'they love'

Inflection serves to relate parts of sentences more distinctly to other parts. If, as in Latin, nouns are inflected in the nominative and accusative, like English pronouns with the *I/me, he/him, she/her,* and so on, distinction, the precise relationships between nouns and verbs, is clear. As in the maxim of Chaucer's Nun, *Amor vincit omnia,* there can be no question of the role of any of these words if one knows the Latin inflections: *amor,* nominative singular masculine, can only be the subject; *vincit* 'conquers,' third singular present indicative active, must be the accompanying verb; *omnia* 'all things,' neuter plural nominative or accusative, must be the object. The sentence therefore can only mean: 'Love conquers all things.' If adjectives are inflected for case, number, and gender, noun phrases are precisely indicated.

Since nouns and verbs are the primary categories that undergo inflection, languages with SVO order have less need of inflection than do VSO and SOV languages, in which two nouns stand side by side. The hackneyed newspaper headline *Man bites dog* is more readily understood in an SVO language like English than it would be in a VSO language: *Bites man dog,* or an OV language: *Man dog bites.* SVO languages, like English and Putonghua, accordingly tend to have little inflection. The OV language, Turkish, on the other hand has rich inflection for both nouns and verbs. But particles may also signal the functions of verbs and of nouns in sentences, as they do for nouns in Japanese.

The parts of speech and their inflection in any language are closely interrelated with its typical sentence structure.

4.4 Patterns of Arrangement for Bases and Affixes

Words are commonly analyzed into two large sets: (1) **roots** or **bases** and (2) **affixes,** that is, morphemes attached to roots or bases. Affixes are subclassified by their position with regard to bases. If they precede the base, as does *a* in Sanskrit *abhavam* 'I became,' they are called **prefixes.** If they follow the base, as does *mi* in *bhavā-mi* 'I become,' they are called **suffixes.** If they are placed inside the base, as is *na* in Sanskrit *yu-na-j-mi* 'I yoke,' they are called **infixes.** The base, here *yuj*, is then said to be discontinuous.

Affixes may also be suprasegmental; in some verbs of Proto-Indo-European, for example, the accent is on the base in the singular, on the endings in the plural; a survival of this pattern is still found in the *s/r* contrast of *was/were*. Affixes consisting of pitch or stress are called **superfixes.** Superfixes are prominent in many African languages.

SOV languages tend to have suffixed inflectional elements, as we note in Section 4.6 for Japanese verbs. In VSO languages, on the other hand, inflectional elements tend to be prefixed. English, as an SVO language, has very few inflectional elements.

Affixes, however, are widely used in English for derivation, both prefixes and suffixes. Among the many prefixes are *pre-, re-, un-* as in *prepare, rearrange, unlock.* Among the many suffixes are *-tion, -ment, -able* as in *preparation, rearrangement, unlockable.* When we examine such suffixes we find a variety of formations, as for words ending in *-an* meaning 'pertaining to.' One group is formed from proper names: *Elizabethan* 'pertaining to (the age of Elizabeth),' *Lutheran* 'pertaining to Luther,' *Ohioan* 'pertaining to Ohio.'

At one time *-an* was commonly added to bases ending in *y* or *ia*, for example, *Asia Asian,* some of which were in turn modified, for example, *Italy Italian.* A separate suffix was then produced and used with bases having no final *y: Spenser Spenserian, Shakespeare Shakespearian, Milton Miltonian.* It was also added to others with further changes of the base, for example, *Canada Canadian.* These examples illustrate how affixes may be extended in form.

Even more extensive forms of the suffix have developed, as in *geometrician,* on the pattern of *mathematician* and similar forms. Instead of using the suffix *-ian,* as in *historian* from *history,* a suffix *-ician* was taken away from the supposed base and fitted onto *geometry.* This process is known as suffix clipping. The resultant suffix has become widespread, as in *beautician* and *mortician.* Similarly, the suffix *-arian,* as in *librarian* (based on *library*), has been extended to nouns without *-ary,* for example, *unitarian* from *unity* and *humanitarian* from *humanity.*

These examples may serve to illustrate how affixation is used to enlarge the stock of words in language, as well as to indicate inflectional relationships. Affixation is a highly important process in inflected languages like Latin, Greek, and Sanskrit. Much of the time required to master Latin and Greek is taken up by learning the inflectional paradigms. The emphasis of traditional grammar on morphology can be understood when one notes that such grammars were designed in the description of these languages.

4.5 Modification of Morphemes

The shapes of base and affix morphemes may vary in accordance with their environments. The English variants of the third singular present suffix: [z s əz] in *lives, sniffs, hisses* may serve as illustration. In structural grammars such variants are known as **allomorphs.** English inflectional endings may be used to provide further examples.

Few affixes are used throughout all forms without modification, that is, without more than one allomorph. English *-ing* is an example of a morpheme with one shape, although many speakers use a variant [ɪn], especially after bases like *ring* that end in [ŋ]. The third singular present morpheme has three forms in accordance with the preceding phoneme. After sibilants, as in *hiss, whiz, rush, rouge, clutch, budge,* the allomorph is [əz]. After voiceless phonemes other than [s š č], the allomorph is [s], as after /p t k f θ/, for example, *rap, hit, back, laugh, sleuth.* After other voiced stops and fricatives and after resonants and vowels, the allomorph is [z]. Variants determined in accordance with the preceding sounds are said to be phonologically conditioned.

The past tense morpheme also has three principal variants. After the phonemes /t d/, as in *butt, bud,* the allomorph is [əd]. After voiceless phonemes other than /t/, the allomorph is /t/, as in *rap, back, laugh, sleuth, hiss, rush, clutch.* The allomorph /d/ occurs elsewhere, except in the irregular verbs. These follow various patterns that cannot be determined from their phonological structure; such variations are then said to be morphologically conditioned. In most of the irregular verbs in English there is internal variation of vowels. One of the largest subclasses is made up of verbs ending in nasals or the nasal /ŋ/ plus /k/, for example, *swim, begin, spin, ring, sing, spring, drink, shrink, sink, stink.* Here the internal change consists of /ɪ/ going to /æ/; the replacement may be represented by the rule: /ɪ/ → /æ/ before /m n ŋ ŋk/. As in our irregular verbs, morphologically conditioned allomorphs often are the result of processes in an earlier stage of the language.

In structural grammars modifications of bases and affixes in morphological processes are known as morphophonemic changes, and their study as morphophonemics.

4.5.1 Assimilation

The most widespread type of modification is assimilation. In **assimilation** one or more sounds come to be articulated like another sound. English verbal endings in the third singular present and in the past show assimilation to the preceding sound, whether voiced or voiceless. The past tense affix of Japanese verbs also undergoes assimilation. When the base ends in *n*, for example, *shinu* 'die,' the past is *shinda;* the *t* of the suffix *ta* has assimilated to the preceding voiced sound [n]. Assimilation in which a preceding element modifies a following is called **progressive.**

When the base ends in *r*, for example, *toru* 'take,' the past is *totta.* The *r* is devoiced in accordance with the following voiceless stop and is modified to a stop. Assimilation in which a following element modifies a preceding is called **regressive.**

When the base ends in *m*, as in *sumu* 'live,' the place of articulation of [m] is modified to that of the [t], and the [t] is voiced like [m], yielding *sunda*. Assimilation in which both elements are affected is called **reciprocal.**

In these examples the assimilation involves contiguous elements. Assimilation may also be noncontiguous, as we may illustrate with Proto-Germanic, the earlier form of Old English and Old High German. Back rounded vowels of stems were fronted, yielding front rounded vowels, as in standard German *Hüte* 'hats' versus *Hut* 'hat,' *Götter* 'gods' versus *Gott* 'god,' and *Mäuse* 'mice' versus *Maus* 'mouse.' The low back vowel was fronted, as in *Männer* 'men' versus *Mann* 'man.' The contrast was widely extended in German, especially to indicate noun plurals, while in English it was largely abandoned. By the time of Old English, rounded front vowels were lost; relics of the earlier plurals are found in *geese* versus *goose, brethren* versus *brother, mice* versus *mouse,* and *men* versus *man.* This kind of assimilation is often referred to by a term borrowed from German, **umlaut.**

In describing assimilation it is useful to note the characteristic features of sounds as presented in Chapter 3, Section 3.2, for in the modification of one or more features assimilation is brought about. Examples of the past tense of verbs in Japanese provide illustrations. Assimilation may be made in place of articulation, as when the base *sum* becomes *sun* in *sunda* 'lived.' Assimilation may be made in manner of articulation, as when the resonant *r* becomes a stop in *totta* from *tor-* 'take.' Assimilation may be made in the articulation of the vocal folds, as when *t* becomes voiced in *shinda* 'died.'

Modification may also be made between words. The common form /gɔ́nə/ of *going to* shows assimilation in place of articulation of [ŋ] to [n] before [t]; the [t] then is lost. The forms [kǽnčə wónčə] of *can't you* and *won't you* show assimilation in manner of articulation, as well as in the use of vocal folds; [y] in the sequence [ty] becomes devoiced and narrowed to a fricative [š], yielding [tš č]. In the sequence *give me* there is often assimilation in velic articulation to the pronunciation [gɪmi]; the fricative first becomes nasalized, and the sequence is simplified as in the pronunciation indicated here.

Since articulation of sequences is simplified in assimilation, it is accounted for by articulatory moves towards ease of articulation.

4.5.2 Other Processes of Modification

Dissimilation is a type of substitution in which two phonemes become less like each other. It may be accounted for through psychological rather than articulatory processes. When two complex activities must be carried out, we find it simpler if they differ slightly. In keeping with this observation, dissimilation generally affects complex phonemes, such as the aspirates or the resonants. As an example, the English word *turtle-(dove)* is a dissimilated form of *tur-tur*, the name given the bird after its call. Another example is the word *purple,* based on Latin *purpura.*

When dissimilation leads to loss of an entire syllable, it is called **haplology** (literally, the simplifying of a word). Examples may be found in English adverbs ending in *-ly*. From *slow* we may make an adverb *slowly*. But if the base already ends in *-ly*, for example, *lively, friendly,* we do not maintain the second *-ly,* but simplify the word to *lively* as in *He stepped lively.*

Metathesis is change in the order of phonemes. In the West Saxon dialect of Old English, for example, *r* is metathesized after vowels in many words, such as *birnan* 'burn' (compare Gothic *brinnan,* German *brennen, hors* 'horse' compare Old Saxon *hross,* German *ross*), and so forth. Metathesis may be understood if we note the phonological patterning in a language. In West Saxon, sequences of short vowels followed by *r +* consonant are one of the standard patterns, as in verbs like *weorpan* 'throw (formerly, and now), warp,' *beorcan* 'bark,' and so on. It is natural then for verbs like earlier **brestan* to become *berstan* 'burst' in agreement with the predominant pattern.

4.6 Japanese Verb Forms

Japanese verb inflection is useful to examine for further examples of morphological processes, because the classes and categories are relatively simple, the arrangement and modifications relatively straightforward. There are two subclasses of *u* verbs in Japanese: those whose bases end in vowels (for example, *ne* 'sleep') and those whose bases end in consonants (for example, *tor* 'take').

For each subclass we list four simple forms (example 12). The labels give a general indication of each form's use. As is clear from the forms of *neru* 'sleep,' when endings are added to the vowel subclass, there are no changes in the base or the affixes.

12.			
	Indicative	*ne-ru*	*to-ru*
	Infinitive	*ne*	*to-ri*
	Past	*ne-ta*	*tot-ta*
	Participle	*ne-te*	*tot-te*

In the consonant subclass, however, both the final consonant of the base and the initial consonant of the ending may be changed. To determine the underlying form of the base, it is useful to start from a derived form, the negative. This form has the ending *-anai.*

After identifying the base of the consonant subclasses from examination of the negative, we may examine the modifications from the indicative, the infinitive, and the past. For *toru* 'take' we set up two allomorphs of the base, *tor tot.* Apart from the infinitives of bases ending in *t s w* the modifications are found in the past. The past exhibits various kinds of assimilation of both the suffix and the base. Bases ending in a voiced consonant other than *w* assimilate the *t* of the past affixes to voiced *d.* The dental of the past affix, on the other hand, brings about assimilation of the labials of *tob, nom, kaw.* Velars, as in *kik, kag,* on the other hand, are dissimilated to vowels. In this way even the simple verb system of Japanese illustrates several types of modification.

13. Bases ending in:

	Indicative	Infinitive	Past	Negative
t 'wait'	matsu	machi	matta	matanai
n 'die'	shinu	shini	shinda	shinanai
b 'fly'	tobu	tobi	tonda	tobanai
m 'drink'	nomu	nomi	nonda	nomanai
k 'hear'	kiku	kiki	kiita	kikanai
g 'smell'	kagu	kagi	kaida	kaganai
s 'speak'	moosu	mooshi	mooshita	moosanai
w 'buy'	kau	kai	katta	kawanai

Japanese has many derived forms. In these the affixed endings are added to one another with little modification and in transparent arrangements. A language with such a structure is called **agglutinative.** By contrast, English, Sanskrit, Greek, Latin, and the Semitic languages are known as inflectional languages because their affixes usually merge in part with the base, as in *gives, gave,* and so on.

Among the derived forms of the Japanese verb are the following, given with their affixes indicated. The causative is made by suffixing *saseru* to vowel verbs and *aseru* to consonant verbs, for example, *nesasaru* 'cause to sleep' and *mataseru* 'cause to wait.'

We may also note forms of the *i* class of Japanese verbs, for example, *takai* 'be tall,' as in *ki ga takai* 'the tree is tall.' As the past indicates, these have the same inflection in this category as the *u* verbs.

14. Indicative   *takai*
      Adverbial   *takaku*
      Past   *takakatta*

In further secondary forms, the negative and the desiderative, the inflectional endings are like those of *i* verbs, for example, *matanai* 'does not wait' and *matanakatta* 'did not wait.'

Japanese verbal inflection then may illustrate not only how a part of speech like the verb may share similarities with that in other languages, but also how it has characteristic features of its own.

4.7 Selected Categories of Inflection

Many general categories of inflection are widespread, though, as we have noted for the Japanese verb, details may differ from language to language. In some languages, however, the categories differ considerably from those we know in English. In some Amerindian languages the inflected verb form must indicate whether the subject is sitting, standing, or lying; or it may indicate whether the object is within sight, not within sight but within hearing, or neither. The precision in information that such inflections afford also occasions large numbers of inflected forms; an estimate for the Oneida verb is more than a million.

In dealing with categories we must note that they are linguistic rather than natural. Linguistic categories can be related in general to logical or natural categories, as is gender with sex: Masculine, feminine, and neuter generally correspond to male, female, and neither. But one scarcely learns more than a few words of German before noting that all words ending in the diminutive suffixes *-chen* and *-lein* are of neuter gender (compare English *-kin* as in *lambkin, catkin* and *-ling* as in *darling*). Accordingly *Mädchen* 'girl' and *Fräulein* 'young lady' are neuter. Similar examples could be cited from Latin, Spanish, French, and other languages with gender classes.

Gender is a congruence category; that is to say, it requires marking words that accompany nouns, such as articles and adjectives, in this way showing those elements of sentences that go together, indicating that they are congruent. The reasons for membership in any such category are various, partly historical, partly based on patterning in classes because of form or meaning. For any inflectional category one must first determine the linguistic usage and then relate this usage to natural and logical classes.

One must not be misled by the terminology of the grammars, such as *masculine* or *feminine*, or *present, past, future* in verbs. Such terms have been introduced into the study of language in attempts to provide graphic terminology, but they do not apply in a concrete way to all uses of the forms in question. As frequent expressions indicate—such as *We go to town tomorrow*, in which the present tense indicates future time, or *If we went to town tomorrow*, in which the past tense indicates future time—labels given to categories indicate only partially their natural and logical meaning.

4.7.1 Inflectional Categories Associated with Nominal Elements

Categories widely found with nouns, pronouns, and adjectives are case, gender, and number. The two last may also be found in verbal inflection. In the following sketch of these categories the distinction between linguistic and natural categories may be further observed.

Number is apparently a straightforward category, referring to quantities. Yet the use of number is often nonlogical, as examples from well-known languages may illustrate. In a simple number system we might expect a category for one, singular, and a category for more than one, plural. Some number systems have a category for two, dual, for example, ancient Greek and Sanskrit. A few number systems have a category for three, **trial.** For a general analysis of number systems we would need to speak of categories for countable nouns, such as English *cat, compass, meaning,* and for uncountables, such as English *cattle, compassion, tact.* The use of these nouns in English is evident not only from their inflection—*cat, cats* but not *cattle, *cattles*—but also from their relationships to other syntactic entities: *He has no cats* versus *He has no cattle* and *He has a cat* versus *He has cattle;* the syntactic entities *no, a* function differently with each.

Relationship, as we have noted, is important for determining linguistic classes. Besides the relationships pointed to in the previous paragraph, specific relationships determine which nouns can be classed together for counting. We may say *A cat and a dog are animals*. But we do not class together *a cat* and *a hair,* saying, for example, **A cat and a hair are on the sofa*. In this way linguistic expression determines what can be counted or associated in a given language.

In English, for example, the word *cousin* refers to males and females: We can therefore say *John and Mary are cousins*. In German there are distinct words for 'male cousin' *der Vetter* and 'female cousin' *die Kusine/Base*. Hence one must say *Hans und Marie sind Vetter und Base*. Conversely, for 'brother' and 'sister' German has a collective, *Geschwister*. Accordingly, to correspond to *John and Mary are brother and sister* German permits *Hans und Marie sind Geschwister*. One may also compare such simple items as *scissors,* a plural in English but a singular in German, *die Schere;* or *glasses* versus *die Brille;* or conversely *hair* versus *die Haare,* a plural in German.

Such minute variations are often neglected by polyglots. For example, the words for *vacation* is plural in Latin, *feriae*. The word was borrowed into German and is used as plural, *die Ferien;* similarly, in French the term is plural, *vacances*. Nonnative speakers of English with French or German as their native language will frequently speak of their *vacations*. Speakers of German may also seek *informations,* on the pattern of German *Auskünfte*. All of these examples illustrate the importance of linguistic rather than "natural" categories in language.

But it is scarcely necessary to go beyond one language to illustrate the primacy of linguistic categories in linguistic patterns. If John ate several oranges for breakfast, his admirable dietary practice may be reported either with a plural, *He ate more oranges than one,* or with a singular, *He ate more than one orange*. Whether the linguistic report uses a plural or a singular, John ate the same number of oranges. In spite of the difference between linguistic categorization and natural or logical groupings, some speakers confuse the two. On the basis of such confusion they may modify their own usage and try to influence others. The application of the word *gender* for 'sex' is one example of this attitude to language.

The nouns exemplified previously can be counted and are therefore often referred to as **count nouns.** By contrast, **mass nouns** cannot be counted, or if they are, the reference is to separate items, for example, *money, sugar, experience*. Each of these may be used after *He didn't have much . . . ,* though a count noun like *book, shoe, idea* may not. If we say *There are several sugars in those jars* it is understood that the reference is to several kinds of sugar. We may also use auxiliary nouns like *kinds of sugar, types of money, head of cattle* with numerals, for example, *two kinds of sugar, three types of money, seven head of cattle*.

In some languages, for example, Chinese and Japanese, all nouns must be treated in this way. Rather than speaking of two pencils, one must say *ni hon* 'of pencils' in Japanese. *Hon* is used in counting long round objects. For flat things like sheets of paper one must say *ni mai* 'of paper'; for humans, *ni jin* 'of people'; for birds, *ni wa* 'of birds'; and so on. Such auxiliary nouns are known as **numeral classifiers.** Comparison with English mass nouns may provide some understanding of Chinese and Japanese nouns. The latter are neither singular nor plural, simply aggregate.

Gender is a congruence category, as we noted above. By means of gender, nouns and their modifiers are linked together. In the first line of the *Odyssey,* for example, there is no question about the noun modified by *polútropon* 'experienced.'

15. *ándra moi   énnepe, moûsa,   polútropon,*   *hòs mála pollà*
     man   to-me   tell-of, oh-muse,   experienced,   who very many
     'Tell me of an experienced man, O muse, who (suffered) very many
          things'

As a masculine accusative singular, it must modify *ándra* rather than *moûsa.* Gender in this way indicates associations in selection classes and permits greater freedom of arrangement. Both classical Latin and Greek permit freer placement of adjectives than does English.

Case is a category that specifies selection of nouns in greater deatil. Noun systems may have two cases, as in English, four as in German, six as in Latin, eight as in Sanskrit, or even more, as in Finnish and Hungarian. Cases may refer primarily to grammatical relations (for example, the Sanskrit nominative and accusative) or primarily to locational relations (for example, the Sanskrit ablative and locative), or they may single out entities, for example, the vocative. In general, the nominative is used in Latin and Sanskrit to indicate the subject of the action, the accusative to indicate the object. This widespread use of the accusative led to the label 'objective,' which is common in English grammars for this case, for example, *me, her, him, us, them,* as compared with the nominative *I, she,* etc.

Languages may use cases to express differences in meaning that are expressed by lexical entities in other languages. In the following Latvian examples the difference between a single present action and a general mode of behavior is indicated by a contrast between the dative and the accusative cases:

16.   (*es* 'I'; *klausīt* 'obey'; *says* 'own';
            vecáki 'parents')
     a.   *Es klausu saviem vecākiem.* (dative)
          'I am obeying my parents (now)'
     b.   *Es klausu savus vecākus.* (accusative)
          'I always obey my parents.'

Like surface grammatical categories, then, case forms must be analyzed and described for their uses in the language concerned.

4.7.2 Inflectional Categories Associated with Verbal Elements

Categories widely found with verbs are voice, tense, aspect, mood, person, and number.

Voice is a category specifying the relation of the subject to the action expressed by a verb. Latin has two voices: an active, indicating that the subject performs the action expressed by the verb, for example, *He reads many books;* and a passive, indicating that the subject undergoes the action expressed by the verb, for example, *Many books are read by him*. Classical Greek has another voice, the middle, which is also found in Sanskrit; the middle voice indicates that the subject performs an action for his or her own benefit. An example is *édomai* 'I eat (for my own benefit).'

The active/passive distinction of English, Latin, and other languages seems natural to us. Active sentences select the nominative for the subject, in parallel with the use of the nominative as subject for intransitive verbs.

> 17a. *She arrived early.*
>   b. *She met him at the gate.*
>   c. *He was met by her at the gate.*

The contrast between nominative and accusative uses as found in English is clearly important only in the last two sentences.

If one were designing a language, the form of the subject in the first sentence would not need to be nominative, but could as readily be like the accusative, that is, like sentence 17d.

> 17d. **Her arrived early.*

A great many languages are structured in this way. To avoid confusion in describing them, different terms are used for the contrasting forms. The form used in the subject of transitive sentences is called **ergative;** the form used for the subject of intransitive sentences and the object of transitive is called **absolute.** Languages with this alignment are known as **ergative,** as opposed to **nominative/accusative** languages like English. The principal languages of Europe are nominative-accusative. Basque and many languages of Asia, the Americas, and the Pacific, including Australia, are ergative.

Although the ergative alignment may seem strange to us, some English verbs have been interpreted as having ergative value, as when we say:

> 18a. *The story developed beautifully.*
>   b. *Their money increased by leaps and bounds.*

Compare:

>   c. *She developed the story beautifully.*
>   d. *The story was developed beautifully by her.*

As in an ergative language, sentence 18a has the object of the transitive verb (cf. 18c) used as subject with no need for an agent. Although not distinguished by inflection, the subject of verbs like *develop, increase* is comparable to the absolute of ergative languages.

By examining language, as illustrated with example 18, we observe elements that are relatively central, like the verb relation to objects and subjects, and others that are less central, like the morphological marking of these relationships. Speakers of ergative languages find their morphological markings as clear as do speakers of nominative/accusative languages. The observation of such more fundamental matters in contrast with the less fundamental has given rise to the distinction between surface and deep structures.

Surface structures are close to actual utterances. Deep structures, on the other hand, reflect semantic and logical relationships. As with the nominative/accusative distinction, surface often refers to inflectional morphology. Many examples can be cited to illustrate that this is not of primary importance. As we observed above, English has been gradually losing inflections, maintaining accusatives only for a few pronouns. Because the deep structure characteristics are more fundamental, recent linguistic study has been primarily concerned with them and with the categories found to be general in language.

Tense is a category specifying the time of the action. Latin tense categories are as rational as any that might be expected: present, past, and future. Old English has no tense for the future; instead the present tense is used, as today in *We go there tomorrow*. Modern English expresses future tense by using the auxiliaries *shall* and *will*.

Tense is a grammatical category. The relationships expressed by tense forms may not refer to time. The past tense form in the sentence *If she did her homework regularly, she would make a B* indicates unreality rather than activity in the past. Compare also: *If he went next Monday, . . .* where the past tense form refers to a possible future action. More examples of the necessity to regard tense as a linguistic rather than a natural category could readily be cited, comparable to those cited in Section 4.7.1 concerning **number.**

Instead of tense, or coexistent with tense, many languages have a category referred to as aspect. **Aspect** indicates the status of the action as viewed by the speaker rather than its time relationships. An action may be completed or incompleted. If completed, the aspect is called **perfective;** if incompleted, **imperfective.**

Aspect categories are prominent in the Slavic languages. The Semitic languages also have verb inflection for aspect. In biblical Hebrew, for example, *qɔtal* means 'killing has been completed by him,' and *yiqtol* means 'killing by him is not yet completed.' The perfective frequently corresponds to a past tense, so that *qɔtal* is often translated 'he killed,' and the imperfective *yiqtol* is often translated as the present tense or with a future 'he will kill.' Yet the uses of many aspectual forms may not be compatible with the verbal relationships of a tense system. It is instructive and engaging to compare translations from Hebrew into languages that have tense, such as Latin and English. Saint Jerome's translation of the opening of Psalm 121 reads *Levāvī oculōs* 'I have lifted up my eyes'; the King James version by contrast reads 'I will lift up mine eyes.' The translators differed in their interpretation of the Hebrew aspect form.

Some verb systems have highly subtle inflectional categories. Other languages include such subtleties in the lexicon, as we noted for the English "ergative" verbs above. English *look at,* for example, corresponds to a perfective form in *I looked at him,* whereas *see* corresponds to an imperfective, as in *I saw him.* When one compares additional forms—for example, *I am looking at him* and *I am seeing him*—the complexities of aspectual languages may not seem unduly forbidding.

Mood, or mode, is a verbal category that reflects the manner of the action, often also the attitude of the speaker. The indicative indicates that speakers present the material with assurance; the imperative that they command or request some action. If an inflectional system includes a subjunctive mood, it may suggest uncertainty; an optative suggests some sort of volition. Yet the precise meaning is determined by the categories found in a language. The early Indo-European languages gradually reduced the number of modal inflections. In early Sanskrit, these four moods exist side by side in the present tense of the active and the middle voices; in later Sanskrit the subjunctive is lost. In Latin the optative is lost, leaving the indicative, the imperative, and the subjunctive. In Germanic the subjunctive is lost, leaving the optative, but the use of the Germanic optative is remarkably parallel to the subjunctive of Latin, and in handbooks it is generally labeled the "subjunctive." German has maintained a subjunctive inflection, but in English, Norwegian, Danish, and so on it is lost. Where other languages express modes by means of inflection, these languages use modal auxiliaries, such as *may, might, should.*

Besides these categories verbs may be inflected for number, such as singular, dual, and plural, and for person. Simple systems have three persons: The first corresponds to the speaker, the second to the addressee, and the third to others. Verbs may also be inflected for gender. In Arabic and other Semitic languages there are different forms for the second and third person singular masculine and feminine.

4.7.3 Overlapping of Parts of Speech

Nouns and verbs may seem to be distinct parts of speech. Yet they have overlapping forms, such as the verbal nouns and adjectives made from verbs. These are called nonfinite to distinguish them from the finite forms, which are inflected for such categories as tense and person. Infinitives are often used as nouns, for example, *To study was one of her greatest pleasures.* In such a use they retain something of their verbal force, as is noted by the accompaniment of adverbs, for example, *To play brilliantly requires long practice.*

Other nonfinite forms are participles; they are often used as adjectives, for example, *On any given day you could see the swirling winds kick up dust there.* Used as nouns, participles may be referred to as gerunds. The English *-ing* form provides examples, such as *dancing, eating, singing, writing,* and many others. These are used not only as nouns but also as adjectives and members of verbal phrases.

Nouns, on the other hand, may be modified to verbs, often by means of auxiliaries. In Japanese, for example, many words borrowed from Chinese and English are treated like verbs through combination with the verb *suru* 'do.' Thus the Japanese noun borrowed on the basis of English 'type' *taipu* is converted into various verb forms, such as *taipu suru* 'she types' and *taipu shita* 'she typed.'

In English the boundaries between parts of speech have long been slender. Shakespeare abounds with examples like *But me no buts*. Like the conjunction *but* here, prepositions, interjections, and virtually any part of speech may be used as nouns or as verbs: *The ins were jubilant, The ayes have it, He upped the ante*. Parts of speech may be defined and distinguished from one another, but their members are by no means frozen and fixed in a living language.

4.8 Compounds

Compounds are words consisting of two or more bases which are treated as units in inflection and accentuation. To simplify discussion, most of the examples presented here contain only two segments, such as *lighthouse* and *greenback*, rather than three or more segments, such as *lighthousekeeper* or *greatgrandfather*. The formation of larger compounds is generally based on those of two-element compounds: *lighthousekeeper* is constructed from *housekeeper* and *light-(house)* in much the same way as *housekeeper* is constructed from *house* and *keeper*, which in turn is a complex noun built up of *keep* and *-er*. The longer compound could also be made up of *lighthouse* and *keeper*, each of which can be further analyzed. Accordingly, longer compounds can be classified like compounds of two elements. Four common types of compounds are coordinative, subordinative, possessive, and synthetic.

In *coordinative* compounds the two elements are parallel. Some coordinative compounds have one element repeated with little change in meaning, as for example, *papa, mama*. In such Japanese compounds the effect is accumulation, collectivization, or pluralization. Thus *yama-yama* means 'a group of mountains.' Numerous Japanese adverbs indicate an intensification of the action represented, for example, *para-para* 'pit-a-pat,' *poka-poka* 'again and again.' A similar effect is observed in English compounds like *pitter-patter* and *flim-flam*. Here too the effect is intensification. As exemplified by these English compounds, modification may accompany reduplication.

Some coordinative compounds are additive, for example, *thirteen* 'three + ten' and Japanese *eibei* 'England and America.' Sanskrit grammarians named coordinative compounds **dvandva** from a typical additive compound meaning 'two plus two.' The name *dvandva* is often used for additive compounds even in grammars of languages other than Sanskrit.

Other types of relationships may be found in coordinative compounds. For example, in Japanese some such compounds are composed of opposites, such as *umu* 'being–not being = existence.' As illustrated by *umu*, or by *zehi* 'yes–no = propriety,' the meaning represents a balance between the two opposites.

In **subordinative** compounds one element modifies the other. The modifying element may precede, as in *tapeworm* 'a worm shaped like a tape,' or it may follow, as in *hippopotamus*, literally 'horse (of the) river.' The subordination may be of various types. And differing classes of elements may occupy either position in the compound, as we can illustrate with the first element in some English compounds: nouns, as in *clotheshorse;* adjectives, as in *greenhouse;* pronouns, as in *she-pony;* and verbs, as in *rowboat.*

Most English compounds are subordinative, with the first element modifying the second. Compounds with the second element modifying the first are characteristic of VSO languages, such as Irish and Welsh; compare the names *Macadam* 'son (of) Adam' or *Pritchard* (Welsh *ap* 'son') 'son (of) Richard.' As Hebrew names illustrate, for example, *Ben-Gurion* 'son (of) Gurion,' this pattern is also found in the Semitic languages. Greek probably based the word *hippopotamus* on a Semitic or a Hamitic designation for the animal, for both of these groups had VSO structure.

Subordinative compounds may well be the most widespread of all compounds, as they are in English.

In **possessive** compounds the relationship between the elements does not provide the essential meaning of the compound; rather, possession of the stated characteristics is central. For example, a *greenback* is not a back of a given color but rather an object that possesses a green back, a bill—usually a dollar bill. *Blockhead, tenderfoot,* and *whiteface* are similar. Such compounds were very frequent in the early Indo-European languages. In modern English their connotation is often derogatory, as in *redneck, baldhead, bigmouth.* The Sanskrit term for these compounds, *bahuvrihi,* literally 'much rice,' is also used as a designation for them; it is an example of the class meaning 'a man who possesses a great deal of rice.' In the course of their history, possessive compounds have been greatly reduced in the Indo-European languages.

Synthetic compounds are compact expressions. They may be unabbreviated; the name of the flower *forget-me-not* is a complete imperative sentence. But commonly synthetic compounds are shortened clauses. For example, *pickpocket* reflects a clause like 'He picks pockets.' Other examples are *show-off, good-for-nothing.*

Synthetic compounds are found in ancient Latin, Greek, and Sanskrit. Latin *artifex, artificem* 'art-maker = artificer' is composed of a form of the words for 'art' and 'make.' In some synthetic compounds, such as Greek *Menelaos,* the verbal element precedes; the first element means 'upholds,' the second 'people.' When used as names, synthetic compounds had marked order; they indicated a desired attribute of the person so named, as *Menelaos* does for a king.

Compounds may be interpreted as abbreviated clauses or parts of clauses. Japanese supports such an interpretation. It includes compounds made on the one hand with native Japanese elements, on the other with Chinese elements. Each type observes the word order of the language providing the elements. An example is *hara-kiri* 'stomach-cutting,' which reflects the Japanese OV sentence pattern; the Chinese equivalent of *kiri* 'cutting' is the first element in the synonym *seppuku* 'cutting-stomach.' Both words refer to a traditional form of committing suicide. Another example supporting the analysis of compounds as reflexes of clauses may be taken from the compounds like Japanese *umu* discussed above. These are based on a Chinese pattern, as in *da-xiao* 'large-small = size.' They reflect the Chinese disjunctive sentence pattern, as in the normal greeting: *hao bu hao* 'good not good = How are you, Hello.' The compounds concerned are made up of one positive, one negative element, just as the disjunctive sentence pattern consists of one positive, one negative clause.

If accounted for as reflections of typical sentence and phrase patterns, coordinative compounds are compact expressions for phrases combined with a coordinating particle, such as 'three and ten' for 'thirteen.' Subordinative compounds are abbreviations of phrases in which one element modifies another, such as 'a horse for clothes' for 'clotheshorse.' Possessive compounds are abbreviations of sentences expressing possession; when one recalls that the early Indo-European expression for 'have' was made with the verb 'be,' the relationship between a clause like 'to him is much rice' and 'much-rice = a man who possesses much rice' can readily be understood. Synthetic compounds are scarcely disguised reductions of sentences.

4.9　Syntax in Analytic Grammars

Both traditional and structural grammars treat sentences by analyzing them for their constituents. The primary constituents of such analysis are subjects and predicates. The term for such analysis is **immediate constituent analysis** (IC) and the elements so determined are called immediate constituents. After analysis for subjects and predicates, predicates are analyzed for verb and possible objects. Thereupon the modifiers of these primary constituents are identified.

In the treatment of syntax, sentences are often diagrammed. This is a graphic procedure to illustrate successive analyses for immediate constituents. It may be illustrated as follows:

19.

a.	The	army	crossed		the	Rubicon
b.	subject		predicate			
c.			verb		object	
d.	article	noun			article	noun
e.			base	past tense		

As we have noted above, syntactic analysis for immediate constituents is readily carried out for simple sentences. In analytic syntax, a sentence is analyzed for its constituents at various levels. In 19e the analysis is carried further to the morphology.

Compound sentences are distinguished for coordinate or subordinate relationship. Coordinate clauses are parallel in form, for example:

20.　*Caesar crossed the Rubicon and marched on Rome.*

Subordinate clauses are dependent on a principal clause, for example:

> 21. *Caesar crossed the Rubicon, so that he could take over Rome.*
> 22. *When he wanted to take over Rome, Caesar crossed the Rubicon.*

Coordinate clauses are generally straightforward in patterning, like simple sentences. Subordinate clauses are often modified from the simple forms, either in arrangement or selection. Special verb forms may be found in subordinate clauses, such as the subjunctive forms of German, French, and Latin. These have gradually been lost in English, surviving only in forms of the verb *be*, for example:

> 23. *If Caesar were emperor, the Romans would lose many rights.*

English also employs modals like *might, could, should, would* and past tense forms with present or future meaning where other languages employ the subjunctive.

> 24. *If he took his vacation next week, he might have fine weather.*

Subordinate clauses are generally discussed in two groups, relative and adverbial clauses. Relative clauses modify nouns; adverbial clauses modify verbs. The analysis and classification of subordinate clauses generally make up much of the syntactic section of analytic grammars.

These grammars, especially traditional grammars, devote much of their syntactic discussion to uses of forms. If nouns are inflected for case, uses of each case are described. The same procedure applies to verb forms and to other parts of speech. Structural grammars also concentrate on analysis, but give special attention to intonation patterns.[3] Such presentations of syntax are in keeping with the theoretical bases of analytic grammars. They start with a selected corpus, whether the works of an author like Homer or those of an entire period, such as Middle English. They identify the forms in the corpus and describe how they are used. Syntax in this way is an extension of morphology.

As an example, we may review the treatment of subordinate clauses in traditional grammars. These, as we have noted, are equated to parts of speech. The subordinate clause of sentence 25b is comparable to a simple object, and accordingly it is called an "object clause."

> 25a. *We expect their arrival at noon.*
> b. *We expect that they will arrive at noon.*

Because of this treatment of syntax, parallel constructions are treated at different points in the grammar rather than under one heading. The following two sentences

---

[3] For an example see Archibald A. Hill, *Introduction to Linguistic Structures*, pp. 336–405.

are parallel to sentence 25b; the segments after *expect* may be considered reduced variants of that in 25b.

> 25c. *We expect them to arrive at noon.*
>   d. *We expect their arriving at noon.*

Since the verbal element in sentence 25c is an infinitive, traditional grammars treat such patterns with other infinitive constructions. The verbal element in sentence 25d is a gerund, and this variant is treated under gerunds. Users of such grammars must track down the parallel constructions in several places of the work.

Transformational grammars, by contrast, regard sentences 25b, c, and d as embedded variants of the simple sentence:

> 25e. *They will arrive at noon.*

These grammars group the three variants together as different forms of complements in English.

Besides different approaches to syntax, the two procedures illustrate differing regard for surface and deeper structures. Traditional grammars and structural grammars devote their attention to surface structures.

4.10 Advantages and Shortcomings of Analytic Grammars

With their attention to surface matters, traditional grammars are able to provide exhaustive descriptions. The most comprehensive English grammars follow this pattern, as do the authoritative grammars of other modern languages, of Latin, Greek, and many other languages. An example is the comprehensive *Modern English Grammar* by Otto Jespersen; another comprehensive work, devoted solely to syntax, is *An Historical Syntax of the English Language,* by F. T. Visser. These grammars deal in great detail with the patterns of English, providing many examples. Pedagogical grammars draw on them as do linguists who produce grammars and monographs concerned with deeper structures.

Analytic grammars and dictionaries based on the presentation of analytic grammars are especially useful to native speakers. These have an intuitive understanding of their language. In using grammars, dictionaries, and other handbooks they may simply be interested in verifying details. Nonnative speakers may, however, find such works less helpful, for they must learn how to express themselves, for example, to master the possible ways of producing "object clauses" after verbs like *expect*. Nonnative speakers find grammars treating these several ways under one heading more helpful than one that treats them separately under their morphological elements.

Grammars treating under one heading constructions related to each other are also of greater interest to many scholars concerned with language. Investigators of language acquisition favor them, for infants learning to speak master linguistic patterns in sequences reflecting their interrelationships. Psychologists also favor generative grammars, for they are concerned with deeper structures, assuming these to be comparable with the patterns stored in the brain. In attempts to comprehend language, analytic grammars do not enjoy the attention of the grammars treated in the following chapter. But anyone concerned with the facts of languages must use traditional grammars until linguists of other theoretical approaches produce equally comprehensive works.

QUESTIONS FOR REVIEW

1. Cite evidence to support the view that speakers recognize morphemes as well as words.
2. Identify selection, arrangement, modification/sandhi, and discuss their role in morphology.
3. How are parts of speech identified? What does it mean to say that they are selection classes?
4. What is meant by *declension?* Cite categories found in declensions.
5. What is meant by *conjugation?* Cite categories found in conjugations.
6. Discuss the function of inflection. In what type of language is it especially prominent?
7. Define the following: *base, affix, prefix, suffix, infix, superfix.*
8. Discuss and exemplify *reduplication* and some of its varieties.
9. Sketch briefly inflection in English—the parts of speech inflected and the categories for which inflection is introduced.
10. Discuss the use of affixation in making derived words in English.
11. Describe the modification for the third singular present morpheme in English verbs. For the past tense morpheme.
12. What is meant by *morphophonemics?* By *morphophonemic change?*
13. Define *assimilation,* and cite examples from the Japanese verb to illustrate assimilation in the prime articulatory processes.
14. Account for the following pronunciations in rapid speech:
    a. [hiz] for *he is*
    b. [hǽftə] for *have to*
    c. [díjə] for *did you*
    d. [kǽnčə] for *can't you.*
15. Illustrate several types of modification, using examples from the Japanese verbal inflection.
16. Discuss the significance of the observation that grammatical categories do not

correspond precisely to natural categories. Cite further examples showing that gender is a grammatical category and not a natural category.

17. Make a sentence in English with a past tense form that does not indicate past time. With a present tense verb form indicating future time.

18. Cite verbal forms that are used as nouns or adjectives.

19. What is meant by a compound? Cite an example of a coordinative, a subordinative, a possessive, and a synthetic compound in English.

20. What are the procedures of traditional grammars in dealing with syntax? Of structural grammars?

21. Define *immediate constituent*.

22. Discuss the difference between traditional grammars and generative grammars in treating sequences like the following: *She noted that the child swam capably*.

23. Cite advantages of traditional grammars. Cite disadvantages.

PROBLEMS FOR REVIEW

1. Just as *gasohol* is based on a suffix derived from *alcohol*, so *workaholic* is based on *alcoholic*. But the implication of the two suffixes *-ahol, -aholic* differs greatly. Account for the production of two such differing suffixes from essentially the same element, both developing in very recent times.

2. In *Through the Looking-Glass* Lewis Carroll includes a poem entitled *Jabber-wocky*, which contains many words he made up. The first stanza reads as follows:

> 'Twas brillig, and the slithy toves
>   Did gyre and gimble in the wabe;
> All mimsy were the borogoves,
>   And the mome raths outgrabe.

   a. Identify the nouns, verbs, and adjectives, giving the basis for your identification.

   b. Can you determine without ambiguity the part of speech for *brillig?* (It might be a holiday like *Christmas,* or a period of time, like *early* or *morning.*)

   c. How did you identify the last three words? (In his own identification Carroll takes *outgrabe* to be a verb form like *gave;* the word *outgribe* means "something between bellowing and whistling, with a kind of sneeze in the middle," by his explanation. But is there any formal way of determining whether it is a verb?)

3. English nouns are inflected in four forms, which may be labeled for *goose* as

follows: nominative singular /gus/, genitive singular /gúsəz/, nominative plural /gis/, genitive plural /gísəz/. These forms may be analyzed for base and suffix, as indicated here: base: /gus//gis/; genitive /əz/. In preparation for analyzing the four forms of each of the following nouns, write them in transcription:

	Nom. Sg.	Gen. Sg.	Nom. Pl.	Gen. Pl.
1. mother	_____	_____	_____	_____
2. student	_____	_____	_____	_____
3. dog	_____	_____	_____	_____
4. chief	_____	_____	_____	_____
5. girl	_____	_____	_____	_____
6. duck	_____	_____	_____	_____
7. horse	_____	_____	_____	_____
8. judge	_____	_____	_____	_____
9. wife	_____	_____	_____	_____
10. house	_____	_____	_____	_____

    a. Determine the bases of the nouns and also possible allomorphs, as in items 9 and 10.

    b. Indicate the allomorphs of the affixes for the genitive singular, the nominative plural, and the genitive plural; then state the arrangement of the markers in the plural.

4. English verbs are inflected in five forms, as follows: *save saves saved saved saving*. These forms may be analyzed for base and suffix, as indicated here:

Base: /sev/

Suffixes: /z/ /d/ /d/ /ɪŋ/

In preparation for analyzing the five forms of each of the following verbs write them in transcription:

1. sin	_____	_____	_____	_____	_____
2. live	_____	_____	_____	_____	_____
3. slip	_____	_____	_____	_____	_____
4. gaze	_____	_____	_____	_____	_____
5. need	_____	_____	_____	_____	_____
6. rock	_____	_____	_____	_____	_____
7. lay	_____	_____	_____	_____	_____
8. bathe	_____	_____	_____	_____	_____
9. state	_____	_____	_____	_____	_____
10. push	_____	_____	_____	_____	_____

    a. After determining the base for each verb, indicate the suffixes for each of the four last forms.

    b. Determine the morpheme for each of the inflections and indicate the distribution of possible allomorphs.

5. The following are further English verbs. Analyze them for base and affix, as in Exercise 4. It is important to start from phonetic transcriptions for all forms.

1. read   ____   ____   ____   ____   ____
2. drink   ____   ____   ____   ____   ____
3. take   ____   ____   ____   ____   ____
4. tear   ____   ____   ____   ____   ____
5. lead   ____   ____   ____   ____   ____
6. sing   ____   ____   ____   ____   ____
7. ride   ____   ____   ____   ____   ____
8. shake   ____   ____   ____   ____   ____
9. wear   ____   ____   ____   ____   ____
10. rise   ____   ____   ____   ____   ____

    a. After determining the base for each verb, indicate the affixes for each of the four last forms.

    b. Indicate the processes involved in the inflection of these forms.

6. Selected Japanese verb forms are listed below. Give the bases and the affix for each of the four inflections, describing the morphophonemic patterning and stating its conditioning.

	'dig'	'hold'	'call'	'write'	'row'	'fly'
Indicative	horu	motsu	yobu	kaku	kogu	mau
Infinitive	hori	motši	yobi	kaki	kogi	mai
Past	hotta	motta	yonda	kaita	koida	matta
Negative	horanai	motanai	yobanai	kaganai	koganai	mawanai

7. Arrangement is important for the meaning of compounds and phrases made up of a verb + adverb/preposition such as *putout* versus *output*. Examine the sequences of *over* with *come, ride, take*. What differences in meaning do you find when the verb stands before the adverb in contrast with adverb + verb order?

FURTHER READING

Bloomfield, Leonard. *Language*. New York: Holt, 1933.

Gleason, Henry Allen, Jr. *An Introduction to Descriptive Linguistics*. New York: Holt, Rinehart & Winston, 1961.

Hill, Archibald A. *Introduction to Linguistic Structures*. New York: Harcourt, Brace, 1958.

Hockett, Charles F. *A Course in Modern Linguistics*. New York: Macmillan, 1958.

Jespersen, Otto. *A Modern English Grammar on Historical Principles*. 7 vols. Copenhagen: Munksgaard, 1909–49.

Jespersen, Otto. *The Philosophy of Grammar*. London: Allen & Unwin, 1924.

Kittredge, George Lyman, and Frank Edgar Farley. *An Advanced English Grammar*. Boston: Ginn, 1913. Reprint, Folcroft, Pa.: Folcroft, 1973.

Lyons, John. *Introduction to Theoretical Linguistics*. Cambridge: At the University Press, 1968.

Marchand, Hans. *The Categories and Types of Present-Day English Word-Formation*. 2d ed. Munich: Beck, 1969.

Matthews, Peter H. *Inflectional Morphology*. Cambridge: At the University Press, 1972.

Visser, F. T. *An Historical Syntax of the English Language*. 3 vols. Leiden: Brill, 1963–.

CHAPTER FIVE

Generative Grammars

5.1 Grammars as Theories of Language

Grammars of the Greeks and Romans, as well as Panini's grammar of Sanskrit, were designed in part for practical purposes, as we have noted in the preceding chapter. Panini needed a grammar that could be memorized. The Greeks and Romans set out to teach the complex inflections of their literary languages when these were being lost in the spoken language. As linguists came to deal with many languages toward the end of the nineteenth century and in our own, they examined the purpose and aims of grammars rather than practical concerns. The examination resulted in part from attention to languages different in many ways from Sanskrit, Greek, and Latin. Study of such languages led to the endeavor to devise grammars that would capture the essence of a language. One result of that endeavor is the understanding that a grammar is a theory.

By this approach a grammar aims to account for language much as a theory of physics aims to account for natural phenomena—energy and matter. Both the physicist and the grammarian or linguist deal with their data in accordance with general propositions. For some time physicists and other natural scientists have been explicit about the propositions they assume, but linguists have been so only recently. As a result grammars have been produced in accordance with a specific explicit theory of language only in recent decades.

97

The theory that has been dominant in linguistic study for the past two decades was developed by Noam Chomsky. Grammars produced under the theory are known as generative and transformational. Both of these terms have a technical sense, which we will now examine.

5.2 Generative Grammars

The term **generative** means that a grammar accounts explicitly for the data of language. Like many linguists, Chomsky takes sentences as the basic units of language. A generative grammar sets out to provide a complete description of all sentences that are acceptable to a native speaker of a language as grammatical, whether these are simple like sentence 1a, or more complex, like sentences 2, 3, 4, and 5. (Sentences like 2 and 3 are known as 'clefts' because the additional elements [*who, is*] cleave the basic sentence. Sentence 4 contains a relative clause; 5 is a command.)

> 1a. *The father drives a convertible.*
> 2. *It's the father who drives a convertible.*
> 3. *What the father drives is a convertible.*
> 4. *The car he drives is a convertible.*
> 5. *Drive yourself to the concert!*

Such a grammar also rejects as ungrammatical sentences like 6. As is done here, ungrammatical sequences are indicated with an asterisk (*).

> 6. **Drives yourself to the concert!*

The description in a generative grammar states the structure of sentences by means of rules that apply throughout the language. Moreover, in contrast with traditional grammars, which treat languages as bodies of data, generative grammars treat them as processes. Structural grammars speak of a **corpus,** which a linguist examines. The material for such a grammar is accordingly regarded as in a state of existence. For generative transformational grammars, a sentence is treated as if it were in the process of becoming.

Generative transformational grammars view sentences as they are produced by speakers. In this process speakers apply a series of rules; we will limit ourselves here to the syntactic and lexical rules, disregarding for the time being phonology and semantics.

The syntactic rules for sentence 1a indicate that this sentence is made up of a noun phrase (NP) followed by a verb phrase (VP). Each of these has constituents. The VP consists of a verb (V) and an NP. For the analysis here we disregard the two constituents of *drives:* the verb root and the suffix. Each NP in sentence 1a consists of an article and a noun (N). Articles belong to a class of words known as determiners. This class is labeled *Det* (pronounced [dɛt]) for determiner, though some handbooks use the label Art (pronounced [art]) for article.

The following syntactic rules may be given to account for sentence 1a *The father drives a convertible:*

$$7a.\ S\ \rightarrow NP\ VP$$
$$b.\ VP \rightarrow V\ \ NP$$
$$c.\ NP \rightarrow Det\ N$$

The arrow in these rules means 'may consist of.' When such rules are spoken, the arrow is also read 'is rewritten as.'

To complete the description of this and similar sentences, the lexical elements must be listed for each simple category. The rules of example 8 are known as **lexical rules.** Lexical rules for sentence 1a may be given as follows:

$$8a.\ V\ \ \ :\ \ \ drives$$
$$b.\ N\ \ \ :\ \ \ father, convertible$$
$$c.\ Det\ \ \ :\ \ \ the, a$$

The rules of example 7 state the structure of the sentence by phrases and words. Such rules are known as **P-rules** (phrase rules) or as PS-rules (phrase structure rules).

Various conventions are used to make rules general. To have example 7c apply to proper nouns or mass nouns, Det is given in parentheses: NP → (Det) N. This convention indicates that such an element is optional. If *Henry* were included in example 8b, this form of rule 7c would still apply to generate the sentence: *Henry drives a convertible.* (See Exercise 1 in the problems at the end of this chapter for an example.)

Another device employs braces: { }. This device permits alternate elements, such as pronouns rather than nouns. Thus, the following form of example 7c introduces pronouns, for example, *he,* as in *He drives a convertible.*

$$7d.\ NP \rightarrow \begin{Bmatrix} (Det)\ N \\ Pronoun \end{Bmatrix}$$

Similarly, example 7e introduces forms of *to be* followed by an adjective.

$$7e.\ VP \rightarrow \begin{Bmatrix} V\ (NP) \\ is\ Adj \end{Bmatrix}$$

The rules may be listed as above or in tree form. When trees are depicted, lexical elements are given as the final elements.

The following tree is equivalent to example 7 plus the lexicon of example 8:

9a.

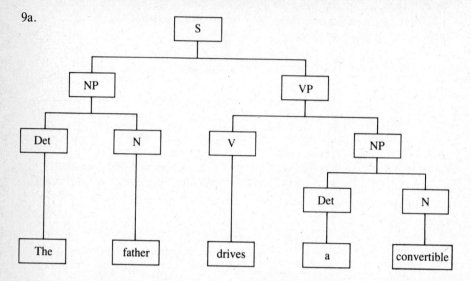

It may be noted that the traditional terms 'subject' and 'predicate' are not used. Generative grammars consider NP and VP preferable because they are more general; NP applies in example 9a to the object as well as to the subject. Moreover, both the P-rules and the tree indicate subject and predicate relationship by position in the rule or in the tree. If the traditional terms are used in a generative transformational grammar, they are given as 'subject of' and 'predicate of,' to indicate their use as relational terms.

The P-rules of example 7 can generate a huge number of sentences, given a fuller lexicon than that of example 8. Even the addition of elements in class 8c, such as *this, that,* increases the output of this small grammar, not to speak of the many nouns that could be added in class 8b and the many verbs in class 8a. Phrase structure grammars are accordingly very powerful.

In fact, they are too powerful; the rules given here would generate some unacceptable sentences, even with this small lexicon. The following sentence could be generated by the grammar but would be rejected by native speakers.

10. *The convertible drives a father.*

And the following sentence would be questioned or considered unacceptable; it implies that every father typically drives a convertible.

11. *A father drives a convertible (?)*

To prevent such ungrammatical and unacceptable sentences, elements of the lexicon are labeled for features. Some of these have long been used in grammars, such as the feature 'transitive/intransitive' for verbs. Examples of well-known features for nouns are 'common,' as for *father*, and 'proper,' as for *John;* also 'animate' for both *father* and *John,* 'inanimate' for *convertible*. In a thorough lexicon, *drive* would be characterized for features that would block sentences like example 10.

Even a lexicon indicating 'animate' and 'inanimate' nouns would be insufficient to generate only acceptable sentences for the verb *drive*. A grammar must also block sentences like example 12:

> 12. *The duck drives a convertible* (*?*)

It could do this by including the feature 'human.' In this way all items in the lexicon would be labeled precisely for features.

An explicit and precise lexicon defines words by feature classes, indicating by $(+)$ if they have a feature, by $(-)$ if they lack it. The nouns in example 9a would then be further identified as follows:

> 9b. father   convertible
> $\langle +$common$\rangle$ $\langle +$common$\rangle$
> $\langle +$human$\rangle$ $\langle -$human$\rangle$
> $\langle +$male$\rangle$ $\langle +$vehicle$\rangle$
>   etc.   etc.

If instead of *father* a proper noun would be the subject, for example, *George*, it would be labeled $\langle -$common$\rangle$. This label would block the use of a Det, so that the ungrammatical sentence, **The George drives a convertible,* would not be generated.

Lexical features in this way label classes that speakers recognize. The dictionaries we use do not list all such features, assuming that native speakers have mastered them as they learned the language. A generative grammar and its lexicon, on the other hand, set out to be completely explicit, approximating the control or competence of the native speaker. Both a generative grammar and a native speaker control the language so thoroughly that only grammatical sentences are allowed.

5.3 Transformational Grammars

Even large sets of P-rules and lexical features are inadequate for proper analysis of many sentences. The most widely cited examples in support of this statement are the following:

> 13a. *John is eager to please.*
> b. *John is easy to please.*

In a traditional analysis, *John* is subject of each sentence. But on more thorough analysis, *John* is indeed subject of *please* in sentence 13a but its object in 13b.

For 13b is actually a variant of the sentence: *It is easy to please John*. A traditional grammatical analysis accordingly produces a description that does not reflect the meanings of these sentences.

Moreover, speakers recognize many sentences as variants or combinations of others, such as the examples given earlier:

> 1a. *The father drives a convertible.*
> 2. *It's the father who drives a convertible.*
> 3. *What the father drives is a convertible.*

Sentences 2 and 3 are variants of 1a, with the same meaning but with a slight difference in emphasis. An economical grammar ought to treat language in accordance with this observation.

Yet, though sentences like 1a, 2, and 3 have the same meaning, traditional grammars analyze each of them differently. In sentence 2 they treat *it* as the 'grammatical subject.' They then provide a special label, such as 'expletive' or 'filler' *it*. They also state that the 'real' or 'true' subject of the thought is *father*, recognizing in this way the interpretation of speakers. In sentences like 3, *what* may be explained as equivalent to 'that which' and having a 'double construction' equivalent to *That which the father drives is a convertible*. By such analyses sequences like sentences 2 and 3 are presented as having grammatical structures that do not agree with their interpretation. A more economical grammar would relate these variants to the simple sentence with the same meaning.

Transformational grammars accord with this aim. They have a totally different way from traditional grammars of accounting for such sentences. Instead of treating them like simple sentences, they take them to be generated by the further type of rule, which gave the name of these grammars. A T-rule (transformational rule) "transforms" the output of a P-rule, without appreciably modifying the meaning.

In accordance with this way of examining language, transformational generative grammars include rules that affect the output of P-rules. Some sentences, like sentence 1a, are essentially outputs of the P-rules. Others, like sentences 2 and 3, result from transformational modifications after the P-rules have applied. A further such variant is the passive in English, as in the following example.

> 14. *A convertible is driven by the father.*

Sequences like sentences 2, 3, and 14 are therefore secondary, as may be noted by the use of a two-shafted arrow ($\Rightarrow$) in T-rules. We will examine selected T-rules in greater detail below. Here we briefly illustrate the passive transformation, by which sentence 14 is derived.

First, however, we will amend rules 7 and 8. These rules did not take account of the inflected form of the verb. Comparing with *drives* the progressive form, as in *is driving*, the simple present may be represented as having an auxiliary-like element *s*.

> 1b. *The father is driving a convertible.*

Both 1a and 1b would then result from a sequence consisting of four elements:

$$15.\ \text{NP} - \text{Aux} - \text{V} - \text{NP}$$
$$\quad\ 1\qquad 2\quad\ 3\quad\ 4$$

A T-rule operates on such elements, supplying surface characteristics of the derived sentence and often rearranging the elements, as does the T-rule labeled passive. The passive T-rule is stated as follows:

$$16.\ \text{NP} - \text{Aux} - \quad\text{V}\quad - \qquad\qquad \text{NP}$$
$$\quad\ 1\qquad 2\qquad 3 \qquad\qquad\qquad 4$$
$$\Rightarrow\ 4,\qquad 2,\quad be + en + 3, 0 + by +\ 1$$

By indicating that item 4 replaces item 1, this rule makes the object of a simple sentence, e.g., *a convertible,* into the subject of the passive sentence. By indicating that *be + en* is added to the verb node, the rule changes the active verb, e.g., *drives,* to the passive, *is driven.* Finally, it deletes the old object slot, replacing it with *by* plus the agent based on the subject, e.g., *the father,* of the simple sentence. Compare sentence 14 with sentence 1a to note the effect of this transformational rule.

In this way any passive sentence in English can be equated with its simple form, as in the following:

17a. *Tides are caused by the moon* =
     The moon causes tides
  b. *Music was provided by a combo* =
     A combo provided music
  c. *The dinner was enjoyed by all* =
     All enjoyed the dinner

One T-rule thus accounts for a large number of complex sentences, relating them to their simple counterpart. The simple sentence is then readily generated by P-rules. In this way a transformational generative grammar simplifies the analysis of many sentences of a language. Moreover, it recognizes the understanding among speakers that passive sentences are somehow secondary—modified forms of active sentences. Further, it reflects the acquisition of language by children; they first use active sentences. Then they learn passives and other variants like those illustrated in sentences 2 and 3.

As this discussion indicates, generative transformational grammar views the production of sentences by means of sets of rules. The P-rules are prior to the T-rules, or "deeper" than they in the derivation. This approach makes use of the constructs, **deep structure** and **surface structure.** Deep structure refers to sequences that provide the basic meaning of a sentence. Surface structure refers to sequences closer to actual utterances. But surface structures are not equivalent to actual utterances; they still include abstract elements like *en,* which then are interpreted by phonological rules.

The term **deep structure** as well as the passive transformation illustrates that generative transformational grammars employ greater abstractions than do traditional grammars. Such grammars indeed deal with abstract classes like noun, verb, plural, present tense, past participle, and so on. But transformational grammars include elements like *en;* this represents any past participle ending, whether in *driven, worked, bought, set,* etc. Another abstract element is Aux, which has various outputs, such as *is, may, could,* but may also lead to no overt marker, as in the sentence *I drive a convertible.* With their greater use of such abstractions, generative transformational grammars speak of **formatives** rather than morphemes.

Generative transformational grammars employ additional devices, which we will examine in greater detail below. One such device is ordering of rules; some cannot operate before others or they would cause ungrammatical sequences. The T-rules generating examples 2 and 3 apply after the passive T-rule; otherwise, sequences like 18a rather than 18b would result.

> 2.   *It's the father who drives a convertible.*
> 18a. **It's the father a convertible is driven by whom.*
>   b. *It's a convertible which is driven by the father.*

Clearly the passive of sentence 1 must be made before the *it*-form is generated. The *it*-rule is accordingly ordered after the passive rule in a grammar.

In general, speakers permit only certain patterns regulated in part by the sequence in which rules are applied. Rules must then be ordered in accordance with some principles. In keeping with its aims to be completely explicit, a generative transformational grammar sets out to determine those principles.

When more complex sentences such as 19a are examined, we find that speakers must employ even further devices.

> 19a. *They expect you to drive yourself to the concert.*

The reflexive *yourself* must be derived before its clause is included in the matrix sentence, for reflexives apply to the subject, which in 19a is *they.* Yet a native speaker of English would not allow 19b.

> 19b. **They expect you to drive themselves to the concert.*

Consequently the reflexive must have been introduced to the embedded clause before it is modified to the sequence in 19a. This sequence is a reduced form of a string like:

> 19c. *You drive yourself to the concert.*

Thereupon, in the generation of 19a the subject of *drive* is deleted when 19c is added to a sequence like:

> 19d. *They expect something.*

The analysis of sentences like 19a suggests that a series of rules applies first to "lower sentences" like 19c, and then to the remainder of the sentences in a compound string. To account for such application, transformational grammars include the notion of the **cycle.** In a compound derivation "lower sentences" are first generated by means of a cycle of rules; the cycle is then applied to higher sequences. We will now examine in greater detail the use of abstract categories, of rule ordering, and of the cycle in transformational grammars.

5.4 Abstract Categories: Aux and Selected T-rules

Transformational grammars set out to determine highly general rules. This aim has led to the assumption of some abstract categories that are not posited in traditional grammars. One such category is Aux; Aux is an abbreviation of auxiliary but is widely used now as a technical term. English examples may illustrate its usefulness.

When we examine frequent sentence patterns in English we find many with auxiliaries preceding the verb, for example:

> 20a. *We are taking the train.*
> b. *We will take the train.*
> c. *We may take the train.*
> d. *We don't take the train.*

Others lack such an auxiliary but have a different marker:

> 20e. *She takes the train.*

To provide a general P-rule for all such sentences, transformational grammars assume that they are based on a sequence:

> 7f. S → NP Aux VP

This rule is in accordance with the view that each of the surface sequences of sentence 20 is generated from one underlying structure. The differences in surface arrangements result from the application of transformational rules as the actual utterances are generated.

For sentences 20b and 20c the assumption of Aux has no problems, generating readily the modals *will* and *may*. But for 20e, the position of the surface element *s* after the verb must be accounted for. Similarly, in 20a and 20f we must account for other sequences: *be -ing* and *have -en*, and in 20g where the surface element is zero.

> 20f. *She has taken the train.*
> g. *We take the train.*

To generate these and many other sequences, transformational grammar makes use of various kinds of rules.

One kind of transformational rule moves elements, as in generating sequences like 20h.

20h. Will Doris take the train?

In 20h, Aux yielding *will* is adjoined before the initial NP. Placed directly under S, this process is referred to as daughter-adjunction.

We may assume an initial output for 20h like 21a:

21a. N (Doris) – Aux (will) – V (take) – NP (the train)

A movement rule transforms this output to that illustrated in 21b. It shifts the Aux before the subject, replacing the Aux position with zero in the surface string.

21b. Subject-Auxiliary Verb Inversion

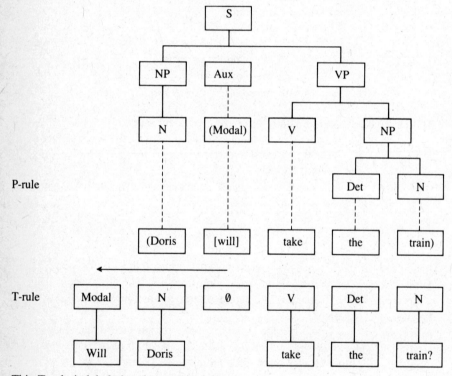

This T-rule is labeled and stated as follows:

21c. Subject-Auxiliary Verb Inversion

$$NP - \begin{Bmatrix} \text{Modal} \\ \text{be} \\ \text{have} \end{Bmatrix} - X$$

$$\begin{array}{ccc} 1 & 2 & 3 \\ \Rightarrow\ 2+1 & 0 & 3 \end{array}$$

Since this T-rule involves only the first two elements of the underlying string, the remainder is treated as a nonpertinent variable, symbolized by *X*. It could be of varied length and could include various sequences, such as: *take the train after work, take the train when she goes on vacation.* Following the practice of texts on logic, such variables are labeled *X, Y, Z,* and so on.

This rule also yields strings leading to sentences like the following:

> 21d. *Is Doris taking the train?*
>   e. *Has Doris taken the train?*

Like many T-rules, 21c includes deletion, as the zero replacing 2 indicates. T-rules then specify deletion as well as movement processes.

T-rules may also bring about substitutions. Relative clauses, for example, are derived from sentences embedded in others. A complex sentence may be made of two separate sentences, as in 22c:

> 22a. *John takes the train.*
>   b. *John likes the old days.*
>   c. *John, who likes the old days, takes the train.*

Here the relative pronoun *who* is substituted for *John* of the embedded sentence.

Sentences 22a and b would be generated with a tree like that given in 9a. A further tree, diagrammed in 23a, illustrates how 22b is embedded in 22a. A triangle is included in the derivation rather than a total analysis of some phrases, to simplify statement of the procedure for deriving relative clauses. Similarly the Aux node is not shown in the tree.

23a.

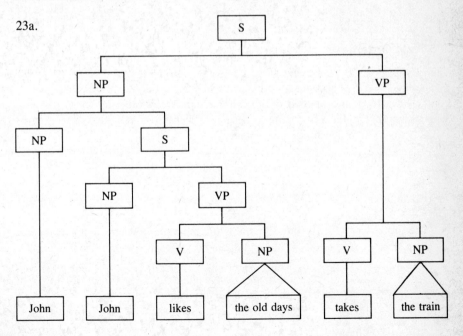

Relativization is brought about by embedding on an NP a sentence with an equivalent NP. That is, the person referred to in 22a must be the same as the person in 22b. What is important is that the embedded sentence is indicated next to the NP, as in 23b. Moreover, in stating the rule only the pertinent elements are noted; others are represented by the symbols for variables: X, Y, Z, W.

23b. Relative Clause Formation
$$X - [NP - [Y - NP - Z] \ ] \ - W$$

	NP	S		S NP	
1	2	3	4	5	6

Condition: 2 = 4
$\Rightarrow$ 1, 2, *who* + 3, 0, 5, 6

In the formation of relative clauses, as the stated condition indicates, a relative marker replaces one of two equivalent NPs. The remainder of the two strings is unaffected as the variables and the brackets indicate. The rule could be applied to any equivalent noun in an embedded sentence, such as 23c:

23c. *We gave the goblet to John.*

Application of the relative clause formation rule would yield:

23d. *We gave the goblet to John, who likes the old days.*

This rule, as well as those given earlier, illustrates how T-rules lead to surface forms through processes involving movement, deletion, and substitution.

5.5 Rule Ordering

Grammars set out to account for a language in the most compact manner possible. One of the procedures applied to achieve this aim is rule ordering.

English examples illustrating ordering of rules are provided by reflexive constructions, as in the following sentences:

24a. *Tom prides himself on his skill in fly-fishing.*
　b. *Help yourself to the candy.*
　c. (= 5) *Drive yourself to the concert.*

The process of reflexivization requires the presence of equivalent NPs within a clause. Earlier strings of 24a, b, and c can be represented as follows:

24d. *Tom$_i$ prides Tom$_i$ on his skill . . .*
　e. *You$_i$ help you$_i$ to the candy.*
　f. *You$_i$ drive you$_i$ to the concert.*

Indexes like $_i$ and $_j$ are used to identify items with equivalent or differing reference. Thus 25a implies two individuals:

25a. *She$_i$ helped she$_j$ to the car.*

The output of 25a would be 25b and not 25c:

25b. *She helped her to the car.*
  c. *She helped herself . . .*

By contrast, 25d implies one individual, leading to the sentence of 25e:

25d. *She$_i$ helped she$_i$ to the candy.*
  e. *She helped herself to the candy.*

In accordance with the requirements of generative transformational grammar for explicit derivation, sentences like 24b are derived from strings like 24f by two transformations: reflexivization and *you* deletion. These are given in rules 26 and 28.

26. Reflexivization
$X - NP - Aux - V - NP - Y$
1   2   3   4   5   6
Condition: 2 = 5
$\Rightarrow$ 1, 2, 3, 4, 5 + Reflexive, 6

The condition in this rule states that as noted above reflexivization only applies when two NPs stand in the same clause. Under this condition the rule generates all reflexive constructions in English, such as the following:

27a. *You drive yourself to the concert.*
  b. *Joan likes to sing to herself.*
  c. *Janet prides herself on her piano playing.*

When such sequences are requests or commands, a subject is not essential. It can be deleted by the *you*-deletion rule.

28. *You* Deletion
$X - $ *you* $- Pres - $ $V - Y$
1   2   3   4   5
$\Rightarrow$ 1,   0,   3,   4,   5

By this rule, sentences like the following are generated:

29a. *Drive yourself to the concert.*
  b. *Help yourself to the candy.*
  c. *Pay for the tickets for yourself.*

In generating sentences like those of example 29, these two rules must apply in a specific order. Since reflexivization requires an equivalent NP in the clause, it must apply before the subject is deleted, for otherwise there would be no possibility of the form *yourself*. In the transformational segment of a grammar, then, the reflexivization rule must apply before the *you*-deletion rule. Other rules as well must apply in a specific order.

Ordering of rules brings about greater economy in a grammar. A rule might indeed be written that would specify the condition for reflexivization even if it applied after the deletion of *you*. But the rule would have to be complicated. It would then conflict with the ideal requirements of a transformational generative grammar for simplicity and economy as well as explicitness.

5.6 Ordering by the Cyclic Convention

In the previous section we have noted that reflexives are introduced if a clause contains a further NP equivalent to another NP in it, as in 30a.

> 30a. *John expects himself to win.*

In some sentences, however, reflexives are found that do not refer to the actual surface subject, as in 30b:

> 30b. *John expects you to drive yourself to the station.*

Both of these sentences are derived from earlier strings, which we may represent as follows:

> 30c. *John expects something.*
> d. *John will win.*
> e. *You will drive yourself to the station.*

Without presenting the details involved in generating these and still more involved sentences, we may note that the simplest description of sentences like 30b requires reflexivization before application of the T-rule introducing 30e into the matrix sentence 30c. That is to say, T-rules are applied first to any lower string in a tree containing more than one S. Thereupon they are applied to higher strings.

In this way reflexivization applies to the lower string represented in 30e before it is combined with 30c. It does not, however, apply to the structure representing 30a until 30d is incorporated in it. Such a sequence of application is referred to as the **cyclic convention.**

We may illustrate briefly the derivation of 30b. In examining it, we note that verbs like *expect* may take object clauses of three types, known as **complements.**

> 31a. *I expect that he will go.*
> b. *I expect him to go.*
> c. *I expect his going.*

As suggested above, these might be accounted for by proposing that *expect* may be followed by indefinites like *something;* this then is deleted as the embedded clause is introduced.

By another procedure, the bar-X convention, the VP is assumed to have as "object" an S, under which sentences may be embedded. The S element is equivalent to a complementizer, either (*for*) *to* with an infinitive, or a possessive + *-ing,* or *that* plus a clause. Such a derivation may be illustrated by example 32a. See page 112.

In such a string the subject of the lower sentence is "raised" to the higher string by means of a T-rule known as subject raising. This brings about the sequence: *John expects you S.* Now S is left with the following structure:

32b.

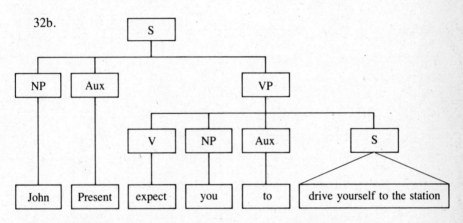

If reflexivization had not applied before *you* was raised from the lower string, there would be no possibility of generating *yourself.* To avoid such an impasse, the cyclic convention was developed.

The rules and patterns examined here illustrate the procedures applied to syntactic strings in transformational grammar. A complete transformational grammar would include rules for all patterns of language. As one further illustration we may examine the use of the bar-X convention in extraposition.

As in 32a, S is a node under NP. Three variants of 33 are therefore readily generated.

    33a. *That Tim plays Haydn delights Ann.*
       b. *Tim's playing Haydn delights Ann.*
       c. *For Tim to play Haydn delights Ann.*
      (d. *See page 113.*)

The transformational rule for extraposition is as follows:

    33e. Extraposition
$$[S] \quad X$$
$$1 \quad\quad 2$$
$$\Rightarrow \quad it, \quad 2 + 1$$

32a.

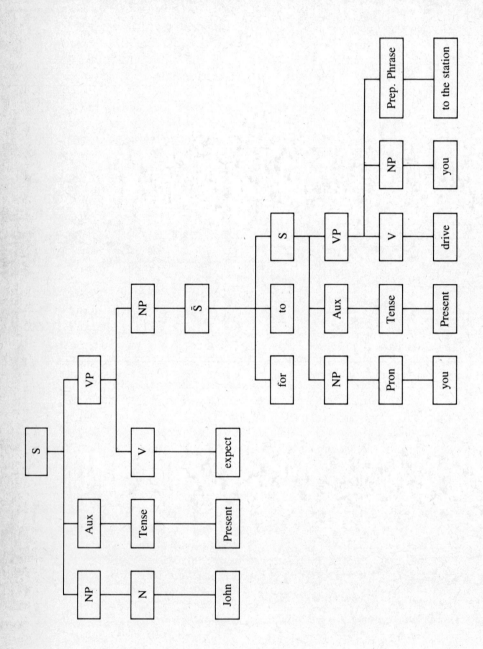

33d

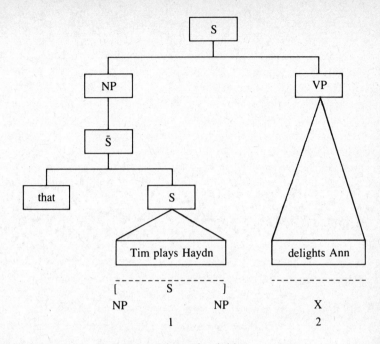

Applied to 33a and c the extraposition rule yields:

> 33f. *It delights Ann that Tim plays Haydn.*
>   g. *It delights Ann for Tim to play Haydn.*

In this way, the bar-S device yields transposed structures with a single rule. Moreover, these examples may illustrate how transformational analysis points up patterns that are treated by specific rules and those that are not.

Extraposed patterns themselves may be treated by further rules, as illustrated in example 34.

> 34a. *To catch bass in this lake is easy.*
>   b. *It is easy to catch bass in this lake.*
>   c. *This lake is easy to catch bass in.*
>   d. *Bass are easy to catch in this lake.*

The imaginative labeling applied to such matters has given rise to the label *Tough movement* for the process illustrated in 34d. This is the transformation applied in the often cited sentence: *John is easy to please.* By Tough movement an object is raised to a higher sentence. The number of adjectives that permit sequences like 34c is small, including a few like *tough, easy.* Determining the best analysis of such patterns has contributed to the extension of transformational theory. It has also led to revisions in the theory. Details may be found in handbooks like Baker's *Introduction to Generative Transformational Syntax.* Despite revisions, the approach to the study of grammar has been maintained, as summarized in the following section.

5.7 The Pattern of a Generative Transformational Grammar

As we noted above, a generative transformational grammar views language as a process. Moreover, the sentence is the basic unit. Grammars, then, present the production of sentences by speakers. They also set out to understand the processes involved in acquiring a language.

Further, syntax is treated as the central component of human language. Of all the known communication systems—those of bees, of birds, of other animals— only human language has a highly developed syntax. Through it human beings are able to express much broader and more complex meanings than are their fellow creatures. Accordingly, grammars might well give the central position in language to syntax.

Transformational grammar places high store on other human capabilities, such as that of infants to acquire any language, to learn it rapidly and in accordance with well-documented stages, as we noted in Chapter 2. Because these observations are true of any human infants learning any language whatsoever, generative transformational grammar assumes a common grammatical segment for all languages.

The common segment consists of lexical elements and P-rules. The P-rules generate basic strings, such as those given above. The lexical elements are features, which languages combine into words. The features may be variously combined from language to language; for example, in one language a word *cousin* may be neutral with regard to the male/female feature, whereas in another language this feature distinguishes words, as in our kinship terms *uncle/aunt, niece/nephew*. Together the P-rules and lexical elements lead to deep structure.

The deep structure entities are further processed by the set of rules known as transformational. Application of T-rules leads to surface structures. Expression of these in sentences is brought about by phonological rules, as discussed in Chapter 3, Section 3.7.

The grammar then consists of the follow components:

35.
   PS-COMPONENT
   LEXICAL COMPONENT
      DEEP STRUCTURES   SEMANTIC COMPONENT

   TRANSFORMATIONAL COMPONENT
      SURFACE STRUCTURES

   PHONOLOGICAL COMPONENT
      SENTENCES

The rules of these components encompass the speaker's activities in producing utterances.

The sketch of a transformational grammar presented here is in accordance with an early form of the theory, published by Chomsky in 1965 and often referred to as the Standard Theory. After 1965, modifications were made in the theory, to account for structures that caused difficulties for the Standard Theory; among these modifications is the bar-X convention. Others have to do with analysis of stylistic features. Some American speakers, for example, speak with a nasal twang, but they have the same phonological, transformational, and syntactic rules as those who do not. Such characteristics are treated in a stylistic component, after the phonological.

The semantic component includes rules that have to do with the expression of meaning. These deal with spheres that have long occupied logicians; they assure the proper logical form of sentences. We may take an example from quantifiers, *some* and *any*. These two quantifiers have been interpreted by some scholars as variants: *some* is used in positive sentences like 36a; *any* in negatives like 36b.

> 36a. *Yes, I want some.*
> b. *No, I don't want any.*

But like much of language, the situation is not quite so simple, as a few illustrations indicate.

In the following sentence, *some* is quite acceptable.

> 37a. *The clerk was quite surprised when I told him I didn't want some of the imported caviar.*

Here *some* stands in a negative sentence, but it is used because the sentence is produced from the point of view of the clerk, rather than the speaker, who may well have said:

> 37b. *I don't want any of the imported caviar.*

In a similar fashion, a mother may urge a child to eat by saying 38a rather than 38b.

> 38a. *Don't you want some potatoes?*
> b. *Don't you want any potatoes?*

The rules for such patterns are treated in generative transformational grammar as being applied by speakers in parallel with the rules discussed above. A recent form of the theory, called the Revised Extended Standard Theory, sets out to determine these as well as syntactic and phonological rules.

A component including such rules may be included in figure 35 after the deep structures. Thus a semantic or logical component would regulate quantifiers and other elements having to do with meaning much as transformational rules regulate the form of sentences like 2 and 3.

In producing sentences, then, a speaker employs a variety of processes. Besides the syntactic devices sketched in this chapter are those for the phonological

component, outlined in the last sections of Chapter 3. Here, too, processes are
heavily emphasized. These rules employ features as indicated in Chapter 3, Section
3.7. Distinctive features and lexical features are the smallest entities of language;
they are manipulated by rules to produce the sentences used in conveying
information.

5.8 Other Forms of Generative Grammar

As theories, generative grammars are based on certain assumptions. Differing
assumptions may accordingly lead to different grammars. In contrast with the
assumptions maintained by Chomsky on central position for syntax, some linguists
assign central position to semantics. Such linguists are known as *generative
semanticists;* their approach is referred to as *generative semantics,* in contrast with
generative syntax as advocated by Chomsky.

Differences in approaches also have to do with sentence generation. The
standard theory, as we have seen, proposes as initial strings highly abstract
sequences, such as S → NP Aux VP. These lead to actual utterances through a
series of further rules, among them T-rules. The massive use of transformations
resulted in various problems, such as the interrelationships of T-rules. We have
examined devices for clarifying these, such as rule ordering and the cyclic
convention. Even these devices have not solved all problems. Moreover, psychological experiments have been unsuccessful in determining the validity of transformational rules. The failure of such experiments when applied to the transformational component has led to skepticism concerning it and, consequently, also to
grammars attempting to reduce the scope of transformational rules. Such grammars
may set out from surface strings rather than from abstract structures.

Unlike traditional grammar, which also begins with surface strings, these
grammars apply at the same time rigorous rules to account for the syntax and the
meaning of sentences and their constituents. The sentences are described in a
panoply of rules, providing a rich but also a highly complex analysis. Approaches
of this sort are now under development; see now Dowty et al. and Katz.[1] Even an
introduction to them would unduly extend an elementary presentation of generative
grammar. Students concerned with such approaches may build on the generative
grammars of the past several decades.

5.9 The Impact of Transformational Generative Grammars

Generative transformational grammar strongly affected theoretical studies of
language. Linguists holding the theory explored syntactic problems, attempting to
clarify relationships between syntactic patterns as traditional grammars had clarified
morphological relationships. Patterns like "raising" were scrutinized repeatedly;

[1] David R. Dowty et al., *Introduction to Montague Semantics* (Dordrecht: Reidel, 1981), and Jerrold
J. Katz, *Language and Other Abstract Objects* (Totowa, N.J.: Rowman and Littlefield, 1981).

if grammars were to account for the total structure of language economically, they might hope to solve with one set of rules the process involved in raising subjects equivalent to the subject of the matrix verb, as in 39a, and those differing from it, as in 39b and c.

> 39a. *I expect to come.*
> b. *I expect him to come.*
> c. *I expect that he will come.*

Intensive investigations of such problems led not only to various solutions but also to great concern with syntax. That concern is a major contribution of transformational grammar.

Moreover, the emphasis placed on syntax has brought this segment of language greater prominence. A new large-scale handbook on English places far more emphasis on syntax than on morphology or phonology.[2] Yet this grammar does not adhere closely to the theory proposed by Chomsky. The effects of transformational theory may, then, be indirect, in focusing emphasis on syntax without determining the procedures used in presenting syntactic patterns.

Transformational grammar has also exerted an influence on the teaching of language. An example is the use of "sentence combining." In learning to write, students often set down one simple sentence after another, without using devices like cleft sentences to indicate emphasis, without subordinating matters that are less essential, and so on. "Sentence combining" instructs such students in understanding such relationships. As we have noted, transformational grammar treats cleft sentences as variants of simple sentences, such as sentences 2 and 3 as variations of sentence 1. Similarly, relative clauses and other subordinate clauses are embedded through transformational rules. By applying this view of such complex sentences, teachers of rhetoric have been successful in improving the writing skills of many students.

A major impact of generative transformational grammar has had to do with psychological investigations involving language. Earlier psychological study of language was often limited to externals, in keeping with the attention linguists gave to surface forms. Investigations were carried out on possible recall of lists of words. These yielded little information on language or on its control by the brain. The deep structures proposed by transformational grammar, on the other hand, offered possibilities of studying patterns of far greater interest. Cognitive psychologists thereupon undertook to determine the reality of such constructs as subjects and predicates of clauses. Investigators of language acquisition examined the sequence of mastering complex structures, such as passive as opposed to active sentences. Such investigations are continuing, not only on language acquisition but also on language loss, as in speakers with brain injuries, on language difficulties, as with neurotic and psychotic speakers. Investigations of all these kinds are carried out to determine the common features of language.

[2] Randolph Quirk et al., *A Grammar of Contemporary English.*

Features and characteristics common to all languages have come to be known as universals. They receive support from such observations as the ability of all infants to acquire any language. That ability must rest on basic features underlying all languages. One readily observed universal is the existence of sentences in all languages. Another is the universal use of consonants. But investigators seek more specific universals, as we have noted earlier and will see further in Chapter 8. The interest in universals has been heightened by better understanding of control of language by the brain, especially by greater knowledge of areas that control semantic, syntactic, and phonological functions. As such understanding has been increased, further problems have been disclosed, among them the modifications of sentences in longer sequences, known as discourse, or text. These problems will be examined in the following chapters.

QUESTIONS FOR REVIEW

1. State implications of the statement that a grammar is a theory of a language.
2. Define *generative* in reference to grammars.
3. Define *NP,* comparing it with the terms *object* and *subject.*
4. Define *VP, Det,* and *Art.*
5. How is → interpreted when it occurs in rules? How is :? How is ⇒?
6. What is a P-rule (PS-rule)? A lexical rule? List some lexical features.
7. What is a transformational grammar? A T-rule?
8. Give examples of English sentence patterns that are readily accounted for with T-rules.
9. Define *deep* as opposed to *surface* structure.
10. Define *formative.*
11. Cite various elements generated from Aux.
12. State the subject-auxiliary verb inversion T-rule and indicate what it does.
13. Discuss three kinds of effects of T-rules.
14. Give a full explanation of the relative clause formation rule 23b, indicating the purpose of each symbol contained in it.
15. State the purpose of adding conditions to T-rules, illustrating with the condition in the relative clause formation rule.
16. State evidence in favor of assuming rule ordering.
17. State evidence in favor of the cycle.
18. How is the bar-X convention used? How does it contribute to simplicity of the grammar?
19. Sketch the pattern of a generative transformational grammar.
20. Discuss some of the impacts exerted by generative transformational grammar.

PROBLEMS FOR REVIEW

1. The following is a phrase structure grammar of a portion of English:

$$\#S\#$$

$S \rightarrow NP \quad VP$

$NP \rightarrow \begin{Bmatrix} (Det) & N \\ Pronoun \end{Bmatrix}$

$VP \rightarrow \begin{Bmatrix} V \ (NP) \\ is \ Adj \end{Bmatrix}$

Det: the, this
N: editor, girl, Tim, organization
Pronoun: it
V: saw, remembered, wrote
Adj: energetic, impossible, courageous

   a. Make ten grammatical sentences with this grammar.
   b. Two categorial elements are given in parentheses, Det and NP in the VP rule. Would the first ever be utilized in this exercise? If so, under what conditions?
   c. Would the second element in parentheses be used? If so, make five such sentences.

2. The following are selected English sentences.
   1. The books vanished completely.
   2. His notes disappeared suddenly.
   3. Their records dropped alarmingly.
   4. Her glasses broke completely.

   a. Construct a phrase-structure grammar that will generate these sentences.
   b. Make four additional sentences that are acceptable, using your P-rules and this lexicon.

3. Illustrate the use of the passive transformational rule given in example 16 of this chapter with one of the following sentences. First produce a tree of the sentence you select and then apply passive.
   1. Joe rotated his tires after the picnic.
   2. The players enjoyed their game in spite of the rain.
   3. Yesterday Alice took her dog to the vet.

   After producing your passive sentence, apply the T-rule given in example 21 to make a question.

4. The following include relative clauses. Using the rule given in example 23b, indicate the simple sentences from which these sentences were produced. Illustrate the formation of the relative clause in any one of the examples by drawing the appropriate tree.
   1. People who throw stones shouldn't live in glass houses.
   2. This is the cat that worried the rat that ate the cheese.
   3. He couldn't find the street on which the garage was located.
   4. Help yourself to the sandwiches that are on the upper shelf.

5. In accordance with the T-rule for reflexivization (example 26), determine the strings for the following before its application.
    1. Jack hurt himself on the court.
    2. If they saw themselves as others do, they would retire.
    3. Don't take yourself so seriously.

6. Give the deep structure of one of the following sentences and the transformations to derive it.
    1. He expected them to take the dog.
    2. Did she think that he built the birdhouse?
    3. They were surprised by her driving.

7. Examples 1 to 4 at the beginning of the chapter illustrate clefting in English. This device points up segments of sentences. If *that* is used, such patterns are known as clefts; if *what*, they are known as pseudoclefts. In addition to the first four of this chapter, here are further examples:
    1. Joe wore the blue cap.
    2. It was the blue cap that Joe wore. (Cleft)
    3. It was Joe who wore the blue cap. (Cleft)
    4. What Joe wore was the blue cap. (Pseudocleft)
    a. Discuss the effect of these patterns, indicating the segment to which they give prominence.
    b. As the preceding sentences 2 and 3 illustrate, clefts can apply to objects as well as to subjects. To what element of the sentence do pseudoclefts apply?
    c. If sentence 1 above is modified in the following way by a pseudocleft, which element receives focus?
        5. What Joe did was wear the blue cap.
    d. How do these sentence variants compare in meaning with passives, as in the following sentence?
        6. The blue cap was worn by Joe.

FURTHER READING

Akmajian, Adrian, and Frank Heny. *An Introduction to the Principles of Transformational Syntax*. Cambridge, Mass.: MIT Press, 1975.

Baker, Carl L. *Introduction to Generative Transformational Syntax*. Englewood Cliffs, N.J.: Prentice-Hall, 1978.

Burt, Marina K. *From Deep to Surface Structure. An Introduction to Transformational Syntax*. New York: Harper & Row, 1971.

Chomsky, Noam. *Syntactic Structures*. The Hauge: Mouton, 1957.

———. *Aspects of the Theory of Syntax*. Cambridge, Mass.: MIT Press, 1965.

Quirk, Randolph, Sidney Greenbaum, Geoffrey Leech, and Jan Svartvik. *A Grammar of Contemporary English*. London: Longman, 1972.

CHAPTER SIX

Beyond the Sentence

6.1 Shortcomings of Sentence Grammars

In the past, linguists concentrated on the study of sentences. Longer sequences, such as entire texts, were of concern to the discipline known as *rhetoric* in the Middle Ages, to literary scholars in the modern university. This division of interest is now changing. On the one hand, many widely admired literary scholars, such as Tzvetan Todorov and Roland Barthes, have incorporated linguistic procedures in their treatment of literature. And many linguists are discussing texts rather than sentences as the basic units of communication. The broader concern has raised new questions and placed some old questions in a new light. When we limit ourselves to the study of sentences, many features of language are left out of consideration. Almost any text will disclose some of these, such as the following passage from Chapter 3 of *Alice in Wonderland*.[1]

> 1. *This question the Dodo could not answer without a great deal of thought, and it stood for a long time with one finger pressed upon its forehead . . .*

[1] *The Complete Works of Lewis Carroll,* Introduction by Alexander Woollcott (New York: Random House, n.d.), p. 38.

What we hear or read:	Why, *she*, of course.
Our literal interpretation:	Why, ? , of course.
What we understand from the preceding material:	Why, Alice . . . , of course.
What we understand from the text:	Why, Alice is to give the prizes, of course.

Figure 6.1 Deriving Meaning

An illustration of the use of the entire text to achieve understanding of a statement. Without the text, the statement is almost meaningless; we do not know what ''she'' refers to. If we have the preceding material, we substitute ''Alice'' for ''she.'' But only from the entire text do we know the entire meaning.

> *while the rest waited in silence. At last the Dodo said* ''Everybody *has won, and* all *must have prizes.''*
> ''*But who is to give the prizes?''* *quite a chorus of voices asked.*
> *''Why,* she, *of course,''* *said the Dodo.*

In this text, the first two words represent the object of *answer,* in contrast with the normal word order:

> 2. *The Dodo could not answer this question.*

Grammars deal with such sentences. In transformational grammar such a shift of the object before the subject is known as ''Yiddish movement'' because this word order is common in Yiddish. From the point of view of discourse the interest lies in the specific force linking the sentence directly to the previous sentence and on the reasons for using such order at this point in the text.

Similarly, the next paragraph, beginning with 'But who,' has the object clause initially rather than after 'asked.' Moreover, 'the rest' can only be interpreted if we know an earlier section of the story. Further, if it is to be understood, the last statement 'she' must be supplemented by 'is to give the prizes,' as illustrated in Figure 6.1. In addition, by his italics the author has indicated prominence for *Everybody* and *all,* presumably to signal the enthusiasm of the speaker as well as the unexpectedness of such a decision. All of these features of language have meanings, meanings that cannot be determined or studied rigorously by dealing with each sentence alone. The devices employed to link sentences in longer sequences and to relate them with their users are now receiving widespread attention.

Linguistic investigation of sequences longer than sentences is known as **discourse analysis** or **text linguistics.** Investigation of relationships between users and language is known as **pragmatics.** Some aims of these approaches will be examined in the following sections.

6.2 Sentences in Texts and Functions of Their Constituents

Patterns like that found in the initial sentence of our *Alice in Wonderland* passage first attracted attention among scholars who were especially concerned with the function of words and grammatical patterns rather than with the forms themselves. The most prominent of such scholars carried out their investigations in Czechoslovakia. Their approach is often known as **functionalism.** To them also we owe the elaboration of the phoneme concept, as it developed in classical phonemics. Phonemes are sound units identified in part by their functions. Syntactic and semantic units were to be investigated in the same way.

When we examine passages like example 1 for functional entities, we find that these may be assigned by different rules from those applying to syntactic entities. For, as in this passage, an object may have a more important function in one position of a text than a subject. Typically we think of English sentences as placing subjects first, then verbs, and later still objects; linguistic rules, such as S → NP VP, imply such an arrangement. But any examination of texts, whether written or spoken, shows that the arrangement is not rigidly followed. Rather, we place first the entities referring to the topic or theme of discourse.

Handbooks on style also recommend that writers avoid repeated sentences of the pattern *subject, verb, object.* The recommendation is made in the interest of writing paragraphs and essays characterized by "unity" and "coherence." Sentences are to be linked by a number of devices: by varying arrangements, by the use of pronouns referring to constituents of previous sentences, by omissions, and so on. As we have seen, these devices were employed by Carroll in example 1 above. All of them are concerns of functional linguistic study.

Among devices that help to avoid a succession of "monotonous" sentences is the use of the passive and of *there* with forms of *be.* Grammars treat both of these constructions, as well as initial placement of the object, as variants of simple sentences. Besides the arrangement of the first clause he used, Carroll might have chosen:

> 3a. *This question could not be answered by the Dodo . . .*
> b. *There was this question the Dodo could not answer . . .*

A transformational linguist would relate these variants to the simple pattern given in example 2. The "derivation" of 3a and 3b as well as Carroll's version would then be specified by transformations, as we have noted in Chapter 5, Section 5.3. But the connotation of the modified sentences would be left for others to study.

Text linguists seek to move beyond this restriction to syntactic analysis. Their broadened concern recognizes that the variations are not merely syntactic; rather, they change the meaning as well as the form of the normal sentence. Investigations of the meaning carried by segments of a sequence, regardless of their syntactic role, employ the terms *theme* and *rheme.* Instead of *theme,* some scholars use *topic;* instead of *rheme,* they use *comment.* The **theme,** generally the initial element, identifies the principal item of content in a sentence. The **rheme** tells us something about the theme, generally something new. The theme, on the other hand, often refers to old material, already introduced in earlier portions of a text. Placement of the grammatical object initially in example 1 illustrates how writers employ various elements as themes to relate the sentences in a text and to highlight those elements.

A functional approach to analysis of the passive illustrates the usefulness of examining sentences for theme and rheme. Passive sentences in English put the natural syntactic object as the subject, by these means identifying it as an element previously mentioned or intended as the center of attention. The theme is highlighted, singled out as a topic to be further elaborated. When we regard the English passive in this way, we see that it is a construction for emphasizing the object of active sentences and downplaying the subject, as in example 3a. In German, the passive can also highlight the verb when an impersonal pronoun is used as subject:

> 4. *Es wurde getanzt.*
>   'It was danced = Dancing was going on.'

In languages with the adversity passive, the verb is also highlighted, as in Japanese.

> 5. *Kare ga tsuma ni shinareta.*
>   he (*sub*) wife   by was-died
>   'He suffered the death of his wife.'

Analysis for function as well as syntax in this way sharpens our understanding of constructions found in different languages and also of the force of a given construction in any text.

6.3 Concerns of Text Linguistics and Rhetoric

Text linguistics is concerned with all such devices and their meanings. Other possible transformations of example 2 are pseudoclefts, as in 6, and clefts, as in 7.

> 6a. *What the Dodo could not answer is this question.*
> b. *What the Dodo could not do is answer this question.*
> 7a. *It was this question that the Dodo could not answer.*
> b. *It was the Dodo that could not answer this question.*

Both of these constructions imply that the text will go on with commentary on 'this question' or on 'answering this question,' explaining in some way the Dodo's inability. Investigation of such patterns and their functions informs us of subtleties of our usage. It is the task of rhetoricians to apply such findings, as in the generally required "Freshman English" courses.

Handbooks on rhetoric advise writers to avoid the passive. Further consideration of its implications in English illustrates the reasons for their concern, but on the other hand also the reason for the preference among many scientists for the passive rather than the active. William Strunk's classic recommendations give as reason for avoiding the passive that "the active voice is usually more direct and vigorous than the passive."[2] Yet Strunk is vague about the basis of the indirectness and lack of vigor. A few lines later, however, he intimates that they result from the constituent used as subject. Since a subject of an active verb is often animate and the object inanimate, as in example 2, active sentences are indeed more direct and vigorous.

Scientific writing, on the other hand, is often condemned because of overuse of the passive. But scientists favor it for the very reasons identified by Strunk. Scientific results are supposed to be impersonal. The facts are to speak for themselves, with no involvement by the writer. How better to succeed in this aim than by using the passive! Yet the impersonality welcomed by scientific writers lacks appeal in general essays and in literature. Consideration of language in its various applications, then, keeps us from blanket condemnation or approval of any one construction. Linguistic analysis shows us the reason for the effect. Rhetoricians suggest the preferable patterns to achieve a given effect.

This discussion of the passive in English illustrates that text linguists and functional linguists deal with somewhat the same facts of language as do rhetoricians and "Freshman English" teachers. Text linguists and functional linguists identify and describe patterns that bring about coherent texts; rhetoricians and teachers of English advise writers on their uses.

6.4 Sentences in Various Uses: Performatives

Recent study of language has drawn on logic and its wider field, philosophy, to deal with problems of language. Here again, disciplines that have had differing concerns ever since the founding of universities are joining. The initial curriculum of the medieval university concentrated on three disciplines: grammar, rhetoric, and logic. They made up the trivium, literally 'three ways' to deal with communication: grammar with its forms; rhetoric with effective expression; logic with the use of reason in expression. Scholars from the three disciplines are now collaborating in seeking deeper insights into communication.

One of the highly influential scholars in this collaboration was the late J. L. Austin. Much of his impact came through a small book of essays, *How to Do Things with Words,* published posthumously. Austin pointed out a considerable difference between normal utterances and utterances like the following:

8. *I name this ship the* Queen Elizabeth.
9. *I give and bequeath my watch to my brother.*

[2] William Strunk, Jr., *Elements of Style,* 2d ed. With revisions, an introduction, and a chapter on writing by E. B. White (New York: Macmillan, 1972), p. 13.

These and many other utterances, such as the marriage vow, differ from simple statements by involving the performance of an action as well as the production of an utterance. Accordingly, Austin labeled them **performatives.** Among other characteristics of performatives is their role in an activity; example 8 can only be used meaningfully when a ship is christened, 9 only in a will. Moreover, if we do not carry out the action appropriately, the performative statement is not regarded as false but rather as made "in bad faith."

If, for example, the following utterance were made and not followed through, we would say it was a false statement:

> 10. *I gave my watch to my brother*.

But if upon reading a will no watch is discovered, we describe 9 not as erroneous but rather as deceitful. Austin's book led to great interest in performatives and also to the more general study of relationships between utterances and the persons involved.

6.5 Speech Acts

Austin went on to distinguish many such utterances, designating them as locutionary acts of various types. They are now more often referred to as **speech acts.**

Some speech acts are scarcely more than expressions of effusiveness.

> 11. *Boy, it's hot today*.

Others are **illocutionary;** "in saying something, we do something," such as informing, ordering, or warning someone.

> 12. *I advise you not to roller-skate at your age*.

Still others are **perlocutionary.** By saying something we bring about an activity in someone else.

> 13. *I persuaded her to go roller-skating*.

The study of performatives in this way led to identification of three kinds of utterances: simple locutionary, illocutionary, and perlocutionary. Austin went on to deal with subsets of these, which we will not pursue here. He also made it clear that seemingly simple sentences are often highly complex, and that they include a great deal of implicit information. Such complexity Austin illustrated by examining in detail some apparently simple statements.

One of his examples is often cited:

> 14. *The cat is on the mat*.

While syntactically simple, this statement involves a complex set of assumptions and attitudes. First of all, the utterance of such a sequence "presupposes" the existence of a cat, of a mat, and so on. And if the cat is on the mat, this "entails" the fact that the mat is under the cat. Moreover, speakers uttering the statement "imply" that the situation is true, that the cat is actually located on the mat. On the other hand, if a hearer does not believe the statement, such lack of belief does not imply that the cat is not on the mat; the belief may simply be wrong. In this way, Austin explored features associated with locutionary acts, such as presupposition, entailment, and implication.

Since Austin called these matters to general attention, they have been intensively studied. If we are concerned with the meaning of utterances, we must deal with such subtleties, not simply with the relationship between a word and an object in the outside world. Many utterances of ours, even a routine statement like 14, impose such requirements for understanding; their entailments, implications, and presuppositions must be known by the hearer as well as the speaker.

We may examine the requirements for understanding even a simple statement like the following:

15. *The Mississippi is 1,470 miles long.*

Among other things this statement presupposes that there is such a river. Further, it entails the conclusion that the speaker is dealing with the Mississippi River proper, rather than the Mississippi-Missouri, which is much longer, one of the longest rivers in the world. Moreover, the statement implies that rivers are objects that can be measured in miles. Our use of language and our knowledge of English involve mastery of such subtle information, also about our attitudes and beliefs when we speak.

Texts employ devices that are rich in implications. If we encounter a text beginning: *There was once a . . .* , we know immediately that the text is a folktale. If on the other hand someone says: *Have you heard the one . . .* , we know that the speaker is about to tell a joke. Each of these phrases has its implications. One implication has to do with the special kind of text. When the phrase *Once upon a time* is used, we do not expect a factual report. Rather, the phrase puts us in the frame of mind for a fanciful account. Other languages have devices to communicate such implications. German fairy tales commonly begin: *Es war einmal* 'There once was.' In Sanskrit, folktales begin: *asti* 'there is,' and continue with identification of the site or the characters involved. Children soon come to understand such devices and their implications. They also come to know the structure of texts and may protest if the text does not fulfill their expectations—that is to say, if it disappoints their presuppositions concerning certain language patterns.

Interpretation of language, then, calls on more than grammatical or lexical knowledge. We have texts from the past that we can analyze completely for their words and forms, but we do not know what they mean. Among these are some of the runic inscriptions from the first centuries of our era. A relatively transparent one is given in Chapter 10, Section 10.3. Literally it say: 'I, Hlewagastir of Holt, made the horn.' Historical linguists derive a great deal of evidence about the language from this inscription and are grateful for that information. But we can only speculate on the real purpose of such inscriptions. We may ask whether the horn has special value because its maker inscribed his name on it. Others speculate on the meaning of elements, such as the third word. Some valuable pieces of metal today have totally different inscriptions on them, such as *In God we trust*. We have clues providing information on the runic texts. But the people who wrote them left no accounts on their purpose, and generations of scholars have constructed scenarios to develop an understanding of these and other inscriptions of the past.

The problems we face in the interpretation of such texts illustrate the importance of knowing both the setting in which language is used and the knowledge of its users. Exploring the extent of that knowledge is now a major concern, along with exploring how we acquire that knowledge. How, for example, does a child ever come to know not only that the noise *cookie* refers to an object in the outside world, but also that speakers mean more than the simple content of a question when they say to the child:

16. *Do you want a cookie?*

Somehow a child has come to know that this statement entails that there are objects known as cookies. It implies among other things that cookies are edible. It carries the presupposition that if the child indicates assent, a cookie will be forthcoming. Clearly, the study of language involves even more than examining an utterance in its text; its relationship to its users, whether speaker or hearer, must also be known.

Study of the relationship between language and its users is known as pragmatics, a designation given it by the American philosopher Charles Sanders Peirce. Peirce identified it as one of the three branches of a new science concerned with the study of signs, which he called **semiotics.**

According to this view signs, whether those of language or any other system of communication, are studied from three points of view:

1. **Syntactics,** the study of relationships among signs
2. **Semantics,** the study of relationships between signs and the outside world
3. **Pragmatics,** the study of relationships between signs and their users, as noted above

The last of these represents an addition to the sphere of language study beyond that outlined in Chapter 1.

Until recently, investigators of language concerned themselves primarily with two of Peirce's groups, *syntactics,* which is to say, linguistics in the narrow sense, and *semantics. Pragmatics* is now being widely studied, but investigators do not restrict its scope in the same way as did Peirce. Current pragmatics involves study of meaning but not truth conditions, which remain in the sphere of semantics. Pragmatics studies how sentences and texts fit into the contexts in which they are produced. To examine more specifically how it achieves this aim, we shall survey the kinds of information carried by speech; thereupon we shall survey these in relation to observations of child language acquisition.

6.6 Approaches and Requirements of Artificial Intelligence

Attempts to simulate the activities of human speakers have disclosed clearly the many kinds of information carried by speech. A close look at the quotation in example 1, especially the sentence in 17, illustrates current activities in the study of language by specialists in **artificial intelligence (AI).**

17. Everybody *has won, and* all *must have prizes.*

Like sentence 17, utterances involve reference to events and things in the outside world. Typically, verbs such as 'won' refer to events, nouns and pronouns such as 'prizes' refer to things. Grammars sort out and describe the relationships of such entities to one another. Additional analysis sorts out the meaningful interrelationships of elements, such as nouns. An active subject, like *everybody* occupies the role of an **Agent.** If the grammatical subject, on the other hand, is the recipient of the action, it may be referred to as **Dative.** In 17, for example, the grammatical subject of *have* indicates recipients of the action rather than the doers, or Agents. This approach seeks out "roles" of nouns in utterances. These have also been called *cases,* and the approach itself has been called *case grammar.* The approach is prominent among scholars who attempt to simulate communication by means of computers.

For that purpose a computer must "know" as much about language as does the brain. It must have the results of a grammatical analysis, which labels *everybody* in sentence 17 for its part of speech as a pronoun and for its sentence function as a subject. It must also deal with role relationships, labeling *everybody* as an Agent. Moreover, it must know the meaning of items and the attitudes of speakers, that is, the semantic and pragmatic features of utterances. Example 17 in this way represents a decision and a command of the Dodo. Both the decision and the command sort out status relations among the participants in the situation. The Dodo is clearly the leader; the audience readily accepts its directives.

A further sphere of pragmatics deals with attitudes to the information in the utterance. Here the Dodo shows no doubt about the accuracy of its decision and the need to carry it out. These attitudes of the speaker are evident in the choice of the theme and the rheme, the choice of which serves to highlight entities. Speakers may also emphasize specific entities by intonation, as in the stress on *all* in sentence 17.

Moreover, the background conditions and presuppositions for understanding an utterance must be known. In the *Alice in Wonderland* passage we must be aware of the fairy tale surroundings, in which the Dodo is recognized as authority. The other participants in the scene agree with the Dodo's decisions because of their presuppositions regarding the status of the Dodo's utterances.

Such a treatment of utterances as used in communication is based on theoretical concerns, as are needed in the attempt to have computers "understand" language. It is also useful for improving our understanding of human uses of language, for example, the acquisition of language by infants. In Chapter 2, Section 2.7, we examined some of the conclusions regarding language acquisition, especially from the time when infants speak. Additional insights are now being noted, especially from observation of infants communicating in their first year of life. These insights support the validity of the views developed in the study of speech acts and artificial intelligence, as we note in the next section.

6.7 Towards Speech in Children

We recall that in his investigation of language Austin distinguished between utterances like:

> 18. *I pronounce "either" with the vowel of "ether."*
> 19. *I pronounce you man and wife.*
> 20. *He pronounced a sentence of thirty years on the accused.*

The three types of sentences are identified as:

1. locutionary, which simply express a concept, like example 18;
2. illocutionary, which involve a social action, like example 19;
3. perlocutionary, which deal with the results of a speech act, like example 20.

Austin and his followers went on to classify verbs involved in such sentences and to describe implications they carry, presuppositions they involve, and so on.

Subsequently John Searle has proposed that all utterances include an illocutionary element as well as the basic locution. Modifications of 18 may illustrate this approach.

> 21a. *Pronounce "either" with the vowel of "ether."*
> b. *You don't pronounce "either" with the vowel of "ether."*
> c. *Why don't you pronounce "either" with the vowel of "ether"?*

The command element of 21a, the negation element of 21b, and the interrogative element of 21c are taken as illocutionary by this point of view. The rest of the sentence is the basic locution. This elaboration of Austin's views is now being tested in study of language acquisition.

How children grasp the notion of communicating through language is a problem of long-standing interest. Infants seem to catch on to the notion when they are about twelve to sixteen months old. But we cannot assume that anyone has taught them the accomplishment, because without language one cannot teach anything intellectually. Most speakers do not remember how they acquired language, though some writers have given their views on the topic. In one of the most remarkable passages of autobiography, St. Augustine recalls how he grasped the notion, almost intuitively. Investigators today are attempting to determine the process more precisely. As we noted in Chapter 2, Section 2.7, children progress rapidly after they grasp the notion of speech. Their vocabulary expands. They learn the grammar. They are often said to have mastered the basic structure of their native language by the time they are five or six years old. But the preliminary process has been obscure. Are we to assume that infants suddenly reach a stage when they recognize the usefulness of speech, or have they gradually been learning this skill?

Recent observations of infants in their first year suggest that the subtler elements of communication, those treated under pragmatics, are acquired earlier than speech. The first such elements are clearly perlocutionary. Through gestures, cries, and so on, infants persuade their parents and others to take care of their wishes from about the age of four months. But observations of the infants' behavior lead to the assumption that they are not aware of their control over the actions of others. The cries, gestures, and so on are therefore not illocutionary, for illocutionary speech acts imply intentional directives.

Intentional commands through cries do not seem to be used before ten months or so. In this second step towards the learning of language, infants come to control illocutionary acts. Their further behavior, including eye contact with adults, suggests that from this time they make intentional demands. These develop towards the use of speech sounds. As a final step in this preliminary process of acquiring language, infants use speech sounds for their requests, finally also just for locutionary acts like 11. At this point they have grasped the notion of language, and they proceed to expand their control of it.

In this way infants are learning the process of communication from a very early age. The pragmatic aspects of communication, which seem more subtle than overt sounds, are acquired earliest. These, then, are fundamental elements of language that we identify in understanding texts as well as in acquiring language.

6.8 Texts and Their Interpretation

The previous sections indicate some of the activities carried on in communication through language. We master these activities so thoroughly that we are unaware of the capabilities we have acquired in learning to communicate with other speakers in our society. These become clearer to us when we find ourselves in a different culture, even when we are in a group of foreigners or, even to some extent, when we are in a different family from our own. We may review them by examining a text from the point of view of the skills we apply in interpreting it.

The text cited here is a story told by the prophet Nathan to King David after David had arranged the death of Uriah the Hittite. David had seen Bathsheba in the bath and coveted her; to add her to his group of wives he ordered her husband placed in the first line of battle, where he was killed. Nathan's story goes as follows:

There were once two men in the same city, one rich and the other poor. The rich man had large flocks and herds, but the poor man had nothing of his own except one little ewe lamb. He reared it himself, and it grew up in his house with his own sons. It ate from his dish, drank from his cup and nestled in his arms; it was like a daughter to him. One day a traveller came to the rich man's house, and he, too mean to take something from his flocks and herds to serve to his guest, took the poor man's lamb and served up that.

David was very angry . . .[3] (The translation is from the New English Bible)

When someone tells us a story like this or even makes a simple observation to us, we are receptive to it. Someone may tell us about a change in the weather, or about an accident, and we believe the speaker when there are no grounds for assuming psychopathic tendencies or some other irregularity. It is a fixed habit of ours to assume that anyone addressing us is sincere and honest. Even when the text is imaginative, such as a parable or a poem, we maintain this attitude; the poet Coleridge referred to it as "willing suspension of disbelief."

David obviously believed Nathan's parable, to judge by his reaction. As a righteous king, he perceived an injustice and condemned the action. Such a reaction results from the coherence of a text, which leads the hearer to assume that the storyteller is reporting the truth.

The construction of a text therefore is important. When we examine this text, or any carefully composed text, we find that the construction as well as the content of its sentences follow definite patterns. The first sentence would not seem in place if it were the third, and vice versa. What the first sentence of this text does is introduce two characters, place them in a setting, and provide the characteristics essential for this story, that is, their economic status.

The first sentence also alerts the hearer to the kind of text, its genre. In upbraiding David for his injustice, Nathan could have delivered a harangue, a brief sermon. But he may have assumed that a parable would be more effective to capture the attention of a king who was also a poet. The first three words identify the genre of our text as a tale.

Texts are held together by many devices. One of the most common is anaphora—using substitutes for content words. The most common anaphoric elements are pronouns. They may be indefinite, like *one* in the first sentence, or definite like *he, it, his* in subsequent sentences. Another device to relate sentences tightly is purposeful omission, as in the second clause of the first sentence of our story. The full forms of these would read: *One was rich. The other was poor.* The verb forms, however, are omitted in a process commonly called **gapping.** Other sentence elements may be gapped, such as *it* in the fourth sentence. Such devices provide economy to the text, reducing possible inattention among listeners.

A thorough analysis of a text would include attention to its sentence patterns, forms, and sounds—in short, a grammar. But unlike grammars dealing only with

[3] New English Bible, 2 Samuel 12:1–5.

sentences, a discourse grammar would relate such patterning to the overall pattern of a text. All these features contribute to the meaning that speakers intend. Discourse analysis, or text linguistics, attempts to account for the meanings conveyed by the larger patterns of a text as well as those of morphemes, words, and sentences. Its procedures involve attention to the syntactic, pragmatic, and semantic features of language.

QUESTIONS FOR REVIEW

1. Define *text linguistics/discourse analysis*.
2. Contrast the treatment of examples like example 2 in sentence grammars and in discourse analysis.
3. Define *theme; rheme*.
4. Contrast a functionalist approach to the English passive with a purely grammatical approach.
5. What is the effect of cleft sentences in English?
6. Why do scientists and literary scholars differ in their view of the passive?
7. Compare and contrast aims of text linguists with those of teachers of Freshman English.
8. What is a *performative?* Give examples.
9. Distinguish between *illocutionary* and *perlocutionary* statements.
10. Discuss *presupposition, entailment,* and *implication,* illustrating their force with examples.
11. Identify the three subgroups of semiotics, according to Peirce.
12. What kinds of information are necessary to understand a sentence like example 14?
13. Sketch the development of an infant's use of communication.
14. What reasons can you suggest for dealing with texts rather than with single utterances in the attempt to understand communication?

PROBLEMS FOR REVIEW

1. The following is the initial part of an essay by Bacon entitled "Of Studies."

    Studies serve for delight, for ornament, and for ability. Their chief use for delight is in privateness [private life] and retiring; for ornament, is in discourse; and for ability, is in the judgment and disposition of business.

    Identify characteristics common in texts, such as gapping and anaphora.

Discuss also the features of the first sentence that make it an unlikely sentence to follow the second.

2. Poetic as well as prose texts are structured by means of special devices. The following lines are from Shakespeare's *Two Gentlemen of Verona*, Act 1, Scene 1. Determine characteristics that provide cohesiveness and economy to this text.

> He after honor hunts, I after love.
> He leaves his friends to dignify them more;
> I leave myself, my friends, and all for love.
> Thou, Julia, thou hast metamorphosed me,
> Made me neglect my studies, lose my time,
> War with good counsel, set the world at nought,
> Made wit with musing weak, heart sick with thought.

3. After determining general classes of verbs, such as transitive and intransitive, we may examine their further meaning. For example, *remember* and *decide* are both transitive and seem parallel in the following sentences.
   a. Jane remembered the issue.
   b. Jane decided the issue.
   When, however, they are followed by clauses, they differ in their meanings, especially the implications they carry. Discuss the differences in meaning of the following: (Does each carry the implication that Jane actually took her lunch?)
   c. Jane remembered to take her lunch.
   d. Jane decided to take her lunch.

4. The following are further examples of such verbs. Determine which imply that the action was carried out, and which do not.
   a. She happened to get her money back.
   b. She wanted to get her money back.
   c. Henry managed to leave.
   d. Henry decided to leave.

5. Examine your own use of such verbs. For example, if you use a sentence like *She deserved to win the prize*, does it imply that she actually won the prize? What are the implications in your speech for the auxiliaries *will, must, may, can?*

6. It is also instructive to examine the implications of such verbs when they are used in the negative. Determine the implications of the two following sentences and compare them with the implications of the examples in problem 3 above.
   a. Jane didn't remember to take her lunch.
   b. Jane didn't decide to take her lunch.
   Discuss also the implications of the sentences in problem 4 above when they are put in the negative.

7. Discuss the implications of such sentences when used as questions, for example:
   a. Did she happen to get her money back?
   b. Did she want to get her money back?

   Examine such sentences also when used with adverbial expressions, such as *yesterday, next week*. Can you use these with either a or b? How do your conclusions agree with your earlier analysis of the implications?

8. The following text is from Shakespeare's *Merchant of Venice*, Act 3, Scene 2. Examine it for characteristics differing from those of the passage above from *Two Gentlemen of Verona,* and also from the prose text of Bacon. Does this text lack examples of gapping and anaphora? In what respect is such a lyric text characteristic?

   > Tell me where is fancy bred,
   > Or in the heart, or in the head?
   > How begot, how nourished?
   > Reply, reply.
   > It is engend'red in the eyes,
   > With gazing fed, and fancy dies
   > In the cradle where it lies.
   > Let us all ring fancy's knell.
   > I'll begin it—Ding, dong, bell.
   > Ding, dong, bell.

9. The following text is of a kind fascinating to children. Discuss elements that may appeal to them. Compare this text with the preceding, which also is lyrical but appeals strongly to many adults.

   > A woman to her son did utter,
   > Go, my son, and shut the shutter.
   > The shutter's shut, the son did utter,
   > I can't shut it any shutter.[4]

10. Select any short text, such as an anecdote, and analyze its structure. Note especially the characteristic features of the first sentence, and thereupon anaphoric and other devices which are possible further in a text.

FURTHER READING

Austin, John L. *How to Do Things with Words*. Edited by J. O. Urmson. New York: Oxford University Press, 1965.

Dressler, Wolfgang, U., ed. *Current Trends in Text Linguistics*. Berlin: de Gruyter, 1978.

[4] From Iona and Peter Opie, *The Lore and Language of Schoolchildren* (Oxford: Clarendon, 1959), p. 30.

Grimes, Joseph E. *The Thread of Discourse*. The Hague: Mouton, 1975.

Longacre, Robert E. *An Anatomy of Speech Notions*. Lisse: de Ridder, 1976.

Ochs, Elinor, and Bambi B. Schiefflein. *Developmental Pragmatics*. New York: Academic Press, 1979.

Pike, Kenneth L., and Evelyn G. Pike. *Grammatical Analysis*. Dallas: Summer Institute of Linguistics, 1977.

Searle, John R. *Speech Acts*. Cambridge: At the University Press, 1969.

Strunk, William, Jr. *The Elements of Style*. 2d ed. With revisions, an introduction, and a chapter on writing by E. B. White. New York: Macmillan, 1972.

CHAPTER SEVEN

Semantics

7.1 What Is Semantics?

The purpose of language is to convey meaning. Utterances may be short, limited to a word or so, as in the requests:

> 1a. *Coffee!*
> b. *Coffee, please!*

Utterances may also have the form of sentences in written texts, as in the requests:

> 1c. *I'd like some coffee.*
> d. *Please give me some more coffee.*

The meaning may be trivial, conveying simply a feeling of friendliness, as in:

> 2a. *Some sky!*
> b. *Nice day, isn't it?*
> c. *That's a fine outfit.*

Or the meaning may be at a high level, as in critical works of literature, scientific discussions of the universe, religious treatises, and the like. Any use of language is designed to convey meaning, whether largely at an emotional level, at a level of factual exchange, at an advanced intellectual level, or some other level. Study of language requires identification of what meaning is and what the devices to convey it are.

As we have seen in Chapter 1, Section 1.3, linguists deal with language at various levels, especially the phonological, syntactic, and semantic. Expression of meaning begins with the syntactic level, relying on forms and words and sentences. As we noted earlier, phonological elements simply are tools used to fashion these implements expressing meaning; they themselves have no meaning, as any examination of a sound unit illustrates, for example, *r* in *rat, rather, tar, tartar, term*. The study of meaning then treats syntactic elements and also larger structures, such as those discussed in the preceding chapter. Moreover, it deals with accompaniments to speech, such as gestures, bodily posture, and any devices used with speech or supplementing it to convey meaning.

The simplest elements used to convey meaning have long been studied. Among the earliest treatments of language that have come down to us are dictionaries from Mesopotamia. Dating back to the third millennium, these were bilingual, designed especially to make the ancient language Sumerian accessible to Akkadian speakers. Such works became prominent once again as Christianity and classical civilization were introduced to northern Europe. Latin had to be made accessible to the speakers of Old Irish, Old English, Old High German, and so on; their languages had to be made accessible to the priests and administrators using Latin. Lists of word-pairs were compiled. They are known as glossaries. These gradually became more comprehensive and developed into the dictionaries we use.

At the same time grammars were concerned with the meanings of sentences and their elements. Books on rhetoric dealt with larger structures and with accompaniments to meaning. Elaborate handbooks were compiled on gestures, especially those used for public speaking. The division of labor has persisted. But if we are to deal with meaning as conveyed by language, the common features of all these devices must be considered together. Such study is carried out in **semantics,** the treatment of meaning in language.

7.2 Semantics and Syntax

Because syntactic constructions have specific meanings, it is difficult to distinguish sharply between syntax and semantics. Syntactic patterns, such as questions and commands, express a consistent meaning, much as do words. Accordingly treatments of syntax and morphology generally include discussions of the meanings of constructions and forms.

Yet the parallelism between syntactic constructions and meaning units is not complete, as may be illustrated by examining paraphrases. Paraphrases are syntactic sequences having roughly the same meaning, though they may differ formally, for example:

> 3a. *He died.*
> b. *He passed on.*
> c. *He bought the farm. (military idiom)*
> 4a. *The dead pilot (adjective)*
> b. *The departed pilot (participle)*
> c. *The pilot who was killed (relative clause)*

Because of the lack of parallelism, different terminology and procedures are used in the treatment of the two levels, syntax and semantics. A detailed account of the procedures of semantics, especially those applied as semantics has become increasingly formalized, is beyond the scope of an introductory handbook. But the general procedures are readily understood and can be briefly sketched.

Rather than sentences (S), semantic scholars treat **predications** (PN). The central element of these is verblike, and known as **Predicate** (P). The nounlike elements associated with predicates are known as **Arguments** (A). Just as a sentence may include several noun phrases, a predication may include several arguments. For convenience these may be numbered.

Predications may be examined by means of rules or tree structures. Example 1 of Chapter 5 would then be treated as follows in semantic analysis:

5.

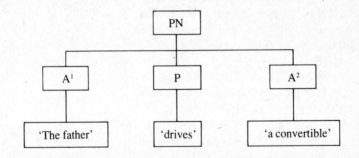

Just as sentences may include embedded sentences, so predications may include "embedded" predications, as for this string:

> 6a. *He knows that the father drives a convertible.*
> (b. *See page 140.*)

In this way semantic analysis can be carried out much like syntactic analysis, though the constituents at the two levels may differ, as illustrated above.

The differences are clear when one encounters "compound" elements like *inform*. This corresponds to 'cause to know.' In semantic analysis the *cause* constituent of words like *inform, manipulate, persuade* may be treated as separate

6b.

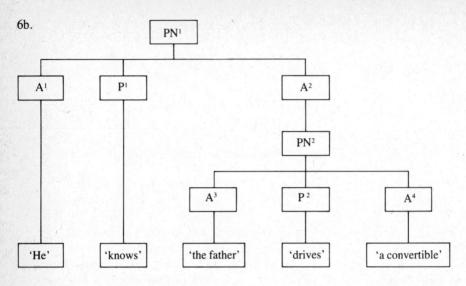

predications, comparable to PN[1] in 6b. This procedure aims to determine the simplest predications, much as syntactic analysis aims to determine the simplest syntactic strings. As a result causatives, modal elements such as *may,* or subjunctive forms are treated in an initial tree, by processes leading to considerably different presentation of utterances when syntactic and semantic analyses are rigorously carried out. Like syntactic analyses, the semantic have terminal nodes consisting of lexical elements and formatives. These are then defined, in ways comparable to standard dictionary definitions.

7.3 Lexical Elements as Treated in Dictionaries

Comparable to linguistic treatment of language, dictionaries define lexical entries at three levels. They provide phonological, syntactic, and semantic information. It is useful to examine lexical entries, to note how they are structured.

The entry *dog* in the *Random House College Dictionary* is first provided with two phonological descriptions, one with the vowel of *caught, dawn,* the other with the vowel of *cot, don.* Then it is identified as a noun or a verb, for which the past tense and present participle are provided. Finally, semantic interpretations are provided. The less central and the transferred meanings are listed after the primary meaning.

When we examine the interpretations, or definitions, we find that they make great use of synonyms and hyponyms. Like *cat* and *horse, dog* is identified by means of the hyponym *animal* or *quadruped.* The learned synonym, *Canis familiaris,* is also given in the first definition. Antonyms may also be cited in definitions, such as *bitch* in the third definition of *dog* as 'male dog.' In addition, descriptors are included, such as *domesticated.*

Such definitions are useful primarily for those who already know the language. If Turkish *köpek* is identified as a *hayvan* 'animal,' anyone not knowing Turkish would profit little from the definition. Dictionaries accordingly use further devices, such as illustrations. These provide evidence for the relationship of the word with an object in the outside world. In this way, our commonly used dictionaries apply the findings of semantic analysis in their definitions.

It is said that the primary use of English dictionaries by native speakers is for checking spelling. This is an important feature of the word, but not, strictly speaking, a linguistic one. Dictionaries serve other uses as well, such as the provision of information for which encyclopedias are produced. Thus *Dodgson,* found a few entries before *dog,* gives the first names of this writer and also the pen name by which he is commonly known, *Lewis Carroll*. The inclusion of such information varies from dictionary to dictionary. All of them assume as their primary purpose the definition of elements, usually words. Their definitions are designed to identify for users the phonological, syntactic, and semantic character-istics of entries.

7.4 Thesauri

Most dictionaries of English and other languages are arranged by the conventional spellings of words. If a writing system uses symbols other than letters, as does Chinese, arrangement must be based on characteristics of these. Chinese and Japanese characters are arranged by an ingenious system based on the number of strokes used in drawing a character. Whatever the basis for arrangement, all such dictionaries list their entries in accordance with external criteria.

Some dictionaries, however, are arranged on a totally different basis, by the meanings of elements. Such a work is known as a *thesaurus,* like Peter Mark Roget's for English. Building on semantic classification of earlier scholars, Roget[1] compiled a thesaurus of a thousand sets. For these, there are six large classes: **abstract relations, space, matter, intellect, volition, affections.** If we examine a kinship term like *mother* in Roget's thesaurus, we find it under set 166, which is labeled *paternity*. *Paternity* is one of eight principal subsets of abstract relations, subclassified under *causative*. *Cat* is listed in set 366, *animal,* itself a subset of *vitality,* which is a subset of *organic matter,* the third subset of *matter*. Set 366 includes the names of all animals, broad classifications as well as specific designations for animals, birds, snakes, even for mythological animals. Such names are cited in groups, with no further definitions; users must supply details in sorting out the various words listed.

Thesauri are based on several assumptions. One is that there must be general categories of meaning, like *space* or *affections*. These are comparable to hyponyms, which embrace a great many words. The categories used by Roget were arrived at

---

[1] *Roget's International Thesaurus of English Words and Phrases.* A Complete Book of Synonyms and Antonyms founded upon and embodying Roget's original work with numerous additions and modern-ization by C. O. Sylvester Mawson (New York: Crowell, 1931).

in the course of philosophical analysis of the universe and its inhabitants. It is assumed that they are universal and might be expected in any language.

When we use thesauri, we generally rely on an index listing the words alphabetically, as in other dictionaries. We might well memorize the six large classes and some of the thousand subclasses, which have been increased in recent editions. But this undertaking would be cumbersome and time-consuming. Thesauri are especially useful when we are dissatisfied with the exact meaning of a word we have in mind and want an alternate. In this way we may seek words suitable for poetry or a given style, as in translating. Examining the sets in a thesaurus illuminates for us nuances of meaning, whether of the word we select or of words that seem less suitable for our purposes at the moment.

7.5 The Treatment of Meaning in Fields

Although thesauri have hit on the device of listing words by sets, the treatment of meaning is difficult because of the large number of words and the huge scope of meanings they must convey if we are to talk comprehensibly about the universe and its inhabitants. In order to deal with a manageable set of items, students of meaning often restrict their attention to specific areas, known as **fields.** The scholar who introduced this term examined the field ''intellect'' in older stages of German. Much attention has also been given to the fields of kinship terms and colors.

Both of these seem straightforward and simple to manage. All speakers have mothers and fathers. They all see blue skies, green plants, and yellow sands. Yet, as we noted earlier, there is no one-to-one correlation between elements of language and objects in the outside world. Kinship systems and sets of color words differ considerably from language to language. A kinship system may include relative age as a feature, as in languages like Japanese, which distinguish older brother and older sister from younger brother and younger sister. A set of color words, like that of Japanese, may include a word like *aoi,* which corresponds to English 'blue' and 'green' and 'yellow.' Even simple sets like these provide many problems for study.

Anthropologists as well as linguists have devoted considerable effort to the determination of principles applying in the fields of kinship and color. In this effort they have sought out components by which individual languages form their set of terms. Kinship terms in English are based on three components: generation (as in *mother, son*), sex (as in *daughter, son*), and lineality (as in *aunt, cousin* versus *mother, sister*). These are not symmetrically applied; the component *sex* is not used in the term *cousin*. In this way sets of kinship terms vary. General types have been determined, such as Omaha, which reflects a close relationship between a maternal uncle and his nephew. As one aim, kinship studies attempt to determine universals as found in semantic sets.

A notable attempt to establish such universals has also been applied to color terms. Examining the large number of studies that have been carried out in numerous languages, Brent Berlin and Paul Kay listed such terms in order of the

$$\begin{bmatrix} \text{white} \\ \text{black} \end{bmatrix} < [\text{red}] < \begin{bmatrix} \text{green} \\ \text{yellow} \end{bmatrix} < [\text{blue}] < [\text{brown}] < \begin{bmatrix} \text{purple} \\ \text{pink} \\ \text{orange} \\ \text{gray} \end{bmatrix}$$

Figure 7.1 An Example of a Semantic Field, with Items Governed by Universal Rules

This chart illustrates the findings of Berlin and Kay in the study of color terms of approximately one hundred languages. A language may have as few as two terms; if so, these indicate white/light and black/dark. If a language has three terms, the further term refers to the color 'red.' And so on, as the chart indicates. English and the languages of Europe have all these terms and even more; a language with only two terms is Jalé, of the New Guinea Highland group.

frequency with which they are found in languages.[2] All languages distinguish between dark and light, black and white. A system made up of only two terms is found in the Jalé language of New Guinea. A three-term system is found in Tiv of Nigeria; it includes a term for 'red,' as do all known languages with more than two color terms. These may have the following further terms, arranged in stepwise fashion: 'green/yellow'; 'blue'; 'brown.' A language with eight or more terms, like English, includes such additional designations as 'orange, grey, purple' (see Figure 7.1). This finding illustrates how semantic sets may be based on universal criteria, in this way supporting the point of view that universals can be determined also at the semantic level. This assumption had earlier been made for the phonological and syntactic levels, as we note in the following chapter.

The universal position contrasts with a relativistic position, as noted in Chapter 2, Section 2.5. The Whorf-Sapir hypothesis, however, applies to particular features in a language rather than to broad principles and deep categories like those determined in studies of kinship and color terms. The two positions are not contradictory. If the Turkish language included only four color terms before the influence of Western science, a Turkish speaker might well have seen the universe in this way rather than with the seven colors of his European counterpart. But his color system was in accord with the conclusions of Kay and Berlin. Both positions, the universalistic and the relativistic, have illuminated our understanding of the semantic level of language and offer many further opportunities for research.

7.6 Connotations and Denotations

Treatments of meaning generally concern themselves with **denotations,** the stock definitions of words. But speakers also have their own conceptions of word meanings, as determined by their past experiences, their life style, and their way

[2] Brent Berlin and Paul Kay, *Basic Color Terms: Their Universality and Evolution* (Berkeley and Los Angeles: University of California Press, 1969).

of looking at things. These are known as **connotations,** and they vary from speaker to speaker.

One example is *convertible*. It denotes a car with removable top. To some speakers the word arouses feelings of a free way of life, as depicted in the novels of Scott Fitzgerald and associated with the Gay Twenties. To others, who may have been invited for a ride in a convertible after or during an unexpected rainstorm, a convertible arouses less attractive emotions. Similarly, those objecting to having their hair tousled may have less than favorable associations with the term.

Varying connotations are found especially with everyday words. One speaker's *hi-fi* is another speaker's headache. *Bacon and eggs* set some salivas flowing, others not. *Waterbed* arouses different reactions from *hair mattress*. Individuals must sort out their own connotations for all such words.

Some speakers are especially aware of general connotations, notably politicians and advertisers. For a while the word *deal* had a highly favorable connotation, attracting many voters, whether it was associated with *new, fair,* or other adjectives. It came to arouse opposition, to be associated with words such as *wheeler-dealer,* and now it seems to have been dropped by politicians. Whether in devising slogans or persuading people, politicians avoid words with negative connotations, as do advertisers. A survey of the ads in any magazine or of the real estate ads in any newspaper provides ample illustrations of the force of connotations in the life of language.

7.7 Metaphors

Language is also molded by metaphors, words or phrases used in transferred senses. Excellent metaphors provide new insights, leading us to view situations differently from our earlier practice. They are especially attractive when applied to abstract entities. Accordingly they are prominent in poetry, which aims to be concrete rather than abstract. Treatments of poetry have discussed metaphors for millennia, examining various kinds in great detail. Yet the basic notion is simple. When computer specialists applied the word *hardware* to their new tool, they were drawing on metaphor. The process has been going on as far back as we can determine, so that language has been called a storehouse of faded metaphors.

Our general language provides many examples. The element 'cide' in *decide* and as modified in *decision* means 'cut.' Some Latin speaker used the word metaphorically and the new use caught on, just as a later English speaker transferred 'cut bait' to the sphere of making a decision, this time a negative one. All the elements of *fish or cut bait* are favored for metaphors, as may be determined by checking them in a dictionary.

Through metaphor, language is renewed. Speakers tire of routine expressions. Some, more inventive than others, innovate. If the transferred use appeals more widely, for example, *home* 'one's native place,' as in *homestead, homeward,* for *house,* speakers may find themselves living in a *townhome* rather than a *townhouse*. If a politician asks for innovative ideas by suggesting that 'a hundred flowers bloom,' the metaphor may even be adopted outside his language. The extent of metaphoric influence on a language may be determined by examining the history of words, which has its own aims, as noted in the next section.

7.8 Etymology

Like metaphor, the study of etymology has a long history. It was pursued by the Greeks and Romans, and also by Indic scholars. But only in the nineteenth century was it fully developed, on the basis of ideas discussed in Chapter 10, especially Section 10.5. By etymology the Greeks sought the "true meanings" of words. Today the term simply means "history of words." In seeking an etymology we determine earlier forms and their uses. Some words go back to Middle English (circa 1050–1450), others to Old English (circa 750–1050), still others to Proto-Germanic (circa 2000 B.C. to A.D. 100) or to Proto-Indo-European (before 2000 B.C.).

The words with most venerable etymologies are those prominent in society throughout four millennia or more, such as *cow, goose, eat, moon*, the numerals, and so on. Words of recent origin are found for technical or cultural innovations, such as *Kodak, quark, coffee, taboo*. By examining etymologies we learn a great deal about the history of our language and about the societies that maintained it.

In presenting an etymology we set out to determine the forms in earlier stages of the language, as we may illustrate with the words *cow, five*.

	cow	*five*
7.		
Middle English	cū	fīf
Old English	cū	fīf
Proto-Germanic	kū-	fimf
Proto-Indo-European	$g^w\bar{o}u$-	$penk^we$

In pursuing the study of etymology, we identify a standard form in each stage of the language, as illustrated in example 7.

Many words, however, cannot be traced back very far. Among these are *boy, girl, cough, lack, spool, tub*. These may have been used only orally, or they may have been introduced in relatively recent times. We can determine etymologies to early periods only if we have adequate texts for those periods.

During times of cultural or social changes, many new words are adopted. To the Scandinavian influence in the Old English period we owe many simple words, such as *egg, husband, sky, window*. To the subsequent French influence we owe a large stock of terms for advanced civilization: in government *country, nation, people*, and many others; in political affairs *jury, justice, privilege*, and so on; in religious affairs *baptism, clergy, prayer, sermon*, and others; in culinary matters *bacon, beef, mutton, pork, veal, dinner, supper* as opposed to the native *breakfast*. Some scholars have jocularly pointed to the older *cow, sheep, pig, calf* as reflecting the social situation of the time; the English-speaking peasants raised the animals and their French masters ate them. Whatever we may think of such proposals, etymology often provides us with our best means of determining the culture of preliterate periods. The words that were in use reflect current cultural and social matters, furnishing us with information on periods that left no historical documents, as we see further in Chapter 10, Section 10.9.

The study of meaning, then, has implications for scholars not concerned with the understanding of language itself. As we will see in Chapter 10, especially Section 10.9, this has been pursued most widely for our own family of languages; much remains to be discovered in the study of others.

7.9 The Carriers of Meaning in Language

As this chapter has indicated, words convey much of the meaning of language. They indicate concepts for items in the outside world. Moreover, the lexicon can be extended at will; a science like chemistry has alone created more than a million technical words. But words do not express complete messages. If we utter a technical word like *polymerization* or a common word like *eat*, hearers will not be able to interpret our intent unless the word is accompanied by a meaningful intonation pattern. We can use *Eat!* as a command, but then it has a specific accent and pitch pattern. In short, we communicate by means of larger entities than words, that is, by sentences and texts.

Sentences are composed of words, meaningfully arranged and, when appropriate, modified as well as accompanied by intonation patterns. They are the basic entities for communication by means of language, its minimal segments conveying meaning. Words and morphemes are of course an integral part of sentences; accordingly, to understand language and communication in general, we must know how words are structured, how they are inflected, what the relations among them are, and how they refer to the outside world.

Many words refer directly to concepts and entities, such as *dog, live, in*. Others have intimate ties with further words, which must be interpreted before they can be understood; examples are *man in the street, out-of-the-way, dog in the manger*. A *man in the street* may be female and far from a street, as one might expect of many 'average citizens.' A *dog in the manger* does not have four legs and may never have seen a manger, though he or she acts like a dog that wishes to take up all of a desirable location. Units like these, with unitary meanings, are known as **idioms.** The existence of idioms in any language supports the analysis of words into morphemes; these reflect the structure of language as well as its treatment by the user.

Whatever the extent of lexical units, whether simple morphemes, words of varying shapes, or idiomatic phrases, we must examine them in the larger patterns they form, that is, in sentences and texts. We must also concern ourselves with the attitudes of speakers if we wish to comprehend the procedures of communication. For all of these activities we set out to determine the widespread or universal features of language. Some of these have been noted above. In the next chapter we will treat patterns that have been of recent concern.

QUESTIONS FOR REVIEW

1. Name some elements used to convey meaning in language.
2. Cite handbooks on meaning in earlier times.
3. Why do linguists propose a semantic level separate from the syntactic?
4. Define *paraphrase*.
5. Identify *predication; argument; predicate*.
6. What is included in the lexical entries of dictionaries? (In answering this question it is instructive to compare the definitions provided in different dictionaries.)
7. Contrast the procedures of thesauri as opposed to those of dictionaries.
8. What is meant by a *semantic field?*
9. List the components on which the English kinship system is based, giving examples.
10. Distinguish between *connotation* and *denotation,* giving examples.
11. Define *metaphor,* citing examples.
12. Define *etymology,* distinguishing its current use from its original meaning among the Greeks.
13. What is an *idiom?*

PROBLEMS FOR REVIEW

1. Compare the definitions in any two selected desk dictionaries, examining them for their phonological, morphological, syntactic, and semantic adequacy. Then compare these definitions with that given in the *Oxford English Dictionary*.
2. After determining the definition of a given word in these dictionaries, find its listing in *Roget's Thesaurus*. Compare the larger sets under which it is arranged with the group in which the dictionary places it. For example, *difficulty* is listed in the thesaurus under "individual volition" as opposed to "intersocial volition." (The *Thesaurus* has been republished by some scholars with considerable modification. You will have to explore your edition for its classification.) By contrast the *Random House College Dictionary* gives as first definition of *difficulty* 'the fact or condition of being difficult'; only the fifth is 'reluctance; unwillingness.' "Fact" and "condition" are listed in several places in the thesaurus, but both are given under "existence." It is interesting to observe the principles applied for given words in the two types of dictionaries and to try to account for differences in classification.
3. Noting the denotation of the following words, indicate their connotations for you: *politician, scientist, humanist, professor, student, democracy, alcoholic, abortion, life, strike, Labor, capitalism*.

4. Examine texts for metaphors they contain. Literary texts may be your readiest source. But it may also be amusing to page through copies of *The New Yorker* magazine, which often prints excerpts under the heading "Block that Metaphor." The excerpts in question usually contain several metaphors that clash with each other.

5. Using one of the standard etymological dictionaries, determine the etymology of some of the following pairs: *adamant, diamond; asphodel, daffodil; banjo, mandolin; beef, cow; brother, friar; catch, chase; cycle, wheel; due, debt; fife, pipe; hydra, otter; joint, junta; mint, money; parole, parable; quaint, coy; shirt, skirt; task, tax; verb, word; zero, cipher.*

FURTHER READING

Leech, Geoffrey. *Semantics*. Harmondsworth: Penguin, 1974.

Lyons, John. *Semantics,* Vols. 1 and 2. Cambridge: Cambridge University Press, 1977.

Malkiel, Yakov. *Etymological Dictionaries. A Tentative Typology*. Chicago: University of Chicago Press, 1976.

Steinberg, Danny D., and Leon A. Jakobovits, eds. *Semantics. An Interdisciplinary Reader in Philosophy, Linguistics and Psychology*. Cambridge: At the University Press, 1971.

Ullmann, Stephen. *Semantics. An Introduction to the Science of Meaning*. Oxford: Blackwell, 1964.

CHAPTER EIGHT

Features Common to Languages; Universals

8.1 Universals

Students of language have long been interested in determining features that are common to all languages. Many of these are obvious. All languages use oral symbols for communication. All make use of sentences as the basic units; these can be analyzed for smaller units of meaning, such as words and morphemes. A small number of sound units is also widely found. Such common features suggest that in spite of their surface differences the seven thousand or so languages that are in use have some features in common. These are now referred to as **universals.**

Human behavior with regard to language supports the notion of universals. An infant can learn any language whatsoever. It acquires the language or languages spoken around it, regardless of the language of its natural parents. As a further well-documented ability, infants rapidly acquire their language, as we have noted. Further evidence is taken from the fact that all languages change in much the same way. They develop dialects—geographical, social, and occupational. Accordingly, the role of language in society supports the position that all languages share common features.

This conclusion and the study of universals raise many questions. One concerns the level at which we should seek universals. There have been attempts to find them in surface structures, but since language is managed by the brain, deep structure universals are far more likely. We are also concerned with the levels at which they are to be found. The phonological level is associated with surface phenomena and accordingly may be composed for the most part of individual characteristics. Somewhat similarly, the semantic level must adjust to external phenomena; therefore, it is less purely linguistic than the syntactic level. The syntactic level, however, is purely linguistic. There are no external phenomena requiring a given structure for sentences. Some languages, like Vietnamese, arrange sentences by means of a succession of syllabic "words," having no inflection. Other languages, like Eskimo, combine elements of an utterance into one large word-like sentence. Still others, like Japanese and Turkish, arrange elements loosely in strings making up sentences. In spite of these differences, all languages have verblike elements and nounlike elements. Sentences are based on arranging these, selecting items from the class of verbs and adding one or more nouns as well as an intonation contour. It is in the syntactic area, then, that the significant universals are found. This chapter will examine some of these, with reference to the other levels as well.

8.2 Phonological Universals

A great variety of phonological systems have been documented. Some languages, such as the Caucasian, have many phonemes; others, like Hawaiian, have few. Some languages, like English, have a large number of vowels. Others, like Latin and Hawaiian, have only five; some Arabic dialects have two. At least one language, Kabardian, has been analyzed as having no vowels. It has a huge number of consonants; resonants accompanied by accents take the place of vowels at the center of syllables. As with vowels, languages also differ in number of consonants. Because of this great diversity it is difficult to posit universals for the phonological level.

Some implicational universals, however, seem well established. An example is the development of nasal vowels. These have generally been related to previous patterns in which a vowel was accompanied by a nasal consonant. As the consonant was lost, the neighboring vowel came to be nasalized. Sound systems also have a kind of parallelism. If a system includes fricatives, such as [f], it will generally have parallel stops, such as [p].

Moreover, as noted most dramatically by the great linguist Roman Jakobson, there are parallels between the sounds an infant first acquires and the sounds that are most widely found in languages and also the sounds that are maintained longest when a speaker has phonological aphasia (see also Chapter 9, Section 9.3). The sounds themselves are easily noted. Infants first acquire stops, e.g., [p t k], nasals, e.g., [m n], and simple vowels, e.g., [i a u]. These are found almost universally. In languages with three vowels, like Arabic, [i a u] are the three. Only a few languages, such as Egyptian Arabic, lack one of these stops, that is, [p]. And studies of aphasic patients lead to the results noted by Jakobson. Accordingly, there seems to be a set of widespread phonological units to which individual languages add others.

In this way, some phonological universals have been proposed. As indicated above, they are not demonstrable for all languages, so they may be better labeled as near-universals.

8.3 Morphological Features

In the nineteenth century considerable attention was given to morphology. Linguistics was making its way as a scientific study, and primary attention was given to the fields of phonology and morphology. As a part of this attention, linguists generalized about morphological types. Many of the generalizations have been abandoned, but languages still may be characterized for their morphological patterning.

One of the earliest classifications distinguished between languages with little or no inflection, like Chinese and Vietnamese, and those with relatively great inflection, like classical Greek and biblical Hebrew. Those with little inflection were called *analytic;* those with much inflection, *synthetic.* Thereupon it was noted that languages like Turkish and Japanese arranged elements loosely together, and a further morphological type was proposed, under the name *agglutinative.* The three terms still have considerable currency.

The characterization of languages by their morphology has, however, been discredited by attempts to relate this to stages in the development of language and society. By one proposal, the earliest language was analytic. Next, elements were arranged together, providing an agglutinative structure. Finally, some elements were lost, and those left were firmly attached to bases; in this way the synthetic languages supposedly arose. For some scholars, then, there was a progressive evolution, with synthetic languages representing the highest stage of development. This was long the authorized view in the Soviet Union, as a result of the deep influence of a linguist named Nikolay Marr. The position persisted, with great persecution of scholars who did not agree with it, until the early fifties, when the Soviet Union had close ties with China. It seemed undignified to be allied with people speaking a ''primitive'' language. Stalin himself rejected the Marrist doctrine, which he had long supported. Such use of morphological ''universals'' hardly brought luster to their proponents.

The problem was compounded by views of other scholars who believed that analytic languages represented the highest stage of development. The great Danish linguist Otto Jespersen looked on English in this way. Today, linguists are highly cautious about expressing such views. Morphological characteristics are held to belong to the surface structure and, accordingly, little likely to represent universals of language.

8.4 Syntactic Patterns of Arrangement

Many syntactic patterns are regulated in accordance with rules directing whether objects stand before or after verbs in a given language. If a language places objects after verbs, it also contains prepositions. Both parts of speech, prepositions as well as verbs, govern nouns; accordingly, it is logical that both occupy the same position with regard to their nouns. English observes this pattern, as do French, Spanish, and many other so-called verb-object (**VO**) languages. Japanese, on the other hand, places objects before verbs; it belongs to the 50 percent of languages that have object-verb (**OV**) structure. In accordance with the general patterning of language, it and OV languages in general also contain postpositions; the part of speech corresponding to English prepositions is placed after nouns. As a cover word for both prepositions and postpositions, the term **adposition** has been introduced.

The following examples illustrate the Japanese pattern and that of OV languages in general. Besides postpositions with meanings like English prepositions, Japanese includes one marking subjects, *ga;* for compactness, this is glossed *sub* below. The marker of objects, *o* is glossed *obj;* the marker of topics, which may be either subjects or objects or some adverbial sequence, *wa,* is glossed *top.* Other postpositions are given English translations below. When the contrasted Japanese and English sentences have the same meaning, no additional translation is given for the Japanese sentence but only its elements are identified. The corresponding English examples illustrate VO patterning.

1. Basic sentence
   OV a. *John ga   inu o   mita.*
           (*sub*) dog (*obj*) saw
   VO b. John saw the dog.
2. Adposition pattern
   OV a. *John ga   inu o   mado   kara mita.*
           (*sub*) dog (*obj*) window from saw
   VO b. John saw the dog from the window.

Another common pattern differs consistently in the two language types, comparison of inequality. Like verbs and prepositions, adjectives used in comparison precede the standard compared in VO languages; in OV languages like Japanese they follow the standard.

3. Comparison of inequality pattern
   OV a. *Inu ga   neko yori ookii.*
           dog (*sub*) cat   than big (is)
   VO b. The dog is bigger than the cat.

Japanese, like many languages, does not include an element corresponding to *-er; yori* 'from = than' is adequate to signal the comparison.

Other syntactic constructions include elements similar to standards. Among such constructions are family names with given names and with titles, as the following examples illustrate:

4. Family names with given names:
   OV a. *Tanaka John*
   VO b. John Smith

```
English                                                      Japanese
           She sees the book.  VO:OV    Hon o miru.
- - - - - - - - - - - - - - - - - - - - - - - - - - - - - - - - - - - -
           Noun relative clause :  Relative clause  noun
       the book that John bought :  John ga katta hon
                  Noun genitive :  Genitive noun
               the book of John's :  John no hon
                 Noun adjective :  Adjective noun
       the book interesting (to John) :  omoshiroi hon
- - - - - - - - - - - - - - - - - - - - - - - - - - - - - - - - - -
                    Preposition :  Postposition
                      to John :  John ni
- - - - - - - - - - - - - - - - - - - - - - - - - - - - - - - - - -
           Comparative construction of inequality
                 bigger than John :  John yori ookii
- - - - - - - - - - - - - - - - - - - - - - - - - - - - - - - - - -
           Interrogative verb :  Verb interrogative
         Does John see the dog :  John ga hon o miru ka
 Interrogative negative verb :  Verb negative interrogative
      Doesn't John see the dog :  John ga hon o mi nai ka
```

Figure 8.1 Comparable Patterns in VO and OV Languages, Though Contrasting in Order (Sometimes Labeled as Mirror-Image Rules)

In all these patterns the essential elements of the English and the Japanese constructions are placed in contrasting arrangement. The illustrations are parallel in meaning, and accordingly the Japanese words may be identified.

> 5. Names with titles:
>   OV a. *Tanaka sensei* ('teacher, professor')
>   VO b. Professor Smith

In keeping with this sequence in names, Japanese arranges addresses from the most general to the more specific elements. In contrast with the well-known English address pattern shown in 6b, Japanese typically uses the following sequence:[1]

> 6. Addresses:
>   a. OV *Nihon (Japan)*
>   *Tookyoo-shi (Tokyo-city)*
>   *Kanda-ku (Kanda ward)*
>   *Surugadai-machi (Surugadai "town")*
>   *ni-choome (2nd street)*
>   *juuroku-banchi ('16 number')*
>   *Tanaka John*[1]

[1] From J. K. Yamagiwa, *Modern Conversational Japanese* (New York: McGraw-Hill, 1942), p. 45.

      b. VO John Smith
              16 Second Street
              Surugadai, Kanda, Tokyo, Japan

This Japanese pattern is now breaking down as international correspondence increases, but you may still receive letters with addresses in this order from Japan and also from the Soviet Union. The replacement of the native pattern provides an illustration of the influence of one or more languages on others.

    As these examples may indicate, the patterns of arrangement differ considerably in VO and OV languages. Since the rules of order are virtually reverse, they are sometimes referred to as mirror-image rules. Having recognized this relationship between rules of arrangement in OV and VO languages, we are able to propose general principles, or universals, governing arrangement.

8.5 Syntactic Patterns of Modification

So far we have dealt with patterns in which one linguistic element controls or governs another. In addition to the process known as **government, modification** is a central feature of language. It too observes different arrangement in OV and VO languages. Modifiers apply to each of the basic constituents, verbs and nouns. If the VO/OV nucleus is fundamental, as these designations for the two language types suggest, we would expect modifiers for both nouns and verbs to stand outside the nucleus. Verbal modifiers would precede the V of VO languages, follow the V of OV languages. The following examples illustrate this principle of arrangement.

    A prominent modifier of verbs is the device to indicate questions as opposed to statements. Many languages have a special marker for interrogation (*int*). Japanese uses *ka*. English uses the dummy verb *do,* which serves in other constructions as well, such as the negative. To make a question of the sentences in example 1, these markers are introduced—after the verb in Japanese, before it in English.

        7. Interrogative:
           OV a. *John ga inu o   mita ka.*
                   (*sub*) dog (*obj*) saw (*int*)
           VO b. Did John see the dog?

    Another verbal modifier is sentence negation (*neg*). This is expressed in Japanese by placing *-nai* after the verb; to avoid complexity, sentence 1a is given below in the present tense. English adds *-n't* to forms of *do* and other auxiliaries, placing this combined expression before the principal verb.

        8. Negative:
           OV a. *John ga inu o   minai.*
                   (*sub*) dog (*obj*) see-not
           VO b. John doesn't see the dog.

The order of *int* and *neg* with regard to each other is also significant. *Int* is placed closer to the sentence boundary both in OV and in VO languages. In this arrangement we also note a universal principle.

> 9. Interrogative + Negative:
> OV a. *John ga inu o   minai ka.*
>   (*sub*) dog (*obj*) see-not (*int*)
> VO b. Doesn't John see the dog?

Other verbal modifiers could be discussed here, such as expressions for obligation, volition, and causation; these too observe the principle stated above, as examples from OV languages like Japanese, Turkish, and Quechua would illustrate. Such discussion would extend this chapter unduly, without contributing materially to the principle or to an understanding of central differences between OV and VO languages. Accordingly those modifiers are left for your future exploration, if you wish to elicit patterns from OV speakers or to examine grammars of OV languages.

8.6 Subgroupings of OV and VO Languages

The examination of verbal modifiers leads to further insights into language structure, especially concerning VO languages. These languages require subjects. Many OV languages tend not to include subjects; sentence 1a would often be expressed in Japanese simply as *Inu o mita*. It is assumed to be obvious from the context or the actual situation who did the seeing. VO languages like English require subjects; they are then subclassified in accordance with the position of the subject as VSO, SVO, or OSV languages. Such languages have complications with verbal modifiers, for these have to compete with subjects for position closest to the initial sentence boundary. OV languages lack this problem, other than the rare OVS type. In OV languages, verbal modifiers can simply be added in their natural order. This possibility is also open to VSO languages, like classical Arabic, biblical Hebrew, Irish, and Welsh. In these the marker for *int* stands closest to the sentence boundary with no interference from the subject; the marker for *neg* can follow, and so on, as the following classical Arabic examples illustrate.

> 10a. VSO Interrogative Pattern:
>   *hal   šāhada ʔalkalba*
>   (*int*) saw-he the-dog
>   'Did he see the dog?'
> b. VSO Negative Pattern:
>   *ma   šāhada ʔalkalba*
>   (*neg*) saw-he the-dog
>   'He didn't see the dog.'
> c. Interrogative Plus Negative Pattern:
>   *ʔamo   šāhada ʔalkalba*
>   (*int + neg*) saw-he the-dog
>   'Didn't he see the dog?'

SVO languages may have special devices to solve the conflict in arrangement between subject and verbal modifiers. That of English is particularly ingenious. English gradually developed the use of *do* for this purpose, also attaching *neg* to it and to other auxiliaries. Shakespeare could still say:

> 11a. *I know him not.*

Less than four hundred years later we find this sequence stilted, using instead:

> 11b. *I don't know him.*

The English change in position of the negative marker is an instance of internal change. Word order became increasingly fixed in accordance with VO patterning. Expression for the negative also came to observe the typical VO order. The same kind of change took place for nominal modifiers, as we note below.

Nominal modifiers, in accordance with the principle stated above, should precede nouns in OV languages, follow them in VO. We will examine briefly three kinds of nominal modifiers. Of these, relative clauses are primary; genitives and adjectives are in a sense reductions of them.

The relationship between these three constructions becomes clear when we observe how relative clauses are introduced into sentences. They result from the incorporation of one sentence into another, which may take place if both contain a noun with the same reference. (See Chapter 5, Section 5.4, examples 22 and 23.) We may utter such sentences in sequence, as follows:

> 12. Relative Clause Formation:
>   a. *John saw the dog. The dog ate the meat.*

In typical speech such sentences would be combined as follows:

> 12b. *John saw the dog that ate the meat.*

In the process of forming relative clauses one of the two equivalent noun phrases is deleted. Deletion applies also if the second sentence in 12a is the principal clause in the combined sentence.

> 12c. *The dog that John saw ate the meat.*

English requires a relative pronoun: *that, which,* and so on. If, however, the deleted noun is the object in its own clause, a relative pronoun is not necessary, as in the following example:

> 12d. *The dog (that) John saw ate the meat.*

OV languages typically make relative clauses without adding a relative pronoun or marker, whether the deleted noun is subject or object in its clause. The Japanese counterpart of 12a and b is:

12e. *John ga inu o mita. Inu ga niku o tabeta.*
  f. *John ga niku o tabeta inu o mita.*

VSO languages also commonly make relative clauses in this way; any internal verb standing after a noun might then introduce a relative clause. The first two words of the Old Testament provide a famous example. These followed by the subject and object are as follows:

13a. bərešiθ   bɔrɔ   Ɂɛlohim Ɂeθ
       haššɔmayim wəɁeθ hɔɁɔrɛṣ
       in-beginning created God (*obj*)
       the-heavens and   (*obj*) the-earth

Not aware of this construction, early translators provided interpretations like that in the King James translation:

13b. *'In the beginning God created the heavens and the earth.'*

Later scholars may treat the bɔrɔ clause as relative with regard to the preceding noun, translating as follows:

13c. *'It was in the beginning that God created the heavens and the earth.'*

The difference may not seem momentous. But the older interpretation suggests that this was the very first act in the history of the universe, while the more recent interpretations take the creation as simply one of the actions in an early period. Application of linguistic knowledge may in this way affect interpretation of texts, whether by literary scholars, by theologians, or by general readers.

Genitive expressions are abbreviated relative clauses. If instead of the second sentence in 12a we embedded the sentence below, we could introduce a relative clause as in 14b. But generally we do not, instead using 14c.

14a. *John saw the dog. It is the dog of his friend.*
  b. *John saw the dog that is of his friend/his friend's.*
  c. *John saw the dog of his friend.*

Japanese equivalents of 14a and c are:

14d. *John ga inu o mita. Tomodachi no inu desu.*
               friend (of)   is
  e. *John ga tomodachi no inu o mita.*
       'John saw the dog of his friend.'

Just as Japanese arranges relative clauses in front of nouns, it also places genitives and possessives there. English as well can have:

> 14f. *John saw his friend's dog.*

This construction is possible if the genitive refers to an animate being. In contemporary English we do not commonly say: *the pencil's point, the house's roof,* and so forth. Yet this was the pattern in English a thousand years ago. Just as English changed its position of the negative, in the same way it changed the position of most genitives.

Adjectives, however, have not changed their position in English, that is, not unless they are themselves modified by an adverbial expression. We therefore distinguish the following:

> 15a. *John saw the dog. The dog is black.*
> b. *John saw the dog. The dog is beloved by children.*

The first may be reduced to:

> 15c. *John saw the black dog.*

But the second must have the adjective after the noun, as is true of most adjectives in the stricter VO languages, French and Spanish, and in the VSO languages like biblical Hebrew.

> 15d. *John saw the dog beloved by children.*

All Japanese adjectives precede their nouns, as the equivalents of 15a and b illustrate:

> 15e. *John wa inu o mita. Inu ga kuroi desu.*
>   black is
> f. *John wa kuroi inu o mita.*

The patterns and examples given here illustrate many of the typical syntactic constructions. They also indicate syntactic universals. As is clear from the reverse arrangements, the universals do not impose a common order on all languages. Rather, they consist of deep-seated principles that establish relative orders. Such are the order of the interrogative marker in relation to the sentence boundary, the negative marker for sentences in relation to the interrogative marker, and so on.

8.7 Semantic and Textual Universals

In Chapter 7, Section 7.5, we noted proposed universals for sets of kinship and color words. Other fields that may also reflect universals require careful study before a proposal can be made.

Such study is now being applied to texts. Folk tales generally have a first sentence that provides the same information, regardless of the language or culture in which they are maintained. Subsequent sentences provide details as the "plot thickens." A punch line concludes the tale. Vladímir Propp has attempted to establish general principles for this genre, and other scholars are dealing with other literary forms.

Such investigations have focused largely on Western texts, as in the books by Andre Jolles and Propp listed in the bibliography. Moreover, they have been directed at short texts, like the folk tale. The energies now being applied in text linguistics may yield insights into universal principles governing longer texts and their structures. To sort out the complexities, literary scholars and anthropologists as well as linguists and specialists in artificial intelligence will need to devote considerable imagination and study to each of the well-known kinds of texts.

QUESTIONS FOR REVIEW

1. What is meant by *universals* in linguistics?
2. In what segments of language are universals most readily identified?
3. Why is it difficult to propose universals regarding vowel systems?
4. Cite an implicational universal.
5. What observations did Roman Jakobson make that have a bearing on phonological universals?
6. What is meant by *analytic, agglutinative,* and *synthetic* languages?
7. What are OV as opposed to VO languages?
8. How are adpositional constructions parallel to clauses?
9. How can the order of comparative constructions be related to that of clauses?
10. What is a *standard?*
11. Illustrate the application of the "standard" in names and in names with titles.
12. In what way is the placement of interrogative and negative markers regulated in accordance with clause order?
13. List three subtypes of VO languages.
14. How are attributive adjective and genitive constructions similar to relative clauses?
15. Discuss the formation of relative clauses in Japanese. How does it compare with some relative clauses in a VSO language like biblical Hebrew?
16. What change has taken place in the position of English genitives over the past thousand years?
17. Compare the position of attributive adjectives in English with that of a stricter SVO language like French. When does English place adjectives after nouns?
18. To what extent can we propose universals pertaining to the semantic and textual areas of language?

PROBLEMS FOR REVIEW

1. The word for 'I have seen' in classical Greek is *dedorka,* a reduplicated form (*de-*) of the root *derk-* followed by the ending *-a,* indicating first person singular indicative active. The corresponding form in Japanese is *mimashita,* from the root *mi-,* followed by the polite suffix *-mash-* plus *-i-,* followed by the past tense ending *-ta.* From a morphological point of view English is analytic, Greek is synthetic, and Japanese is agglutinative. How do these forms support this analysis?

   Other forms in these three languages are 'I have gone,' *bébēka,* and *ikimashita.* Analyze these, indicating how they support the morphological characterization.

2. Names are often patronymics, as in *Johnson,* originally designating 'the son of John,' *Williamson,* and so on. But Irish has names like *MacHenry, MacKendrick,* and so on, where *mac* means 'son.' Welsh has names like *Pritchard,* where *p* is an abbreviated form of *ap* 'son.' Hebrew has names like *Ben-Gurion,* where *ben* means 'son'; Arabic has names like *Ibn Saud,* where *ibn* means 'son.' What kind of syntactic structure would you expect to lead to such names, OV, SVO, VSO, or other?

3. Our word *hippopotamus* is taken from classical Greek; the components literally mean 'horse-river.' If this were a native Greek word, it should mean 'river of the horse' rather than 'horse of the river.' Comparing the names in problem 2, account for this word. Recalling that the animal is not found in Greece, suggest how Greek acquired such an aberrant compound word.

4. The following are Japanese sentences with translations.
   1. *Neko ga inu o mimasu.* 'The cat sees the dog.'
   2. *Inu ga neko o mimasu.* 'The dog sees the cat.'
   3. *Otoko ga inu o mimasu.* 'The man sees the dog.'
   4. *Ane ga inu o mimasita.* 'The older sister saw the dog.'

   After identifying the lexical items in these sentences, that is, the Japanese words for 'man,' 'dog,' 'cat,' 'older sister,' 'see,' state the word order of Japanese clauses in terms of subject, verb, and object. Thereupon examine the following sentences:
   5. *Otoko ga ookii inu o mimashita.*
      'The man saw the big dog.'
   6. *Otoko wa ane no neko o mimashita.*
      'The man saw the cat of his older sister.'
   7. *Otoko wa inu ga kanda neko o mimashita.*
      'The man saw the cat that the dog bit.'
   8. *Inu ga kanda otoko wa neko o mimashita.*
      'The man whom the dog bit saw the cat.'

   What is the position of the relative clause, the genitive construction, and the adjective with regard to the word modified? Compare this position with the order of the comparable entities in English.

5. A pattern pertinent for determining basic word order in a language is that of the 'comparison of inequality.' In an SVO language like English, one finds sequences like the following:

    1. The dog is bigger than the cat.

    In OV languages like Japanese and Turkish one finds patterns like the following:

    2. *Inu wa neko yori ookii*. (Japanese)
       dog   cat   from big
       'The dog is bigger than the cat.'

    3. *Köpek kedi-den   daha* büyük. (Turkish)
       dog   cat from more big
       'The dog is bigger than the cat.'

Account for the differing patterns in terms of the two structures, SVO and OV. Can you relate the comparative construction to the position of the verb with regard to the object?

    In Spanish the sentence is as follows:

    4. *El perro es mas grande que el gato*. 'The dog is more big than the cat'

    On the basis of this comparative construction, would you label Spanish as SVO or OV?

FURTHER READING

Benveniste, Emile. *Problems in General Linguistics*. Trans. by Mary Elizabeth Meek. Coral Gables, Fla.: University of Miami Press, 1971.

Finck, Franz N. *Die Haupttypen des Sprachbaus*. Leipzig and Berlin: Teubner, 1909.

Greenberg, Joseph H., ed. *Universals of Language*. Cambridge, Mass.: MIT Press, 1966.

Jolles, Andre. *Einfache Formen*. 2d ed. Darmstadt: Wissenschaftliche Buchgesellschaft, 1958.

Lehmann, Winfred P., ed. *Syntactic Typology*. Austin: University of Texas Press, 1978.

Propp, Vladímir. *Morphology of the Folktale*. 2d ed. Trans. by Laurence Scott. Austin: University of Texas Press, 1968.

Trubetzkoy, Nikolay S. *Principles of Phonology*. Trans. by Christiane A. M. Baltaxe. Berkeley and Los Angeles: University of California Press, 1969.

CHAPTER NINE

Perspectives on Human Language

9.1 Animal Language

The preceding chapters have examined language itself, its structure, and its mechanisms. We have noted that language has a complex structure—a system of sounds that in themselves have no meaning; combinations of these sounds in a system of sentences used in texts made up of meaningful elements or morphemes; a system of relationships between morphemes in characteristic arrangements and the world outside language. To deal with that complex structure we posit phonological, syntactic, and semantic levels.

Having arrived at such a view of language, we would like to find external evidence for our assumptions—data outside human language, or at any rate outside typical human language, to give us support for our conclusions. Such data are being sought in the communication systems of animals, in attempts to deal with languages by means of computers, and through investigations of unusual types of language, including pathological uses as investigated in neuropsychology. In this chapter we examine some of these investigations and their results, beginning with the study of animal languages for the illumination they provide on human language.

It is quite clear that animals use symbols to communicate, whether through sounds or other devices. Such a finding was beautifully demonstrated by Karl von Frisch, in his investigations of the "language of bees." This, in his description, consists of dances. Messenger bees who have located food perform a wagging dance on a perpendicular honeycomb to indicate horizontal directions and distance to a source of food. While the symbols do not consist of simple gestures, they are direct. A given dance has one meaning, which is not modified to a question, an expression of surprise, an ironic comment. Such a system is then a compact and limited version of the communication system that humans have developed.

To examine human language with regard to more complex communication systems than that of bees, investigators have set out not only to analyze these systems but also to communicate with animals in human language.

In Section 6.7 of Chapter 6 we noted how observation of language acquisition among infants supports the assumption that human language is composite, one segment carrying the central meaning, another indicating its force, whether a statement, a question, a command, and so forth. The communication of animals, on the other hand, apparently consists of simple signals, primarily indicating commands or statements of pleasure or questions challenging a stranger and the like. The territorial calls of birds, for example, like some of the barks, growls, and whistles of other animals, are commands. Other calls are exploratory, seeking to determine whether an interloper is friendly or not. Still other bird songs, barking, and so on are pure expressions of pleasure: The mockingbird actually sings all night long during a brilliant night in spring, hardly to stake out a territory. Animals, then, use sounds for purposes comparable to perlocutionary, illocutionary, and locutionary effects. Many recent investigators have set out to determine whether they also use or can learn to use signals that carry fuller meanings, like the meanings of the proposition segment of human utterances.

The most ambitious such investigations have attempted to teach chimpanzees to learn some form of English. Since earlier studies had found that chimpanzees lack the vocal apparatus necessary for speech sounds, recent investigators set out to teach chimpanzees sign languages. For a time, publications on progress were highly optimistic. The chimpanzees were reported not only to have mastered as many as seventy-five signs but also to have adapted these creatively. That is, besides learning a form of human language, they were able to approximate the ability of humans to devise new combinations. Washoe, Sarah, and other chimpanzees showed their accomplishments on TV. One promising chimpanzee, named Nim Chimsky in honor of the linguist, received intensive instruction from infancy. It was even hoped that the acquired skills might be passed on to the young.

Recently the optimism has been deflated. The skepticism relates to that resulting from disclosure of the supposed prowess of a horse, Clever Hans. For a while around the turn of the century, Clever Hans astounded audiences by adding digits correctly, solving problems in mathematics and musical harmony. He gave his answers by pawing the ground. His trainer even proposed teaching Hans to spell and to perform other wonders. But then it was determined that Hans had no arithmetical, linguistic, or musical ability. His answers resulted from careful observation of his trainer and others, who without design indicated by some physical reaction when Hans had pawed the ground the correct number of times. Such successful communication between animal and master has come to be known

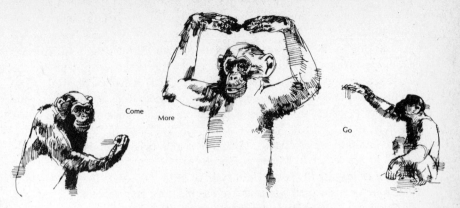

Figure 9.1 Hand Signs Used by Washoe

as the Clever Hans Effect. Animals may indeed interpret their master and other humans correctly; but the process takes place without control of human language or of mathematical symbols.

Critics of the reports on Washoe, Nim, and others now propose that these chimpanzees did not master human language; rather, like Clever Hans, they capably interpret their trainers and then signal the proper responses.

The confrontation of views is recent, and the jury is still out. Supporters of the assumption that chimpanzees have a language ability point to experiments in which animals communicate by means of a typewriter keyboard attached to a computer. Others maintain that they have brought pigeons to teaching one another how to master new signals. Argumentation between the two camps will no doubt continue. Yet the hopes expressed earlier about teaching dolphins, chimpanzees, and other animals to communicate with systems comparable to human language now seem unrealistic.

From the investigations we have, however, gained significant results, as on the importance of the Clever Hans Effect or its equivalent, which is also important in communication between two humans. We convey a great deal of information to close friends and associates nonverbally, as most of us would agree when we recall the preciseness we need to use in speaking to strangers, especially foreigners. Further, we avoid such precision in the family or among close friends. We do so because we can rely on the Clever Hans Effect.

Language, then, is simply one element of communication. When we need to be highly explicit, we speak and we write with great care. But often we leave half the job of communication to tone of voice, gestures, or even the good will of our associates.

9.2 The Language of "Wild Children"

The close relationship between language and other social behavior is demonstrated dramatically by the few known instances of children separated from other humans before they learned language. There may be only two authentic examples, both well described.

The Wild Boy of Aveyron was discovered in southern France in 1800. Unable to speak, unused to clothing and to cooked foods, he was taken over by a physician, Jean-Marie Gaspard Itard, who set out to civilize him. Itard described his aims and also his educational theory, so that we have a good account of his work with Victor, as Itard named him. Victor was to learn to speak, think clearly, and take his part in society. Success in these aims was expected in accordance with contemporary empirical philosophy, which considered social experience rather than innate ideas to be the key to human advancement.

Victor never learned to speak. He may have been born deaf. But he did learn to use letters in order to spell words and to use them for communication. The first word he learned to use in this way was *lait* 'milk'; by spelling out words he communicated with others. His vocabulary remained small. And he never adjusted completely to civilized existence, though he was in the care of a sympathetic woman, Madame Guerin, until his death at about the age of forty. Since many details of his physical abilities remain obscure, we cannot generalize in detail about his limited accomplishments.

In spite of his intensive work with Victor for five years, Dr. Itard was unable to demonstrate the validity of his philosophical views. The relative importance of social experience and innate ideas was not clarified. It is true that Victor's social experiences civilized him to a certain degree. But, whatever the reason, he did not learn language, leaving open the question on its innate basis. His lack of linguistic success does, however, support the assumption that language must be acquired in early childhood or it will remain incompletely developed.

Victor's life story has been described in several accounts, recently by Roger Shattuck; it was also treated in a notable film by François Truffaut: "The Wild Child." While Itard was unsuccessful in his aims, his work with Victor led to improvements in teaching deaf-mutes, including greater use of sign language and instruction in reading and writing. Victor's experience in this way contributed to improved treatment of the deaf, who before the nineteenth century lived out their lives as "deaf-mutes."

We have far more information on Genie, who has been described as a "Modern-Day 'Wild Child.'" Genie was confined by a psychotic father to an upstairs room at the age of twenty months, where she received minimal nourishment but no opportunity to use language. After she was discovered twelve years later, at thirteen years and seven months, a group of eminent specialists gave her the best of training and care. This has been thoroughly documented.

Like Victor, Genie did not speak when discovered. She could comprehend a few individual words but no syntactic sequences. Yet unlike Victor she has learned to speak in sentences and achieved great comprehension of the speech addressed to her. Her own syntactic sequences, however, show gaps. After five years of instruction she did not learn to make passives, nor to shift auxiliaries, as in questions.

Differing interpretations have been made of her language difficulties and of her achievements. Her progress has led some theorists to suggest that the first years are not crucial in language learning. Our information is, however, inadequate to reach such a conclusion; for Genie was not confined to her room before she had heard a considerable amount of language. Further, her confinement there would not have hindered her from hearing all speech utterances. On the other hand, her progress from total nonuse of language is remarkable. But in view of our inadequate information on her early life, we must be cautious in generalizing from it about the process by which humans acquire language.

Other findings from her experience are highly significant. Like Victor, Genie found difficulty with social relationships. Among these is mastery of the distances maintained in social interactions. Typically Americans prefer a distance of a yard or more when speaking with others; Genie maintains much shorter distances.

It is also interesting that Genie has learned language with her right hemisphere. Acquisition of language in infancy may then affect communication generally. A small proportion of speakers, approximately 2 percent, do indeed control language with the right hemisphere, which generally directs spatial control rather than the abstract patterns of language. And as we note below, further discoveries are being made about lateralization. It has been observed that speakers who, like Genie, store language in their right hemisphere are superior in control of vocabulary and in comprehension rather than in speaking. Yet we cannot assert that Genie's reliance on her right hemisphere is a result of her late language learning, for she may be among the 2 percent who naturally use that hemisphere for language.

As from Victor, we have learned a great deal from Genie. We note once more the importance of learning language in the first years of life. We also observe the close relationship between mastery of language and other social conventions. And we may even propose that the syntactic patterns difficult for Genie, like the passive, require grammatical rules that are difficult to acquire at an advanced age. Although we can only speculate on such matters, we note once again the marvelous complexity of human language, as well as the close association between its mastery and other patterns of social behavior. Moreover, from the resilience of severely deprived children like Victor and Genie, we derive no little humility when we compare our own cavalier acceptance of scarcely admirable uses of language.

9.3 Aphasia

Observation of speakers with aphasia has also taught us a great deal about the structure of language. Such speakers may have a variety of language deficits. Their stock of sounds may be reduced, so that their words and sentences are greatly simplified. They may be unable to produce sentences. Moreover, they may use words correctly in sentences, but with incorrect reference; they may say *chair* when they wish to say *table* and so on. These three kinds of aphasia relate to the threefold structure of language—phonology, syntax, and semantics—supporting the view of language presented earlier in this book, for each segment may be separately affected by injury to the brain.

In a brilliant monograph the noted linguist Roman Jakobson proposed a further correlation between aphasia, general sound laws, and child language learning. He observed that speakers with severe phonological aphasia may be left with only a few consonants and vowels. These are consistently stops, like /p t k/, nasals, and vowels like /i a u/, not complex consonants or vowels. Jakobson then pointed out that these are precisely the sounds that infants first master. Everywhere one of the first words acquired by children is *ma, mama.* Other widely found nursery words are *papa, tata* for 'father,' *pipi, pupu,* and so on. In accordance with Jakobson's observation, the stages of phonological loss among aphasics seem to be similar to those of language acquisition. In severe phonological aphasia, those sounds are retained longest that infants learn first.

Moreover, the sounds mastered first are those most widespread in language. Some of the simplest phonological systems are found in the languages of the Pacific, such as Hawaiian. These, as may be observed from place-names like *Oahu, Hawaii, Honolulu,* have few consonants and vowels, typically /p k ʔ h m n l w/ and /i e a o u/. Such a contrast as that between /r/ and /l/ is missing—as it is in Japanese and Chinese. We may then speculate further that when languages have simple phonological systems, they include the sounds first acquired generally by infants.

Observations on phonological aphasia, and also on the other kinds, are increasingly related to the structure of the brain. Specialized speech areas have been identified since the nineteenth century. Aphasia results from localized lesions in those areas, which are now being determined with greater precision not only through sophisticated medical techniques but also by precise observation of patients whose injuries have led to the loss of language.

Among these, a remarkable account of particular language loss is that of a Russian officer wounded by a bullet in World War II, Lev Zasetsky. The bullet entered the left parietooccipital region of his cranium, and the injury was compounded by inflammation. It led to loss of the higher functions of his brain: his knowledge, his memory, and his ability to read, write, and orient himself in space and time. Yet with long-standing encouragement from the eminent neurologist Alexander Luria, Zasetsky began to keep a diary. The work provides an amazing account of courage.[1]

Zasetsky can write only a few words at a time and is unable to read them, for the injury destroyed the area in which we convert perceptions into structures. Some of the other consequences may be illustrated by reports of Zasetsky's difficulties. Observing a picture of human figures, one of which was a "father's brother," Zasetsky made the following remarks: "Father's brother. Here's the brother, and there's the father. Whose father is it? No, whose brother is it? Whose brother is he? I don't understand." As these remarks indicate, Zasetsky regained his ability to interpret words referring to individuals. But he cannot associate them—he did not treat the situation as a whole nor language as a structure.

---

[1] Karl Levitan, "The Teachings of Alexander Luria," *Soviet Life* (September 1980), pp. 27–30, 48–49.

Zasetsky's experience, along with other observations of speech deficits resulting from brain injury, strongly support the view that language is not simply a set of individual items but that these are combined in systems as described above.

9.4 Speech and Lateralization

Some of the most remarkable findings on human control of language have resulted from observation of people with split brains. Operations severing the corpus callosum, which links the two hemispheres, have been performed on epileptics who have uncontrollable seizures; the seizures are then alleviated. Thereupon the speakers concerned have in effect two brains, for after the operation the two hemispheres are to some degree independent. Investigations can then explore differences between them.

Many mechanisms of the brain have long been known, such as the processing of visual sensations by the hemisphere opposite the eye receiving them; the input from the right eye is interpreted by the left hemisphere, and vice versa. Investigations can accordingly provide information to each hemisphere of split-brain subjects independently.

These investigations have found that split-brain speakers comprehend information given to the right hemisphere. But they cannot discuss it. For example, such speakers may be given visual directions through the left eye (right hemisphere) to move objects, such as the buildings of a toy village, but when asked what they have done, they cannot speak about it. These results graphically illustrate the capabilities of the right hemisphere. With it we understand spatial arrangements, but language is largely controlled by the left hemisphere.

The findings are more subtle than this last statement indicates, as may be determined from Gazzaniga's book[2] and other discussions. A great deal of further investigation has been undertaken to determine the extent of lateralization.

One of the most remarkable results indicates differences between the treatment of nouns and verbs by the brain. If nouns like *knife* or *orange* are presented through the left eye to the right hemisphere, patients point out the correct object. If a picture of a house is shown to the left eye, however, without an accompanying verbal cue, patients say that they have seen nothing. But if directed to use their left hand to pick up a card with a picture of a house, they do so. We may conclude that the right hemisphere "understands" the signals provided by nouns and that it can thereupon direct appropriate actions but that it cannot process the verbal signals on its own. Nouns related to verbs, however, are not even "understood" by the right hemisphere. Thus, nouns like *jump* or *locker* are not processed by the right hemisphere, though phonologically similar nouns like *butter* are.

Moreover, when verbs are presented through the left eye to the right hemisphere, no understanding results. While patients point to a knife or an orange and pick up the picture of a house when directed to do so, they do not respond to instructions via visual representations of the words *smile* or *nod* or when requested to *tap*,

[2] Michael S. Gazzaniga, *The Bisected Brain* (New York: Plenum, 1970).

point, or *knock.* When, however, the directions are provided by pictures rather than verbally, the patients perform the actions of smiling, tapping, and so on. The investigators conclude that verbs are "represented poorly if at all in the right hemisphere."[3]

The findings of Michael Gazzaniga and other investigators have important implications for linguistic theory. These findings suggest that the verb is a characteristic category of the communication system developed by humans, that is, of human language. Apparently the right hemisphere, which is similar to the brain of other animals, can process nouns and concepts represented by "pure" nouns. But verbs and their derivatives are processed only in the specially developed speech center of the left hemisphere in humans. Consequently, in grammars and theoretical discussions of language, verbs must be accorded the primary role in sentences. Therefore, grammars that require the inclusion of verbs (though not necessarily nouns) in sentences and their basic rules represent the capacities for speech that exist in the human brain.

This conclusion receives support from the nounless sentences of many languages, including the early Indo-European. In classical Latin the expression for 'it is raining' was simply *pluit,* in classical Greek *huei;* both mean 'rains.'

Research into the processes involved in the perception of language is still in its beginnings, but it promises to increase greatly our understanding of language. Linguists must be grateful to the scholars carrying out such research and realize the need for anyone interested in an understanding of language to keep abreast of future developments. Similar research is being carried out on bilingual speakers and their control of one or more of their languages by the two hemispheres of the brain.

9.5 Bilingualism

The study of bilingualism provides perspectives especially on the use of language and on our capabilities in controlling it. Mastery of one language seems difficult enough, but members of bilingual communities, like the Swiss, the inhabitants of India, and indeed many countries seem to use two or more languages with no appreciable effort.

Often, however, bilingualism raises the problem of language loyalty. Most countries have one official language; use of another may be viewed as betrayal. Such attitudes become acute at times of war. In World War I, many speakers of German were treated badly in the United States; in World War II, the treatment of the Japanese was disgraceful. On the other hand, speakers of two or more languages have great advantages when traveling abroad, in scientific work, and in cultural activities. Fluent speakers of several languages are greatly admired; even the utterance of a single sentence, like President Kennedy's *Ich bin ein Berliner,* arouses widespread acclaim. Attitudes to language in this way become intensified when bilingualism is concerned.

[3] *Ibid.,* p. 121.

The well-known Argentinian author Jorge Luis Borges admirably relates how a perceptive child functions in a bilingual environment. The son of a Spanish-speaking mother and an English-speaking father, he spoke both languages equally from infancy. And as he relates, he was not aware that his situation was in any way unusual. Such an attitude is apparently general among bilingual children.

Such children, however, associate specific languages with specific people; if the same person always speaks the same language, the child has no problems. It is only when they use a different language that the child becomes disturbed. The son of a friend grew up speaking second languages in a multilingual environment. When one day the maid said "Good-bye" to him rather than her usual "Auf Wiedersehen," he shook his fist at her and told her firmly in German that she should not say "Good-bye" but rather "Auf Wiedersehen." Borges reports no such dramatic incident. But he does relate how finally at the age of seven or so he recognized that he was using several languages.

Investigators are now trying to determine how we can control several languages. Do we then employ both hemispheres of the brain? The question is very difficult to investigate, because unlike visual perception, input through the ears is not distinctly related to separate hemispheres. In great part the left ear conveys its information to the right hemisphere and the right ear to the left. But in the process considerable information goes to both sides; as a result, simple tests like providing different messages to each ear do not give clear results.

In examining the problem, Harvey Sussman devised an ingenious means to secure more accurate data based on speech output.[4] First, he asked speakers to tap on a counting device for twenty seconds; in this way he determined the rate of tapping in silence for each hand, as controlled by its hemisphere. Then he asked the speaker to produce some utterances concurrently with finger tapping. When a monolingual speaker was tapping while speaking, the rate of tapping was consistently slower in the right hand only. The left hemisphere was then controlling two actions—right hand tapping and speech.

The crucial part of the investigation measured the difference in rate of tapping when two languages were spoken. Bilinguals showed consistent reductions in both right- and left-hand tapping rates. It turned out to be something of a surprise that bilinguals make considerable use of the right hemisphere for their second language. This is especially true for those bilinguals who did not learn the two languages simultaneously from early childhood.

Such findings have many implications. As we have noted, it has been generally assumed that the left hemisphere controls speech. The assumption is supported by evidence of speech loss as a result of injury to the brain. If, for example, injuries resulting from bullet wounds or vehicle accidents affect the left hemisphere, speech loss often results. The social conditions of today, leading on the one hand to longer life with increased likelihood of stroke and on the other to injuries in vehicle accidents, contribute large numbers of such situations. But relatively few Americans are bilinguals, and accordingly such injuries in the right hemisphere may have

[4] Harvey M. Sussman, Philip Franklin, and Terry Simon, "Bilingual Speech: Bilateral Control?" *Brain and Language* 15 (1982), pp. 125–142.

received little attention. If bilinguals do control one or both languages in the right as well as the left hemisphere, speech loss resulting from left hemisphere injuries may be less crippling to an individual. Investigations like Sussman's are only in their beginnings. We need many more studies on the control of language by each hemisphere. These supplement observations made about the structure of language in applications of linguistics, such as language teaching.

9.6 The Teaching of Second Languages

Teachers of their native language to nonnative speakers invariably state that they themselves have learned a great deal about their own language from their students. Their new insights result from the need they find for detailed analyses of the patterning in their own language, which is required to help their students avoid mistakes or to correct these mistakes. Native speakers master their first language so thoroughly that they are not aware of its intricacies.

Findings from nonnative speakers come in all areas of language. We recognize the extent of aspiration of prevocalic stops when we teach English to a native speaker of French and to native speakers of many other languages. If we teach English to native speakers of Chinese we must devise means for teaching them to distinguish between the voiceless and voiced pairs of *par/bar, tear/dare, core/gore,* and so forth. Their native pattern leads them to use the distinction between aspirated and nonaspirated stops found in *par/spar, tear/stare, core/score.* In the process of our teaching, our own intricate system of allophonic variation in /p t k/ becomes apparent to us.

Speakers of French as well as native German speakers bring it to our attention that 'vacation' for us is one entity, while in their languages it is a plural, as we noted in Chapter 4, Section 4.7.1. Besides telling us of their 'vacations,' native German speakers may give us 'informations,' comment on their 'hairs,' ask for a 'scissor,' and so on. Their language identifies these objects in the outside world differently from ours, and they find our patterns difficult. We, on the other hand, learn that the semantic patterning of English has its particular conventions.

Some of our most trying problems we encounter in the area of syntax. Here we examine briefly classes of verbs and their complements. Instructors teaching English as a second language have problems enough teaching the uses of the verb forms in the following:

> 1a. *We speak English.*
> b. *We are speaking English.*
> c. *We do speak English.*

Most languages have only one such form, comparable to 1a. We must then concentrate on teaching b and c as well. The pedagogical problems are magnified on the introduction of further verbs, some the most frequent in English.

More than a hundred of these do not permit the form in 1b in its normal meaning of a temporary aspect. Some are verbs of perception: *hear, notice, recognize, see, smell;* others are verbs indicating mental activity: *believe, forget, know, understand, remember;* still others refer to emotions: *dislike, like, love, want, wish.* Having learned the use of the form in 1a to indicate duration, in contrast with the temporary aspect of the b-forms, nonnative speakers tend to say:

> 2. **I am seeing the blackboard.*
> 3. **We are knowing our verb forms.*
> 4. **She is liking English.*

The problem is compounded by the use of b-forms for many of these verbs, though with a somewhat different meaning. Students may well be asked by their instructor:

> 5. *How are you liking the course?*

Although the use of the b-form in this question may mislead students, it indicates temporary aspect; the emphasis is on the present.

Until we teach our language to nonnative speakers, most of us do not sort out the special meanings that keep us from using verbs in the b-form. Our problem is compounded with apparently aberrant uses like:

> 6. *We are seeing them next week.*
> 7. *You are always seeing the minuses rather than the plusses.*

We ourselves may comprehend the intricate uses of these three patterns only after a considerable period of teaching English to nonnative speakers.

Another apparently simple situation is found in complementation, the patterning of object clauses. For these, English permits three constructions, as with *expect:*

> 8a. *We expect that they will object to the offer.*
>   b. *We expect them to object to the offer.*
>   c. *We expect their objecting to the offer.*

Many verbs permit object complementation: *hear, recognize, know, understand, dislike, hope,* and so on. Few, however, permit all the patterns, as one may readily determine by using these and other verbs in the three possible complementation patterns. The uses may be intricate, as for *know:*

> 9a. *I know that he likes steak.*
>   b. *I know him to like steak.*
>   c.**I know his liking steak.*
> But: d. *I have known that he likes steak. (?)*
>   e. *I have long known that he likes steak.*
>   f. *I have known him to like steak for breakfast.*

As these examples illustrate, complementation patterning is fully as complex as is the use of the verb forms above. Native speakers somehow master the patterns and use them without difficulty. But when we attempt to determine the rules for such uses, we find that each verb seems virtually to stand in a class by itself.

These examples illustrate that languages follow rules up to a certain point. Thereupon many entities pattern individually. As a result, both grammars and dictionaries are needed to inform us about language. Grammars present the general rules; dictionaries present the individual patterning. When we generalize about language, as in teaching it to nonnative speakers, we instruct them in the broad rules, for most such learners are adults, who have far less time to learn languages than do infants. But the broad rules apply only to a certain extent. When students apply them consistently, they illustrate the shortcomings of the rules, at the same time giving us perspectives on the functioning of our language and of languages generally.

Besides such insights into the structure of language, we also increase our understanding of the use of language when we deal with speakers of different cultures. All cultures seem to need some kind of small talk. When new acquaintances meet, they sound each other out before discussing serious issues. But even then, one has to be wary in choice of topics. Travelers to Ireland have long been advised not to speak about religion. A burning issue in Norway, on the other hand, is the choice of language. Norway has two: *Riksmål,* the language associated with the domination of the country by Oslo and the east and with the long rule of Denmark; *Landsmål,* the language of the west, associated with the free landholders and ancient heroism. Each language has ardent partisans, so that it is well to converse about other topics when meeting a Norwegian.

But even small talk differs. Speakers from Western cultures find discussion of the weather and of one's family uncontroversial. We are taken aback on the other hand if asked about finances, such as our salary or our total income. When in Turkey, we may be asked precisely such questions, where small talk does not exclude them.

Such situations indicate that not only lexical and grammatical patterns vary from language to language, with many effects among bilingual speakers. The total use of language may also differ from culture to culture. As we learn or teach languages, we become aware of our own deep-seated conventions and also of our parochialism, and of the intricate patterning and structure of language and its uses in society.

9.7 Computational Linguistics

In the previous section we have noted that second-language learners instruct us in the intricacies of our language because they tend to apply rules consistently. When we manipulate languages with computers, we find even greater consistency of application. For computers are brutally direct, performing only routines for which they have been programmed, and then with absolute consistency. Much has been learned about language by attempting to use computers in applications, as the course of work in machine translation illustrates.

When computers became available in the late 1940s, one of the suggested applications was automatic translation, generally known as machine translation (MT). Americans are notoriously poor in learning foreign languages. Why not adapt the new symbol-manipulating device for replacing the symbols of one language with those of another?

Initial efforts stayed at the word level. One word in the foreign language was matched with an equivalent in English, and some syntactic rules were included. There was also interest in translating from English into other languages. We illustrate the difficulties encountered with often-cited examples. If a computer is given the sentence, *Time flies like an arrow,* it arrives at various analyses. The word *time* may be treated as a verb, *flies* as a noun, and the entire sentence as a command; obviously, the result does not correspond to a common-sense translation. A computer would also accept *like* as a verb, *time* as an adjective, as in *time-clock,* and interpret the sentence as a description of the tastes of a certain species of fly. Again, the results are scarcely in keeping with those of a native speaker. In fact, few native speakers even thought of such possible interpretations before they were produced by computers.

In setting out to achieve only interpretations acceptable to human speakers, linguists concerned with machine translation introduced ever more detailed rules, designed for the different levels of language. The systems of rules achieved today by no means equal those of a native speaker, for as we have noted in the previous section, even our grammars and dictionaries fail to provide such rules. By now the syntactic rules for the technical segments of languages are pretty well understood. But the semantic sphere is difficult. When our dictionaries inform us of the meaning of a word like *horse,* they provide a drawing of the animal, a procedure we cannot use in computers. A beginning towards semantic analysis has been made by analyzing words not only for their syntactic uses but also for their underlying cases, or roles. The translation systems would then include syntactic rules, as for a verb like *open,* and semantic rules, indicating that it is accompanied by an OBJECTIVE, possibly also by an AGENT and an INSTRUMENT. When a battery of such rules is applied to a sentence, the correct interpretation and translation result.

Current computers are so fast and their programs so highly developed that sentences of technical texts are translated with less cost than by human translators. Soon the voluminous manuals necessary for operating machine tools and mechanical equipment will be routinely translated by computers before these are shipped overseas. The possibilities have great commercial and also social importance. Third World nations will be able to adopt the technologies of communication and other advances that industrialized nations take for granted.

As indicated here, the processes required in having computers use human language provide a clear perspective on its structure. The restriction of efforts to technical language illustrates the realm of pragmatics. The word *bit* has a very specific meaning in computer technology, one that can be precisely defined and reproduced in another language. In the general language, on the other hand, it has a broad array of uses depending on whether the context has to do with *horses, bread, tools,* or other topics. *Bit* may also be a verb. We determine its part of speech by analyzing the entire sentence in which it occurs. We determine its further meaning by analyzing the semantic patterning of words occurring with it, as the following examples may illustrate.

> 10a.　*This bit is too small for my horse.*
> b.　*This bit of butter is too little for my toast.*
> c.　*This bit won't fit in that brace.*

Correct interpretation of any word like *bit* results when we determine its position in the language semantically, syntactically, and phonologically. If we did so consciously when we use language, we would abandon its communicative function, for we would hardly have the time or energy to carry on a discussion. But when we adapt language for a totally blank instrument like a computer, we become highly aware of the various levels of language and of its differing uses as we communicate with differing audiences in differing contexts.

Accordingly, when we examine communication of various types, whether among animals, bilinguals, speakers with deficits, nonnative speakers, or computers, we achieve larger understanding of language. Through such approaches we not only analyze and describe it, but we come to explain it, whether only some portions or only some uses. When we examine particular details, like the plural *mice* of *mouse, feet* of *foot, men* of *man,* or the past tense forms *sang* of *sing, broke* of *break, stood* of *stand,* we can explain these only from their history. The historical study of language also illuminates much of the background of our culture, as we will note in the following chapter.

QUESTIONS FOR REVIEW

1. What is the Clever Hans Effect? What implications does it have for human use of language?
2. Discuss the results of attempts to teach the "wild boy" Victor to use human language. To teach Genie. What inferences may be drawn about language acquisition by infants?
3. What is meant by *lateralization?* What is the normal role of the right hemisphere? Of the left hemisphere?
4. How have effects of aphasia been related to language acquisition? To general properties of language?
5. What has been learned from speakers with "split brains" about the control of language by the brain? To what extent do these findings support given theories of language?

6. Discuss the experience of Borges with reference to bilingualism in children. When does a child become aware of a bilingual setting?

7. The Roman poet Ennius said he had three brains because he could speak three languages: Latin, Oscan, and Greek. To what extent is his statement true?

8. Why do native speakers of French use the plural form 'vacations' when they learn English? Why do German speakers use the singular 'scissor'? What do we infer from such usages about the mastery of second languages?

9. Discuss the problem of teaching verbs like *hear, believe, dislike* to nonnative speakers of English. Why do they have difficulties mastering these?

10. Cite problems faced by a teacher of English as a second language in presenting complementation.

11. Members of some cultures, for example, some Australian aboriginal cultures, do not speak to strangers. How would you make your way into such a culture?

12. The *Analects* of Confucius tells us that he did not converse while eating, nor talk when in bed. Comment on an attempt to maintain such views in modern American society.

13. List the kinds of analyses that must be carried out on language in order to have a computer manage it.

14. St. Augustine tells us in his *Confessions* of his development from an infant. Finding that he was not obeyed when he "sputtered out some words," he turned to crying. He says further that his elders did not teach him how to speak, but he acquired speech by means of his own mind. Eventually he learned the meanings of words by observing the "motion of the bodies" of his elders, as they spoke; he calls this motion the natural language of all nations. To what extent does his analysis of language acquisition correspond with our views?

15. State findings on bilingualism derived from tapping experiments. How do these findings correlate with our general views on lateralization?

16. What has been learned about the structure of language from attempts to translate it by computers? What kinds of analyses are necessary to achieve such translation?

PROBLEMS FOR REVIEW

1. In a letter to *Psychology Today* following an issue with articles on the study of animal communication, the anthropologist S. L. Washburn stressed an important difference between the communication of humans and apes as follows:

> The comparative study of human language has been hindered by the belief that words and grammar are the basic features of speech, and by

paying little attention to the brain. The essential difference between human and nonhuman is that human speech is based on a sound code—short, meaningless sounds (phonemes)—that may be combined into meaningful units (words, morphemes). As in other codes, a few basic elements make possible innumerable combinations. It is this characteristic that makes human language open, allowing the addition of new combinations as needed. The communication of nonhuman primates lacks sound codes. The basic element of all human language is not there, and it is most misleading to use the same term (*language*) for both limited gestural communications and the almost unlimited communication based on the phonetic code. Chimpanzees are taught the meaning of signs; they do not learn to use a code composed of meaningless elements that can be combined in thousands of ways.[5]

State the implications of Washburn's statement for the study of animal communication. Can that study in any way illuminate human language? Assuming that his conclusions are valid, what might be learned from such study about human communication?

2. Washburn goes on to suggest a biological basis for the difference between the communication of humans and apes:

Monkey sounds are controlled by primitive parts of the brain (the limbic system), and massive removal of cortex does not affect the sounds; the same is probably true in apes. Human language is controlled by cortex primarily on the dominant side of the brain. These are two fundamentally different biological systems: the monkey's is primitive, probably not basically different from that of other mammals; the human system is new, from an evolutionary point of view, and vastly more effective than any other mode of animal communication.[6]

Given their biological possibilities, could apes be taught to develop their communication system further?

3. In teaching the chimpanzee Sarah, Premack presented the possessive as follows: *Sarah apple,* not *Sarah's apple* nor *apple of Sarah*. In presenting adjectives, however, he taught the following sequences: *apple red, banana yellow*. If you were teaching animals to acquire a language, what would be your approach to the possessive and the adjective constructions? Would you use two different arrangements, as Premack did? What reasons could be given for presenting the same arrangement in both constructions?

4. By contrast with modern scientists who teach chimpanzees, Dr. Itard set out to teach Victor to speak rather than to use sign language. Assuming that Victor was deaf, how do you regard this approach? Victor learned to communicate by means of cut-out letters; what then is the likelihood that he might have

---

[5] *Psychology Today,* February 1980, p. 5.
[6] *Ibid.*

learned to communicate in French using signs? Support your answer by relating both letters and signs to the elements of speech.

5. In her speech Genie places possessives before nouns; *Vicki car* means *Vicki's car*. In sentences she uses SVO word order. But she does not use pronouns like *which, what*. Accordingly she does not use the relative clauses characteristic of English, though she understands sentences containing them. In view of her possessive constructions, what pattern of relative clauses might one attempt to teach her?

6. In his monograph *Child Language, Aphasia and General Sound Laws*, Jakobson cites sounds that aphasics lose or contrasts that they may fail to make. One is the contrast between [l] and [r]. Another is the interdental fricative, as in *thin, this,* in contrast with [s] and [z]. Some may also substitute [p] for [f] and [t] for [s]; but the reverse does not happen. How can one account for these losses? What relation do they have to child language acquisition?

7. M. S. Gazzaniga and Steven A. Hillyard tested the ability of brain-bisected speakers to interpret sentences with the right hemisphere.[7] After a picture of a boy kissing a girl was flashed to the left eye, two such speakers were asked which of the following was correct: (1) The boy kisses the girl, or (2) the girl kisses the boy. They could not provide an answer. Yet if a picture of a boy were flashed to the left eye, they would be able to select a card with boy on it or to identify the word *boy* among a series of possibilities. What inferences might be made about the capabilities of the right hemisphere to control segments of language?

8a. Teachers of foreign languages encounter many problems that result from the way we perceive language. For example, in teaching French or German to native speakers of English, teachers may pronounce a word with a front rounded vowel, as in French *lune* [lyn] 'moon,' ask students to imitate it, and receive in response a word resembling *lean*. How do you account for this phenomenon? What would you do to teach the proper pronunciation of front rounded vowels?

 b. Another problem faced by language teachers is the production of incorrect grammatical expressions such as **I am knowing it*. For example, native speakers of German (and many other languages) are taught that English has a "progressive present," *I am going,* an emphatic present, *I do go,* as well as a simple present, *I go,* corresponding to the one simple present form in their own language. Account for the production of incorrect sentences, like **I am understanding that,* by such language learners. How would you attempt to circumvent the production of such sentences?

9. If you were preparing a system for translation from English to other languages, what devices would you use to distinguish between the homonyms in the following sentences?

---

[7] M. S. Gazzaniga and Steven A. Hillyard, "Language and Speech Capacity of the Right Hemisphere," *Neuropsychologia* 9 (1971), pp. 273–280.

    1a. They saw the old deer.

      b. They left their saw in camp.

      c. The problem called to mind an old saw.

    2a. It isn't often he wears a white shirt.

      b. It isn't often he tells a white lie.

    3a. His driving sent shivers up and down her spine.

      b. His driving lost him the golf tournament.

10. Following a procedure something like Lewis Carroll's in Jabberwocky, two English scholars, Margaret Masterman and Robin McKinnon Wood, produced a "do-it-yourself kit for writing computerized Japanese haiku."[8] The following is one result.

> All green in the leaves
> I smell dank pools in the trees
> Crash the moon has fled

Comment on the result, indicating whether in your view a poet would produce such a poem. If you think not, what would the poet avoid?

FURTHER READING

Albert, M. L., and L. K. Obler. *The Bilingual Brain*. New York: Academic Press, 1978.

Curtiss, Susan. *Genie. A Psycholinguistic Study of a Modern-Day "Wild Child."* New York: Academic Press, 1977.

Premack, Ann J. *Why Chimps Can Read*. New York: Harper & Row, 1976.

Rumbaugh, D. M. *Language Learning by a Chimpanzee: The Lana Project*. New York: Academic Press, 1977.

Shattuck, Roger. *The Story of the Wild Boy of Aveyron*. New York: Farrar, Straus & Giroux, 1980.

Terrace, H. S. *Nim*. New York: Knopf, 1979.

von Frisch, Karl. *The Dancing Bees*. London: Methuen, 1954.

[8] *TLS*, June 18, 1970, pp. 667–668.

CHAPTER TEN

Language History

10.1 Language Change

In treating the sounds and forms found in words, sentences, and discourse, we produce descriptions or grammars without regard for earlier stages. Many treatments of language are designed in this way; handbooks of English grammar and dictionaries concentrate on contemporary forms and their uses. Such treatments, however, neglect characteristics of language that are of considerable interest, as we may illustrate by examining the word *educate*. It is made up of two Latin elements, *e* meaning 'out' and *duc* meaning 'lead,' as in *duke*, originally 'one who leads.' We may use and describe 'educate,' of course, without knowing its history. But a part of our cultural background is disclosed through the information that *educate* derives from the Greek and Roman practice of having *educators* conduct children from their homes to their teachers. The parallel Greek *pedagogue* literally means 'one who leads a child.' This information by no means completes the story of the interpretation of *educate, educator* in our society.

Some take these words as evidence for their own philosophy of education. By this view a child possesses admirable human qualities; education consists in 'drawing out' those capabilities. This interpretation of the term is historically wrong. Yet many words are wrongly interpreted by their users, as we have seen earlier in dealing with the word *inflammable*. Historical study is concerned with

181

language changes; even historically erroneous interpretations may be the ones that persist.

The word *religion* provides an illustration. It could be derived from either of two Latin verbal roots: that in *legere* 'gather, hold' or that in *ligāre* 'tie, bind.' With the prefix *re-* 'back, again,' the first means 'hold back, restrain'; the second means 'bind, tie to.' The early Christians related the word to the second, thinking that it meant a bond of piety; God through religion binds humans to himself. The earlier Romans, on the other hand, interpreted religion as producing scruples in believers, so that religious persons are those who are scrupulous about their beliefs. By this view religion holds one back from impious actions. Study of the word *religion* in its changing meanings, like historical study of language, tells us much about the development of ideas central in our culture.

Such study also reveals much about our language. We can perfectly well speak of *one* or a *unit,* of *two* or a *duality,* of *three* or a *trio,* and so on, without knowing that these sets came from a single earlier form. The first of each set, *one, two, three,* came directly through the various stages of English from its parent language, Proto-Germanic, and ultimately from Proto-Indo-European. The second, *unit, duality, trio,* has the same ultimate origin, but through Proto-Italic and then Latin. The study of related words of ultimately the same origin, known as **doublets,** illustrates changes that have taken place in form and meaning, for example: *brother/ friar, corn/grain, garden/horti-(culture), steer/Taurus.*

Language in this way provides a record of many past events. We may pursue these by observing changes that have taken place in the forms, patterns, and stock of words and other elements and also by observing the maintenance of elements from the past.

Moreover, the study of language change deepens our understanding of human-kind in general, and its bent for innovation. There is something of a paradox in having a communication system that for its greatest usefulness should be stable and unmodified but, because of the human urge for novelty, for innovation, for new patterns, is always undergoing change. This is carried out in such a way that there is no disruption of communication. The continuity of understanding in the midst of change results from the multilayered structure of language.

Change does not affect all layers at once. The meaning of a word, or its syntactic use, or one or more of its sounds may change. When, for example, the word *jet* came to mean 'airplane,' only the meaning changed, not its use as a noun nor its sounds. The vowel [ɛ] changed before [n] in some dialects of English, as in *pen, pin;* and the verb *set* is widely used as an intransitive, as in *set down.* Each of such modifications is usually quite distinct, so that speakers are not confronted with a situation in which a word like *bet* changes its vowel, its use in sentences, and its meaning simultaneously. Humans indeed introduce change, but not to the point of blocking communication with their social group.

In this chapter we examine some of the major changes in English and its linguistic tradition. We also observe how these permit us to relate modern English first with its older forms, known as Middle English and Old English. To understand its early pattern we compare Old English with other Germanic languages and with other members of the Indo-European family. Through such observations we note the procedures used in the historical study of language and some of its findings. These procedures, as well as the relationships among the Indo-European languages, became clear through a series of insights during the past two centuries.

10.2 Germanic, a Branch of the Indo-European Family

Two centuries ago the relationships between English and Latin, Greek, and other languages were unknown. Then a perceptive man of letters, Sir William Jones (1746–1794), disclosed their relationship. As a British government official in India he learned Sanskrit because it was the language of Indian law. His study opened up a great store of information about ancient India and its culture, which he presented in annual lectures. His lecture of 1786 dealt with the language itself, providing the key that led to understanding of the relationships among the languages now called Indo-European.

In his lecture Jones pointed out a strong "affinity" between Sanskrit, Greek, Latin, Old Persian, Gothic, and Celtic. When the lecture became known in Europe it attracted great attention, leading scholars to the study of Sanskrit and ancient Indian culture. As a result of this study the original language was reconstructed; it is now referred to as Proto-Indo-European (PIE). (The prefix Proto- indicates that a language is not attested. The original language from which English, German, Dutch, Swedish, and others have developed is also unattested; it is referred to as Proto-Germanic [PGmc].)

One of those making use of the new data was Jacob Grimm (1785–1863), the collector of the well-known fairy tales. In Grimm's view, activities of the present could best be explained by studying those of the past, when they were presumably simpler and accordingly easier to understand. Since he also held that activities of the folk maintained many of those simpler practices, he collected fairy tales as reflections of the older literature. He also dealt with law and with the ancient languages.

In 1822 he demonstrated without doubt the relationship between Germanic and the other Indo-European (IE) languages. His contribution consisted in pointing out regular correspondences between the consonants of Germanic and those of the other languages. In Germanic these consonants had undergone a series of changes; the description of the changes is now called Grimm's law. Widely enough known to be listed in desk dictionaries, Grimm's law states the changes between Proto-Indo-European (PIE) and Proto-Germanic (PGmc), indicating at the same time the relationships between the obstruents of the Indo-European languages.

The changes are as follows:

$$
\begin{array}{llllllll}
\text{PIE} & \text{p} & \text{t} & \text{k} & \rangle \ \text{PGmc} & \text{f} & \theta & \text{x} \\
\text{PIE} & \text{bh} & \text{dh} & \text{gh} & \rangle \ \text{PGmc} & \text{b} & \text{d} & \text{g} \\
\text{PIE} & \text{b} & \text{d} & \text{g} & \rangle \ \text{PGmc} & \text{p} & \text{t} & \text{k}
\end{array}
$$

These changes clearly took place in stages over a long period of time. The PGmc *p t k*, which resulted from PIE *b d g,* did not undergo the changes of earlier PIE *p t k,* as they might have if these had not changed earlier to PGmc *f θ x.*

These and further changes separated Germanic from the other Indo-European (IE) dialects, such as Latin, Greek, Sanskrit, and Lithuanian. Words from these languages, rather than the reconstructed PIE forms, are generally used as examples to illustrate the Germanic consonant changes.

The following examples illustrate the change of PIE *p t k* to PGmc *f θ x,* which is the first of the changes:

Gk. pater	Lat. pater	NE father
Gk. treis	Lat. tres	NE three
Gk. he-katon	Lat. centum	NE hundred (h ⟨ x)

The following examples illustrate the change of PIE *bh dh gh* to PGmc *b d g,* which in their early period were voiced fricatives:

Gk. phrater	Lat. frater	NE brother
Gk. (ana-)thema	Skt. dhaman-	NE deed
Gk. khortos	Lat. hortus	NE garden

The following examples illustrate the change of PIE *b d g* to PGmc *p t k:*

Lith. bala 'swamp'	Lat. de-bilis 'weak'	NE pool
Gk. deka	Lat. decem	NE ten
Gk. genos	Lat. genus	NE kin

Many other changes took place in the sounds, forms, and lexicon of Germanic in its millennia of development from the parent language. These led to a language that was no longer intelligible to speakers of neighboring IE languages, such as Celtic, Latin, Greek, and Baltic.

On the other hand, Germanic also maintained characteristics that identify it as IE. Among these characteristics is the internal alternation of vowels, called ablaut, which still distinguishes tense forms in our irregular or strong verbs, as in the following:

bite	bit	bitten
choose	chose	chosen
sing	sang	sung
steal	stole	stolen
give	gave	given

Moreover, the basic stock of words has been kept. Among these are kinship terms: *father, mother, brother, sister,* and so on; numerals; many animal names: *cow, swine, goat, hound.* A particular interrelationship, like that between NE *fee,*

German *Vieh* 'cattle,' Latin *pecus* 'herd,' *pecunia* 'money,' and further examples in the other languages provides evidence for a common origin of these languages. It also points to the pastoral culture of the parent group, where cattle were a medium of exchange.

English and the other Germanic languages, then, still manifest IE characteristics while having undergone considerable change. Subsequent changes brought about distinct Germanic languages, especially as these were established in separate areas where communication between the various groups of Germanic speakers was disrupted.

10.3 English and the Other Germanic Languages

In the fifth century of our era, Germanic tribes of Angles, Saxons, and Jutes settled in Britain. Their earlier home had been the northwestern coast of Germany, extending into Denmark. After they left the other groups of Germanic speakers, their languages underwent separate developments and gradually became distinct. Yet from common characteristics we can determine the special relationships of Old English (or as it is often labeled, Anglo-Saxon) to the other Germanic languages.

Among these, Old English is closest to Old Frisian, another language of the northern coastland of the Continent. With Old Franconian, the ancestor of Dutch, Old Saxon—later known as Low German—and Old High German, it makes up the southern group. These five languages are generally referred to as West Germanic. The North Germanic languages are Danish, Swedish, Norwegian, Faroese, and Icelandic; the oldest form of the last three is often referred to as Old Norse. No survivors of the East Germanic languages are spoken today, but of them, Gothic provides us with the first extensive set of Germanic texts, a translation of the Bible from the fourth century.

The structure of PGmc is still evident in one of the earliest runic inscriptions. This is on one of the golden horns found at Gallehus in northern Denmark; it dates from about A.D. 375. The inscription reads:

> *Ek HlewagastiR HoltijaR*   *horna tawido*
> I   HlewagastiR of Holt   the horn   (did) = made

As with many other such inscriptions, the maker indicates his name to guarantee the object greater authority.

Characteristic of the older language are the full endings. The second element of the maker's name *-gastiR* is related to Latin *hostis,* which also shows the syllabic structure of PIE. In Germanic the element means 'guest'; but in Latin the original meaning 'stranger' came to be 'enemy.' By the time of Old English, the word had lost its final, weakly stressed syllable and was pronounced much as it is today. Similarly, *horna* had been reduced to one syllable in Old English. The loss of endings resulted from a strong stress accent, which was introduced in late PGmc.

As a consequence, final syllables were lost, leading to the monosyllabic structure of many words today in English and also in other Germanic languages, such as Norwegian.

Some of the greatest innovations in English resulted from contacts with speakers of other languages. There were three such groups. The first were the Celts; they made up the principal population of England when the Germanic peoples took over. Many of them gave up their language. Others maintained themselves in the west, where Cornish was spoken into the eighteenth century and Welsh is still spoken today. Few words were adopted from Celtic, only words for items the Germanic speakers met in England, such as *bannock, brock*. Celtic may be the source of the participial form in *-ing*, which has provided English with a set of "progressive" forms in contrast with the other Germanic languages.

The second group of neighboring speakers provided many more loan words, and these at an everyday level. From about A.D. 790 many Scandinavians invaded England; some of them settled there, especially in the north. Only through the vigor of King Alfred (d. 901) were they kept from taking over the entire country. The two peoples lived side by side, and the English speakers adopted many simple words; *anger, fellow, gate, heaven, husband, root, window,* and those beginning with *sk: skin, skill, sky*. In English itself *sk* had changed to *sh*, so that we have doublets like *skirt/shirt*. One of the most striking pairs were the native *ey*, cf. German *Ei*, and the Scandinavian *egg*. The Scandinavian form did not win out until Shakespeare's day; Caxton, England's first printer, notes the two competing words. The long coexistence of English and Scandinavian speech may have contributed to the massive loss of inflections in English, for the language situation must have been similar to that existing when pidgins arise.

The third influence came from French and Latin. When William the Conqueror took over England in 1066, his people spoke French. Originally Scandinavian, they had lived for several generations in Normandy, where they gave up their native language. For centuries Norman French remained the language of the governing group and the upper classes, while English was that of the common people. The situation is still reflected in terms for foods; when these were put on the table they had French names rather than the native English. Compare: *cow/ beef; calf/veal; deer/venison; pig/pork; sheep/mutton*. Many words for government, administration, military, and legal matters were borrowed from French: *country, crown, government, nation, people, state; army, navy, siege; court, crime, judge, jury;* and so on. English became the official language only in 1362, but courts of justice maintained French as the legal language until 1731. As a result of the strong cultural influence, the vocabulary of English is mixed. Only words for everyday matters remain from the Germanic stock, as well as the basic grammatical structure of the language. Because of the influence of the Church, words for religious and educational matters were borrowed from Latin and Greek: *pope, bishop, priest, congregation,* and many others from Latin; *athlete, biology, church, oxygen,* and many others from Greek.

The readiness to adopt foreign words set the pattern for English as an international language. Today its vocabulary includes words from many languages. The extent of its importations may be determined from lists like those in *An Etymological Dictionary of the English Language*.[1]

10.4 From Middle English to Modern English

The Old English period is generally dated from the time of earliest English texts in the late seventh century to about 1050, the Middle English period from 1050 to about 1450. During the fifteenth century the long vowels underwent a massive change, known as the great vowel shift. In this shift, vowels were raised; the two high vowels [ī, ū] became diphthongs, as Figure 10.1 illustrates.

The following list of words gives examples of the long vowels in Middle English (ME) and their counterparts today (New English, NE):

Figure 10.1
The Great Vowel Shift

ME		NE		ME		NE	
wif	[wi:f]	wife	[wayf]	hous	[hu:s]	house	[haws]
seen	[se:n]	seen	[siyn]	spon	[spo:n]	spoon	[spuwn]
sea	[sɛ:]	sea	[siy]	ham	[hɔ:m]	home	[hom]
name	[na:m]	name	[nem]				

In this way the NE sound system is considerably different from the Middle English system. Earlier writers, such as Chaucer (1400), are generally read today in modern English, except by specialists. While the vowel sounds changed, our spelling system reflects the pronunciation of Middle English. When Caxton introduced printing into England in 1476, he adopted the spelling conventions of Middle English. Accordingly our spelling system maintains the values found in Latin and the Continental languages; *see* is spelled with *e*, like German *See*, the vowel of which is pronounced as in *say; name* is spelled like the German *Name*, which rhymes with *comma*. In English, then, the vowel symbols follow an independent convention, leading to difficulties for nonnative speakers who learn to read English and also for English speakers learning foreign languages, which generally observe the Continental values for the vowel symbols.

Apart from the great vowel shift, modern English included no notable change. The language continued to develop towards greater regularity in accordance with SVO patterning. In this development auxiliaries play a large role, especially the dummy verb *do*. Through its use English can maintain SVO order in questions, as in *They find English difficult; Do they find English difficult?* Negatives also are simple, as in *They don't find English difficult; Don't they find English difficult?* Compare the pattern in the King James translation of 1616: Genesis 38.20, *but he found her not*. Moreover, inflections become more regular. Many verbs, such as *bark, climb, laugh* are now regular. Moreover, many irregular plurals were lost in

[1] Walter W. Skeat, *An Etymological Dictionary of the English Language* (Oxford: Clarendon, 1961), pp. 763–776.

nouns; the King James Bible still has *kine* as the plural of *cow*. Other nouns that
have lost the old forms are *book, friend, goat, nut*. And paradigms in general have
been regularized. The genitive of *it* was formerly *his,* as in the King James Version
of Matthew 5.13: *but if the salt have lost his savour, wherewith will it be salted?*
The irregular forms that remain provide a record of earlier characteristics of the
language, including some of the parent language, PIE.

10.5 Methods Used in Historical Linguistics

Besides accounting for change, historical study seeks to establish and verify
relationships between languages. It does this by determining earlier forms. Thus
it is clear that words like NE *guest* and New High German (NHG) *Gast* have
developed from the same earlier form in Proto-Germanic. We have noted a form
comparable to the Proto-Germanic form in the Gallehus inscription: *-gastiR.* Often,
however, such earlier forms are not attested. They are then reconstructed by a
procedure known as the **comparative method.**

By the comparative method two related forms, or cognates, are compared, and
the probable earlier form is proposed. Comparing Greek *genos* and Latin *genus,*
one would have little difficulty reconstructing Proto-Indo-European **genos*. (The
asterisk indicates a form inferred from historical examples but not actually attested.)
The method is often said to be one of triangulation, in which the forms compared
are placed on the base of a triangle and the reconstructed form at its apex:

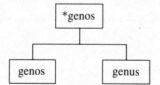

These forms are clearly easy to relate, and the earlier form is easy to reconstruct.
When the relationships are not so transparent, one may draw on one's general
knowledge of phonological possibilities and on the phonological structure of the
languages concerned. For details, a handbook on historical linguistics can be
consulted.

From the forms for 'brother' it would be difficult to decide which initial
consonant to reconstruct for PIE. Greek has a voiceless aspirate, Latin a voiceless
fricative, and Germanic a voiced stop, presumably from an earlier voiced fricative.
Because the Sanskrit is *bhrātar,* and because it is the earliest attested IE language
other than Hittite, the initial consonant is generally reconstructed as *bh.*

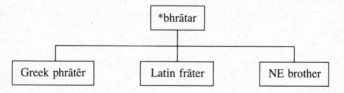

This reconstruction was widely accepted when the PIE obstruent system was assumed to consist of contrasting voiceless and voiced, aspirated and unaspirated stops, for example:

$$
\begin{array}{ll}
\text{p} & \text{b} \\
\text{ph} & \text{bh}
\end{array}
$$

But recent scholarship has led to the conclusion that PIE had no voiceless aspirates. And accordingly, a system with voiced aspirates did not seem realistic. Therefore, assumptions from a general study of phonological systems have led to revisions of the system.

This example may illustrate some of the problems involved in the application of the comparative method. The method is also impossible to use when a language is isolated or when one is dealing with a protolanguage with no known related languages. In such instances a second procedure, known as the method of **internal reconstruction,** is applied.

By internal reconstruction similar morphological items that vary phonologically are examined. For example, roots often have a specific structure in languages. In Proto-Indo-European, most roots have the structure: Consonant:Vowel:Consonant (CVC), as in NE *sit* from the PIE root *sed-, kin* from the PIE root *gen-,* and so on. There are, however, some very common roots with the structure VC, for example, *ag-* 'lead' in Latin and Greek; compare NE *agent.* Assuming that such roots also once had the structure CVC, Ferdinand de Saussure posited for them and other PIE forms some consonants that later were lost. On the basis of internal reconstruction, then, he posited instead of **ag-* a root **heg-.* Advanced in 1879, this hypothesis, for which no further proof existed, was verified when Hittite was discovered around 1906 and found to include the consonants that had been lost.

Internal reconstruction can in this way amplify the conclusions based on the comparative method. Skillful use of the two methods has enabled historical linguists to determine with a high degree of accuracy the relationships of the IE languages and also those of other language families mentioned in the following section.

10.6 Major Language Families

As noted above, English and many other languages belong to a family that since the second millennium before our era extended from India to Europe. Because of this distribution the family is known as **Indo-European (IE).** It consists of nine major branches with modern representatives. Two important early branches, Anatolian and Tocharian, have no representatives today.

1. Indo-Iranian, of which the earliest attested form is Sanskrit. Modern representatives are Hindi, Bengali, and many languages of India, as well as Farsi and many Iranian languages. (See Figure 10.2.)
2. Armenian, spoken by a relatively small number of people.

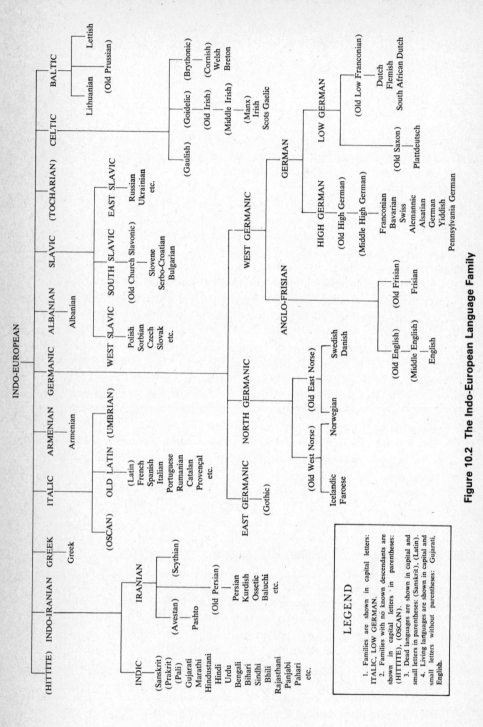

Figure 10.2 The Indo-European Language Family

3. Albanian, also spoken by a small number of people.
4. Slavic, with such modern representatives as Russian, Polish, Czech, Serbo-Croatian, and Bulgarian.
5. Baltic, consisting of Lithuanian and Lettish.
6. Greek, once used throughout the eastern areas around the Mediterranean.
7. Italic, with Latin as an ancient representative and many modern descendants: Italian, French, Spanish, Portuguese, Catalan, Sardinian, Rumanian, and Rhaeto-Romance.
8. Celtic, with Welsh, Breton, Irish, and Scots Gaelic as modern representatives.

In addition to Germanic, the ninth major group, several extinct languages may be noted: Tocharian, and the Anatolian languages, especially Hittite.

These various branches had their origin with a group of people living north of the Caspian and Black Seas in the fifth to third millennia. These people are now identified with the kurgan culture, a term introduced by the archeologist Marija Gimbutas. From their early location the group spread to the east, first to Iran and then India, as well as to the west, where they eventually took over most of Europe. Since they had no writing system, the history of their spread must be determined from archeological records, and inferences must be based on the subsequent distribution of the Indo-European languages.

The basis of their success in taking over such a large area is unclear. But the horse, which they used for their raids into new territory, was doubtless one important factor; another was the chariot. Still another was the use of metals rather than stone for weapons and tools. Moreover, their social system permitted strong administrative coordination, especially in times of emergencies. The account of the Greeks joining forces under Agamemnon in the *Iliad* provides an example. Whatever the details leading to their successes, speakers of the Indo-European languages spread the family over a huge area. The family became one of the most widespread of language families, and much of the theoretical work in historical linguistics is based on investigation of the IE languages.

One of the other major families is the **Afro-Asiatic.** Extending through much of North Africa and adjacent areas of Asia, the family is often referred to as Hamito-Semitic. Some of the earliest attested languages belong to this family, such as Egyptian, attested from the fourth millennium before our era, and Akkadian. Prominent modern representatives are Arabic, Hebrew, Amharic, and Hausa. The account in Genesis of the spread of Hebrew into Palestine is instructive in reconstructing how languages were diffused thousands of years ago.

In central Africa the dominant family is the **Niger-Congo,** with Fulani, Igbo, Swahili, and Yoruba as widely spoken members.

In the southern part of India the principal languages, such as Kannada, Malayalam, Tamil, and Telugu, belong to the **Dravidian** family. Dravidian may have been spoken in north India when the Indo-Europeans invaded between 2000 and 1200 B.C. If so, it was gradually displaced to the south.

In eastern Asia the largest language family is the **Sino-Tibetan.** Its principal members are the Chinese or Han languages, of which there are seven distinct members. Putonghua, also referred to as Mandarin, is now being generalized through the People's Republic of China. This language, based on the pronunciation of the Peking area and the syntax and vocabulary of recent scientific and technical writings, is the native language of more speakers than any other language, including English. Other prominent languages of this group are Cantonese, Hakka, Wu, and Tibetan.

Among other large language families are the **Altaic,** which comprises the Turkic, Mongol, and Manchu-Tungus groups. The **Finno-Ugric** languages include Hungarian and Finnish, as well as languages in the northern areas of Asia.

The most widespread language family in the world, at least until the great expansion of Indo-European speakers, was the **Malayo-Polynesian,** spoken from Hawaii to Madagascar. A member of this group, Malayan, has been adopted as the national language of Indonesia; it is often referred to as Indonesian. Another member, Tagalog, is an official language of the Philippines.

The numerous indigenous languages of the Americas, as well as those of Africa, Australia, and New Guinea, have been classified into families—or stocks, which are larger groups, determined by less specific criteria than are families. Further, there are languages whose relationships are difficult to determine, such as Japanese, Korean, and Basque. Some of these, especially ancient languages like Sumerian, will probably remain isolated unless new sources of data are acquired or until hitherto unread texts will be accessible.

10.7 Writing

Our primary problem in pursuing the history of languages results from the small number and restricted types of texts, as well as the recent introduction of writing for many languages. Only three well-developed systems have been in use: the Egyptian, from which our own system developed; the Akkadian; and the Chinese. The Chinese dates from the second millennium before our era; the two others from the late fourth.

Until recently, no precursors of these were known. Then in a remarkable insight, Denise Schmandt-Besserat identified clay tokens, which had long been found in excavations throughout the Middle East, as figures from which writing developed. The tokens were in the shape of disks, cylinders, rectangles, cones, and so on. Earlier scholars had seen no purpose in them, some classifying them as toys. There now is no doubt that they were used to keep accounts from as early as the ninth millennium and eventually led to symbols such as those which developed into our writing system.

The tokens represented objects and numerals. Disks with different lines inscribed on them indicated sheep, wool, and cloth. Cylinders indicated wood; rectangles, granaries, and so on. In addition to such concrete values, cones indicated numbers of items. The tokens were used to record quantities of animals, cloth, and other possessions.

When sent to market, such possessions were accompanied by clay envelopes containing appropriate tokens. The envelopes were cumbersome, since the items could not be determined until the envelopes were broken. Thereupon, representations of the tokens were made on the clay envelopes, no doubt to simplify checking the items and their quantities. From this step, symbols on clay replaced the earlier tokens entirely. These symbols, initially representations of objects, are precursors of the cuneiform, and of the hieroglyphic system, which is presumably based on it.

Some of the earliest symbols are still transparent in our alphabet, if we examine its shapes and their values (see Figure 10.3). We can readily trace these back through the symbols of the Greeks, the Phoenicians, and the Egyptians. Thus the second letter of the alphabet originally represented the ground plan of a house, without the middle cross line now found in *B*. Its value is that of the first sound of the word for 'house,' in Hebrew *beth;* when the Greeks adopted the alphabet, they changed the word to *beta,* an element surviving as the second syllable of *alphabet*. The first symbol, *A,* represented an ox-head; the third, *C,* a corner of a wall; and so on.

Initially all the symbols represented objects; thereupon, they were simplified and stylized. Selected figures came to be used to represent syllables. Finally, when the Greeks adopted these from the Phoenicians, the symbols came to stand for single consonants and vowels. The Greek alphabet was adopted by the Romans through the Etruscans. From Rome it was introduced to the peoples of Europe and ultimately adopted for most languages of the world.

Writing systems fall into three types: word systems, syllabic systems, and alphabet systems. The word system is represented by Egyptian hieroglyphs, early Akkadian cuneiform symbols, and Chinese. Such symbols are known as logographs. Logographic systems require a large number of symbols, ideally one for each word. The Egyptian and Akkadian systems remained relatively small, but the longer-lasting Chinese system includes over 30,000 characters. Obviously such a system is highly cumbersome. Only small numbers of a society can master it, such as the scribes of ancient Egypt. To provide a speedier means of mastery and also of production, the Egyptians selected twenty-four symbols to stand for syllables. In Egypt, this set of syllabic symbols was used side by side with the hieroglyphs.

Syllabic systems represent a stage towards ease of use. With around eighty symbols, all the words in a language can be written. Such systems have developed from each of the major writing systems. The Phoenicians and other Semitic peoples adopted the Egyptian syllabic system; this is the basis of many other systems, such as the Arabic of today. The ancient Persians adapted the cuneiform to a syllabic system. The Japanese selected Chinese characters for a syllabic system of their own, *Kana;* used in conjunction with Chinese characters for writing Japanese, this exists in two forms, Hiragana and Katakana.

An alphabetic system was devised only by the Greeks. They took over the Semitic syllabic signs, giving each the value of the first sound. Thus the second symbol came to stand for [b], the fourth for [d], and so on. Since the Greeks had no consonant like the first of Phoenician, a glottal stop, they took it to stand for the vowel sound [a]; in this way symbols for vowels were introduced. An alphabetic

Egyptian ca. 2000 B.C.	Meaning	Sinitic ca. 1700 B.C.	West Semitic ca. 1200 B.C.	Ionic Greek ca. 500 B.C.	Early Roman
	Head of ox				
	House				
	Corner of wall				
	Door				
	Man with both arms raised				
	Lotus (possibly man was model here too)				
	Grain of sand				
	Hand				
	Animal of Seth recumbent				
	Open hand				
	Sedge				

Egyptian ca. 2000 B.C.	Meaning	Sinitic ca. 1700 B.C.	West Semitic ca. 1200 B.C.	Ionic Greek ca. 500 B.C.	Early Roman
	Sandy tract, horizon (perhaps not origin of L)				
	Ripples (suggested also for N and even L)				
	Cobra				
	Ornament (often vertical) or weapon				
	Cobra				
	Eye				
	Mouth				
	Animal's belly with teats and tail				
	Head				
	Branch				
	Sandy hills				
	Unidentified cross or "ankh" the sandal strap				

Figure 10.3   Development of the Alphabet

system is clearly the easiest type to learn and use. Any writing system introduced today is alphabetic.

The Roman system was adapted for Old English in the seventh century A.D. Since then it has been essentially maintained without change. We now distinguish between *i* and *j*, and between *u* and *v*, symbols used interchangeably before the introduction of printing. We also use a double form of the last, *w*. But the order of letters, their values, and their use are basically those of Old English and Roman times. There are also external innovations, such as the consistent use of small letters—**minuscles**—and of capitals—**majuscles.** As many older inscriptions and manuscripts illustrate, Latin used only capitals. This situation as developed for English applies throughout western Europe and its sphere of influence in the world.

In eastern Europe, alphabetic symbols were based on Greek letters. While parallel to the Latin, the slightly more ornate forms of these gave rise to Cyrillic, the system used for Russian. The Cyrillic alphabet has been extended to the languages of the Soviet Union. It was also used for languages of the People's Republic of China during its early years; then the People's Republic adopted the Roman alphabet for these. Such symbols are accordingly used for *pinyin*, the official alphabet of Putonghua.

As the Chinese decision illustrates, writing is now considered essential for all citizens of a country. A logographic system interferes with literacy, reducing the contributions of individuals and their participation in society. Writing also assures the maintenance of large numbers of texts, including evidence of a society and its culture wherever it is in use. Its use is then highly important for linguistics and other social sciences, whether focused on the present or the past.

10.8 Names

In a simple society, individuals need only one name. It may be descriptive: *Plato* is someone with a 'broad' forehead or shoulders; *Rufus,* like *Red,* someone with a reddish complexion. It may also imply a special station: *Alexander* 'ruler of men,' *Menelaus* 'guider of the people.' When desired the individual may be further identified by the name of a parent, as is still true in Iceland; this situation has given rise to many family names, such as *Johnson, MacAdam.* In Iceland only one name is used, but telephone directories now routinely provide a patronymic, ending in 'son' or 'daughter.' Elsewhere, only members of royal families still enjoy the privilege of using their given names alone; Queen Elizabeth may be identified as belonging to the House of Windsor, but she has no surname, unlike other widely known personalities, such as Elizabeth Taylor.

The use of single names alone represented the situation throughout Europe until increasingly complex social arrangements, especially taxation, led to more precise identification. At that time, from the later Middle Ages, surnames or family names were introduced. They are of five types: (1) patronymics, such as *Philippson, Thompson;* compare also the Hebrew *Ben-Gurion* 'son of Gurion,' the Irish *MacArthur* 'son of Arthur'; (2) names given for place of origin, for example,

Lincoln, Washington; in German, city names used adjectivally have an *-er* suffix, leading to names like *Hamburger, Kissinger;* (3) names given for a characteristic local site like *Hill, Ford, Roosevelt* 'field of roses'; the family lived near such a site; (4) names given from an occupation, *Miller, Smith, Taylor;* (5) names adopted from the list of given names, *Herbert, Howard, Paul.*

Place-names, which in general have similar origins, may be adopted from earlier peoples by later settlers, in this way preserving information about earlier periods without writing. Many Indian names were taken over in this way as America was settled by Europeans. *Manitowoc* preserves a name for the god *Manitou, Sioux City* the name of a tribe. Like *Texas,* which is a Spanish spelling for the *Tejas* tribe, the original name may be distorted; the [ks] pronunciation was introduced by English speakers who did not know the value of *x* as [h]; the pronunciation [mɛksɪko] has a similar origin.

But despite such distortions, information on a succession of inhabitants can often be obtained from study of place-names. Some American place-names indicate areas controlled by the French in the early period, such as *Prairie du Chien* 'field of the dog,' and *Fond du lac* 'end of the lake.' Others commemorate Spanish areas: *Los Angeles, Santa Fe.* Other place-names were given after the founding cities: *Boston, New York.* Some places were named for local characteristics: *Coon Valley, Hot Springs.* Others celebrate notable figures: *Lincoln, Washington, Jefferson City.* All such names preserve historical evidence.

But names may also be misleading because they were wrongly applied or interpreted. Excavations at the beginning of this century disclosed an important people, who were named Hittites after a biblical group; this people called themselves Nesites, yet the erroneous designation has been maintained. Julius Caesar records the name *Germani* for one of the peoples of northern Europe. The words *German* and *Germanic* derive from this, though Caesar's people may have been Celtic. In any event, the source of *Germani* is unknown; attempts to relate it to *ger* 'spear' as in *garfish* are misguided. Names then may inform us of earlier periods, but they must be carefully studied and interpreted.

10.9 Linguistic Paleontology

The entire vocabulary may be examined to provide information on speakers of a language, for the presence of a word indicates that the object is known. Thus the words *automobile, buffalo, tulip* indicate that these objects are known to speakers of English. Such inferences are particularly important for older languages, where they are referred to as linguistic paleontology. They serve to classify the culture of early speakers or even to identify their location.

Proto-Indo-European has been extensively studied for such evidence. Its vocabulary includes only one word for 'metal,' the etymon of our word *ore.* Because no other names for metals can be assumed, not even for 'gold' and 'silver,' we conclude that the Indo-Europeans were just emerging from a stone-age culture; they had learned about metals but not to the point of identifying different ones.

Names of domestic animals indicate a pastoral rather than a settled, agricultural life. We must posit words for the animals themselves: *cow, sheep, dog,* etc.; but words for *milking, sowing grain,* and so on are later than the period of joint culture around 3000 B.C.

Moreover, words for *horse, chariot, wagon* reflect the means by which the early Indo-Europeans expanded and took over much of Europe and southern Asia.

Scholars have attempted to identify the area from which the Indo-Europeans originated by words for *bee, salmon, beech.* The distribution of these is limited. The beech, for example, is not found east of a line extending southward through central Russia. And bees are not found in desert areas. There has been considerable dispute about salmon, because the earlier habitat of animals may differ from that today. Moreover, animal names may be wrongly applied in new areas, as was the name *lion* to the American panther in *mountain lion* or the name *robin* for a thrush in the New World. Nonetheless, the evidence derived from the Indo-European vocabulary suggests that the early speakers were located north of the Black Sea, an assumption now supported by archeological finds on the kurgan culture.

Language in this way may be used as a source for data on the social groups speaking specific tongues. The study of older periods of any language, such as Middle and Old English, Proto-Germanic and Proto-Indo-European, accordingly has additional aims; it assists us in determining the culture of these periods as well as in explaining forms of the contemporary language. Moreover, even though a language can be adopted by peoples of different cultures, determination of language families helps inform us of peoples who are related or who were at one time contiguous with one another. The differing forms resulting from change also enable us to derive information about differing social groups and attitudes towards language, as we note in the following chapter.

QUESTIONS FOR REVIEW

1. Discuss the relationships between 'two' and 'dual,' indicating the historical details that illuminate the differences between the two forms, especially the initial consonants. Define *doublet*.

2. How did Sir William Jones contribute to our understanding of the history of English and the other Indo-European languages? How did Jacob Grimm?

3. What does Grimm's law describe?

4. What effect did the workings of Grimm's law have on relationships between Germanic and the other Indo-European languages?

5. What evidence can you give to classify Germanic as an Indo-European language?

6. When was English introduced into Britain? Where did its speakers come from?

7. What are the subgroups of Proto-Germanic? The five subgroups of the southern group?

8. State reasons for the importance of the Gallehus inscription.

9. What changes occurred in Old English?

10. Characterize the contacts between the speakers of English and the Celts. What influences did Celtic have on English?

11. Characterize the contacts between the speakers of English and the Scandinavians. What influences did Scandinavian have on English?

12. Characterize the contacts between the speakers of English and the Norman French. What influences did French have on English?

13. How did Latin and Greek affect English?

14. What shift differentiates Middle English from modern English (New English)? Discuss the pattern of the shift.

15. What is the basis of our spelling system? When was it introduced? What is meant by "Continental values for the vowel symbols"?

16. Cite other changes that have taken place in modern English.

17. Describe the comparative method. What are its strengths? Its weaknesses?

18. What is meant by the "method of internal reconstruction"?

19. List the nine major Indo-European subgroups and identify their current location. Identify Hittite; Tocharian.

20. What was the homeland of the Indo-Europeans? How did they succeed in their great expansion?

21. Identify briefly the following language families: (a) Afro-Asiatic; (b) Niger-Congo; (c) Dravidian; (d) Sino-Tibetan; (e) Altaic; (f) Malayo-Polynesian.

22. Outline the earliest steps towards the development of writing.

23. State the origin of our writing system and the major steps in its development.

24. Indicate three types of writing systems, and give examples of their use.

25. What modifications of the writing system were introduced after the time of the Romans?

26. Why is the alphabetic system generally favored?

27. What is the earliest type of name for individuals?

28. How were family names introduced? What are their typical origins?

29. How are place-names devised?

30. What is linguistic paleontology?

31. What inferences have been made for the culture of the speakers of Proto-Indo-European on the basis of their language?

PROBLEMS FOR REVIEW

1. The following are examples of forms indicating the PIE obstruents and their Germanic reflexes:

1.　　　PIE p　　　　　　　　　　　t　　　　　　　　　　　k
　　　Skt.　*pād;* Doric Gk. *pōs*　　Skt.　*tṛnam*　　　Gk.　*kuōn*
　　　OE　*fōt* 'foot'　　　　　　OE　*þorn*　　　　OE　*hund* 'hound, dog'
2.　　　PIE bh　　　　　　　　　dh　　　　　　　　gh
　　　Skt.　*bharati*　　　　　　Skt.　dhitis　　　　Skt.　stighnute
　　　OE　*beran* 'bear'　　　　OE　*dæd* 'deed'　　OE　*stīgan* 'climb'
3.　　　PIE b　　　　　　　　　d　　　　　　　　　g
　　　Lith.　*bala* 'swamp'　　　Skt.　*dvā*　　　　Gk.　*geranos*
　　　OE　*pōl* 'pool'　　　　　OE　*twā* 'two'　　OE　*cran* 'crane'

　　a. Indicate the consonant changes that have taken place between PIE and Germanic.
　　b. Give the NE counterparts of the following. (Since the Germanic counterparts of Sanskrit final syllables were lost, disregard the *-u* in the first form and the *-us* and *-as* in the last two forms).

Skt. *madhu*	'sweet drink'	NE	_____
Lat. *ager*	'field'	NE	_____
Skt. *tanus*	'narrow'	NE	_____
Skt. *pataras*	'flying'	NE	_____

2. Using the comparative method, reconstruct the initial PIE consonant from the following:
Skt. *paśu;* Lat. *pecu;* Gothic *faihu* 'cattle, (fee)'
Skt. *tṛṣyati* 'is thirsty'; Gk. *térsomai* 'become dry'; Goth. *þairsan* 'wilt'
Lith. *kerpu* 'shear'; Lat. *carpo* 'pick'; OE *hærfast* 'autumn, harvest'

3a. In the Middle English period a well-known set of terms for prepared foods was borrowed from French, such as *beef, veal, bacon, pork, mutton, jelly.* On the other hand, native English terms were maintained for the animals in the field, such as *cow, calf, boar, swine, sheep.* Can you suggest the status of the two languages and their speakers from the borrowings and the retentions?

　b. Among other borrowings from French were names for trades, such as *carpenter, painter, tailor,* while simple occupations maintained English names, such as *baker, miller, blacksmith.* How can you use such names to support your conclusions on the basis of the words in problem 3a?

　c. Compare the borrowings from Celtic and possible conclusions based on those.

　d. Cite borrowings from Scandinavian, and discuss inferences based on these concerning the relations between Scandinavian and English.

4. The following are Middle English forms containing long vowels and their New English counterparts in conventional spelling:

rīm	[ri:m]	'rime'
gēs	[ge:s]	'geese'
dǣl	[dɛ:l]	'deal'
tale	[ta:l]	'tale'
bāt	[bɔ:t]	'boat'
mōne	[mo:n]	'moon'
mūs	[mu:s]	'mouse'

Indicate the changes that have taken place between the ME long vowels and their NE reflexes. (Be sure to write the NE forms in transcription.)

5. The following are examples of translations of Matthew 14:15 from three periods of English.[2]

Old English (circa 1000):

> Sōðlīce þā hyt wæs æfen geworden, him tō genēalæhton his leorning-cnihtas, and him tō cwædon, "Ðēos stōw ys wēste, and tīma is forð āgān; forlǣt þās mænegeo þæt hī faron intō þās burga and him mete bicgean."

Tyndale (1534):

> When even was come, his disciples came to him sayinge. This is a deserte place, and the daye is spent: let the people departe, that they maye go in to the tounes, and bye them vytayllis.

King James (1611):

> And when it was evening, his disciples came to him, saying, This is a desert place, and the time is now past; send the multitude away, that they may goe into the villages and buy themselves victuals.

a. Point out differences in vocabulary and grammar between the Old English text and Tyndale's text.
b. Discuss patterns of vocabulary and syntax in the Tyndale and the King James translations that are no longer current.
c. Determine the position of the verbs in the Old English text, indicating their order in each clause.
d. The three texts contain the following forms for 'food': OE *mete;* Tyndale *vytaylles;* King James *victuals.* Compare these with modern forms, as in *sweetmeats* and the pronunciation of *victuals,* and discuss the changes that have taken place.

FURTHER READING

Gimbutas, Marija. "Proto-Indo-European Culture During the Fifth, Fourth, and Third Millennia B.C." In *Indo-European and Indo-Europeans*, ed. by George Cardona, Henry M. Hoenigswald, and Alfred Senn. Philadelphia: University of Pennsylvania Press, 1970, pp. 155–197.

Lehmann, Winfred P. *Historical Linguistics: An Introduction.* New York: Holt, Rinehart & Winston, 1973.

Pedersen, Holger, *Linguistic Science in the Nineteenth Century.* Trans. by John Spargo, Cambridge, Mass.: Harvard University Press, 1931. Reprinted under the title: *The Discovery of Language.* Bloomington: Indiana University Press, 1962.

Schmandt-Besserat, Denise. "The Earliest Precursor of Writing." *Scientific American* 238 (June 1978), pp. 50–59.

[2] From A. G. Riggs, ed., *The English Language: A Historical Reader* (New York: Appleton-Century-Crofts, 1968, pp. 87, 89.

CHAPTER ELEVEN

Dynamism of Language

11.1 Change and Its Effects

Because language is constantly changing, new dialects may arise, as well as new alignments of old dialects or languages and new evaluations of these. When a new technology arises, such as computation, members of the group using it adopt terms that afford them more precise references. Among such terms are *bit, byte, hardware, software*. The new terminology identifies a technical group that is to some extent separated from other speakers by the language. Moreover, the special language may contribute to a feeling of pride among its users. Outsiders may be impressed by the new type of language, or they may be repelled. Those impressed will attempt to adopt the new terms, in this way modifying their own language.

Similar situations and attitudes apply to other varieties of language as well, such as geographical and social. Some of these enjoy high prestige; they are widely imitated and adopted. Others stand in such low esteem that they may be rejected and eventually eliminated. These situations obtain not only among dialects but also among languages existing side by side. Because of them, language is a dynamic activity, rarely stable except when it is fixed by strong social conventions, such as a conservative profession, a dominant literary school, or a powerful learned group.

11.2 Effects of Differing Relations Among Language Speakers, and of Differing Attitudes Concerning Them

Three classic types of language relationships may be exemplified from the history of English. In the first, that of the dominating Germanic speakers and the submerged Celtic speakers in the fifth century A.D., the invaders overwhelmed the natives. In the interplay of languages, only words for new items were adopted into English: *ass* 'a donkey,' *peat* 'vegetable substance of bogs,' and place-names like London. This is the situation that prevailed when European languages were taken to other continents in the great expansion beginning in the nineteenth century. In the United States place-names were also adopted into English from the overwhelmed native languages, for example, *Massachusetts;* words for foods and animals: *pemmican, skunk;* for new concepts: *tomahawk.* Similar adoptions took place in Spanish America, Australia, and elsewhere. The one language enjoyed high prestige, adopting few elements and eventually ousting the languages of the indigenous peoples, or leaving them only remote places in which to continue. Such a result occurs because of overwhelming social and cultural domination by one group or people over another.

In the second type of situation English and Scandinavian existed side by side for centuries, until eventually Scandinavian was abandoned. But it left many effects, especially in the north. In York, for example, the Scandinavian word for street is still found, as even in London: *gate; Highgate,* for example, corresponds to High Street. A similar situation of parallel languages is found in many areas, such as India. Its inhabitants virtually all use two or more languages. This has had a special effect in the south, for the languages concerned may belong to two different families: Indo-Iranian and Dravidian. Since the dominant religion is Hinduism, many Sanskrit words have been adopted in the Dravidian languages. And the Indo-European languages have been modified to Dravidian grammatical structure; Sinhalese, for example, the Indo-Aryan language of Ceylon, exhibits the structure of the Dravidian verb as well as other characteristics. Such mutual influences among languages on an equal plane are also found in the area of the Balkans; here the unrelated languages—Turkish, Greek, Albanian, and Slavic of several kinds—have adopted many similar characteristics. And each of these languages has been maintained. When two languages exist side by side on an equal plane, they may influence each other in any segment of the language, each adopting characteristics of the other. Such mutual influences result from bilingualism of many speakers.

The third type of situation is illustrated by the relationship of English and French from the end of the eleventh century well into the fifteenth. French, as the language of the controlling group, had high prestige, but English was spoken by the great majority of inhabitants. English borrowed many words from French, but unlike Celtic in the fifth century it was not overwhelmed and lost; the preponderance of English speakers was simply too great. A similar situation has applied for Japanese and English for approximately a century now, although the English influence is from abroad. The prestige of English did not result from administrative

Hamlet, Act 3, Scene 1, line 47									
	with devotion's visage/ and pious action we do sugar o'er/ the devil himself.								
Old French	devotion	visage			action	sukere			
Latin	devōtiō	vīsus		pius	āctiō	It. zucchero			
						Arabic sukkar*			
Old English	wiþ			and		we-dōn	ofer	ðe deōfol	him self
								Greek diábolos	
PIE	witero-				ntha-̥		wey-dhō-	uperi	

Figure 11.1 An Illustration of the Diverse Origins of English Words

Almost any stretch of English reflects several origins. This straightforward passage from Shakespeare has four words of Old French origin, one of Latin. One of the Old French words comes from Arabic through Italian, and possibly to Arabic from Sanskrit, sharkarā; hence the * above. (Eight words come directly from Old English; five of these can be traced back to Proto-Indo-European. One was imported from Greek into Old English, with the Christianization of Europe. The two others are obscure in their earlier forms.) The passage illustrates how speakers use their language dynamically, taking over words in accordance with their needs in social communication.

and ecclesiastical dominion, like that of the Normans in Britain, but from technological superiority. Japanese has borrowed words in all spheres, notably scientific and intellectual, but also sports. Moreover, the influence extends to the common language: A former student of mine wrote me bewailing the adoption by children of *mama, papa* in place of native Japanese *haha, chichi.*

This situation exists almost throughout the world today. Even French has not remained aloof from the influence of English. One language can in this way have a strong effect on another. Earlier, Latin enjoyed this role throughout western Europe. Then, from the seventeenth century it was replaced by French throughout the Western world and even in Russia. In Asia, Sanskrit has played a similar role, influencing Burmese, Thai, and other languages as well as the Indo-Aryan languages of today and Dravidian. In east Asia, Chinese was the language of prestige, providing many loan words for Korean and Japanese from the fourth century onward. This situation leads to the massive adoption of words, especially learned words, from one language into another, but the borrowing language maintains itself.

Languages in this way exert a variety of influences on one another, as may be illustrated by a short passage from Shakespeare (see Figure 11.1). According to their prestige among native speakers relative to the prestige of neighboring languages, they introduce changes, largely in the lexicon, though also in syntax and occasionally in phonology. Similar relationships are found among geographical and social groups.

11.3 Relations Among Geographical Groups

When any group of speakers is separated geographically, linguistic differences arise, as we noted in Chapter 2, Section 2.2. Latin was introduced into France and Spain as a unified language. Not only did different languages result in the two distinct areas, but also differing dialects. The speech of Paris differs from that of Normandy, Gascony, and other areas of the country. Although such a tendency towards dialect divisions may be said to be natural, it has social consequences that political unifiers consider unacceptable. Moreover, one dialect, whether that of the political center, such as Paris, London, Madrid, or of the cultural center, such as Florence, usually acquires greater prestige than others. Accordingly, dialects confront each other in ways parallel to those discussed for languages in the previous section.

As nations became centralized in Europe, one dialect came to be adopted in favor of others. The English of London has filled such a role as King's or Queen's English since the days of Chaucer. Parisian French has had similar prestige even longer. In this way national languages arose. When there is no one dominant political and cultural center for an extended period of time, the national language may represent a compromise. Standard German may be characterized as having the consonants of the southern High German and the vowels of the northern Middle and also Low German. This compromise arose among stage groups, who toured the north as well as the south; it was officially adopted only at the end of the last century. The standard language of Italy was long based on the Tuscan dialect spoken around Florence, but now Rome enjoys greater prestige. Whatever the dialect chosen, most countries fix on one language; Switzerland, with three national languages, is a notable exception.

The favoring of one language in a country led to the neglect of their native languages by Germans, Italians, Norwegians, Poles, Swedes, and many other nationalities settling in the United States. All immigrants wanted their children to be fluent in English, even at the cost of losing their ancestral language.

The period of romanticism brought a different attitude. It glorified average citizens, including their speech. Wordsworth set out to write his poetry "in a selection of language really used by men"; Burns wrote most of his in Scots English. Dialects were no longer to be rejected. The change in attitude affected different areas in various ways. For some, like Lithuania and Yugoslavia, it led to stronger feeling for a local national language in preference to a language of another country, whether German, French, or Russian. For others, it led to preference for a dialect used primarily for local communication up to that time; Norway and Greece are examples.

Until 1814 Norway was governed by Denmark. The primary influence on the language came from Copenhagen, so that the standard written languages of the two countries were similar. The language of Oslo, of the new Norwegian government, and of great nineteenth-century writers such as Ibsen, continues this tradition; as noted above, this language is known as Riksmål. However, in the nineteenth century Ivar Aasen, an energetic proponent of Norwegian spoken in the western part of the country, began to propagate a language based on the dialects of western Norway as the national standard. Known as Landsmål, this was recognized as a second language by the Norwegian parliament. Writers from the west selected it for their poetry and literary prose. By law, it had to be taught in all schools of the country. As a result of Aasen's activities, by the end of the nineteenth century Norway had two competing languages. Each had vigorous proponents, and language became a prominent political issue.

Favoring of the language variety used by the Greek people, Demotic, has brought about a similar situation in Greece. The traditional literary variety, Katharevusa, literally "purified," is being challenged. Political support for each is vigorous, as in Norway. In time, the differences may be reduced and in effect one language used for all purposes in Greece.

The necessity of using two languages in a small country—of teaching both to children who need also to learn an international language, of printing government documents and even general materials in both—is clearly a great drain of resources. As a result, efforts are now made to devise one language, often a compromise between competing languages. In Norway, the parliament passes laws directing the features to be adopted at a given point. One example is the sequence in 'twenty-four' instead of that in 'four-and-twenty,' which is still the order in German and formerly was that of English, as in the nursery rhyme: "four and twenty blackbirds baked into a pie." Since such patterns represent a very minor portion of language, they illustrate the gravity that language problems enjoy in Norway.

In most countries dialects have not been promoted to national languages. They may be used in the family, among associates, and in the local community. They may even enjoy wider prestige, as does Bavarian in Germany, the Yorkshire dialect in England, the Texan dialect in the United States. But that prestige may be linked with a regional stereotype. Such dialects, then, have ambivalent prestige, in some respects favorable, in others comical. Yet if their speakers value their own dialect highly, they maintain it regardless of attitudes of others.

11.4 Social Dialects

Well-identified social groups may cultivate their own characteristics, leading to a distinct pattern much like that of geographical dialects. These are also called styles. Among distinct styles is that of the pulpit. Another is literary style. Both of these often favor archaisms. The close relationship of religious as well as literary specialists with earlier periods leads them to prefer traditional patterns. Yet the extent of such preferences varies from time to time. Eighteenth-century literary figures favored the established literary style. Romanticism, on the other hand, as we noted above for Wordsworth, took as model the speech of the common people. Many recent writers have turned to substandard speech. Yet whatever the model, literary language is somehow idealized, not a direct representation of everyday speech.

If formal and daily language are remote from each other, in effect two languages exist. This situation is known as **diglossia.** It arises especially from religious languages but may also involve literary and learned styles. In western Europe, for example, Latin was maintained as the religious language more than a millennium after the Romance languages became independent. In the universities it was used for lectures into the eighteenth century, for dissertations and monographs into the nineteenth; even so recently many professors and students conversed in Latin. As we noted earlier, Latin was the language of the law courts in Britain until 1731. A last stronghold of this diglossic situation has now been eliminated with the decision by the Roman Catholic Church to use local languages in worship.

In eastern Europe, the second language has been Old Church Slavic. In the Middle East, the language of the Koran is still used for religious, legal, and learned purposes. In India, Sanskrit is the language of prestige for learned groups. As in western Europe, these languages are mastered by smaller and smaller numbers of speakers. Eventually, like Latin, they may be used only for academic purposes.

Some social dialects may result from distinct ethnic groups. Black English is a notable example. Blacks were segregated from the time they were captured by Arab traders in Africa throughout their life on southern plantations. Since they came from many distinct tribes, they needed a common language. Just how their special form of English acquired its characteristics is a matter of dispute. Some scholars ascribe the use of forms of the verb *be* characteristic of Black English to patterning in African indigenous languages. Others look for the source in English dialects that blacks encountered in this country. Whatever the origins of its characteristics, Black English is being reduced in breadth of use, like the different immigrant languages brought to this country in the nineteenth century, for the use of different languages, or of different dialects, is often regarded as potentially disruptive in a nation, since they reflect different social groups who may grow increasingly distinct and even antagonistic. Strong social action, such as desegregation in the schools, may then be taken to reduce differences.

11.5 Different Language Varieties Among Naturally Different Groups

Social patterns may also develop in such a way that females speak primarily to females, males to males. Each sex may then have a distinct style.

Japan provides an excellent example. Japanese women pronounce more distinctly than men; they use different verb forms and even different lexical elements, especially when referring to people.

Languages with gender distinction, whether grammatical or lexical, tend to foster such differences. Pronouns are anaphoric as well as deictic. In anaphoric use they refer to nouns; in deictic use they refer to elements in the outside world. Thus *she* is used by sailors to refer to boats, as well as to a name earlier in a text, for example, "Mary left early. She . . ." For generic use, *he* has been in effect in English, e.g., "When carrying out this experiment the student is to proceed cautiously. He . . ." As consciousness of the dual patterning rises, such disparities come to be regarded as sexist; efforts are then made to avoid them.

Lexical patterns are treated similarly. Originally *man* meant 'human' and was used for both sexes, as in the quotation from Wordsworth above in Section 11.3. But in time it came to be used only for males; *woman* from 'wife-man' led to the dichotomy. Such lexical usages are also being avoided today.

Yet repatterning is often awkward. Writers agonize about the possibilities. Many female as well as male writers find alternate forms like *he/she, s/he* clumsy. They are scarcely more receptive to the use of 'they' rather than 'he' or 'she.' In the same way *chairperson, chair* may seem to be poor substitutes for chairman. Even though these innovations have aroused much discussion, for English the problem is relatively simple. Languages like German, French, and Spanish, with gender classification for all nouns, provide far more complex problems in ridding the language of sexist patterns. Generic reference in German, for example, has been made with *man,* a weakened form of *der Mann* 'the man' in contrast with *die Frau* 'the woman.' To avoid sexist reference, some German writers now use *man/frau.* As such "solutions" may suggest, elimination of sexist language will require considerable effort in German or French, not to mention Japanese.

In spite of all the argumentation, much of it carried on with an element of detachment or even humor, the effort to eliminate sexist language represents one of the most successful instances of language engineering applied to English. Today it would be inconceivable for a university press to publish such a sentence as the following: "It must have affected them in much the same way that the impressionistic spelling of a washwoman affects a modern educated person."[1] At best one could compare a member of a poorly educated male group with "educated persons," although such a comparison would encounter objections for social or racist chauvinism.

The effort to eliminate racist language from English has also been highly successful. Even a phrase like "law and order," which has only secondary implications regarding racist attitudes, is now virtually outlawed. Nor would one speak of the Albanians as a race, as did Pedersen.[2] Current standards of usage reflect an increasing awareness of sensitivity to style among general users of language, an attitude that in the past has been prominent primarily among literary figures, politicians, and advertisers.

11.6 Some Disfavored and Favored Types of Language

All languages include words that are socially limited in use. These are known as **taboo** terms, a word taken from Polynesian, where the practice is prominent. The words under taboo differ from society to society; commonly one finds taboos for religious terms, for names, and for hunting terms. Until quite recently, for example, children were not named after a living relative in the Scandinavian area. And when Eskimos died, their personal name was removed from the language; if this were our practice, upon the death of someone named Bill or Penny, new terms would have to be found for 'bills' and 'pennies.' Taboos then differ in the extent of application as well as in the spheres of terms to be avoided.

[1] Holger Pedersen, *Linguistic Science in the Nineteenth Century,* p. 153.
[2] *Ibid.,* p. 188.

The practice arises through association of name and thing, a view that linguists reject but nonetheless is widespread. Thus, articles and books are written about the effect of a name on a person. In accordance with one such publication, the name Clem affects its owner psychologically so that he thinks he's dumb. The name Marilyn leads its owner to think she should be a sexy blond. In some primitive societies, another's knowledge of one's name gave the knower power. The fairy tale Rumpelstiltskin provides an example, because when the girl Rumpelstiltskin wanted to marry finally learned his name, he no longer had power over her, and he tore himself in two. Such primitive ideas are apparently not totally extinct in our modern sophisticated period.

In Western society, prominent areas of taboo were religious terms and terms for the bathroom. These could be used to relieve tension, but only in certain company—males among males, females among females. Hunters avoided the terms referring to their prey, whether birds like 'ducks' or animals like 'bear'; if the spirits of the intended victims overheard the hunters using the names for these, the victims would be warned and would conceal themselves. Tolstoy cites the practice in a short story on bear hunting. Even though terms are tabooed in certain contexts, they remain vigorous. The scatalogical and religious terms that used to be avoided in polite society have long respectable etymologies; some can be traced back to Proto-Indo-European.

The curious attitudes to tabooed terms may lead some speakers, especially the young, to use them to achieve startling effects, often in rebellion; most children enter a period when use of the forbidden terms titillates them. Such effects have also been highly prominent in recent Western society. Deliberate use of tabooed terms is taken to be liberating. Legal decisions forbade the banning of books, like James Joyce's *Ulysses,* on grounds of containing offensive language. It is difficult to predict how long such attitudes prevail. Tabooed usage is closely tied to social attitudes, which change considerably in time. But if the taboo on scatalogical and religious terms is broken in our society, we now have new taboos. There are many racial and sexist terms that we simply cannot use.

Just as strictures on tabooed words may be short-lived, so is slang, a creative development of language, especially among adolescents. Like the use of taboo, slang provides assurance for many who are insecure. The assurance results from having a power through use of new forms of language that are obscure to others. In this way slang is similar to thieves' cant or argot. It is also highly evanescent. Writers of the past who used the slang of their time subsequently require detailed footnotes to be understood. Even slang from the beginning of this century is now largely obsolete. The use of slang illustrates the creativity of language users, however, as well as the stratification of language types among groups of users.

11.7 Manipulation of Language

Politicians have long been expert in the use of language. The notable Greek and Latin orators were read as models for persuasive use of language. Shakespeare illustrates such skill in his lines for roles like Mark Antony in *Julius Caesar,* Act 3, Scene 2; one speech was adequate to change the Roman audience from a favorable to a negative attitude towards Brutus and his associates. In our practical modern times, besides having their speeches written by skilled professionals, politicians are schooled in rhetoric to use or to avoid language that might detract from their standing.

Even politicians may not have reached the sophistication of advertisers. Words with favorable connotations have long been known. Factories with massive production still seek to convey the notion that their bread follows the recipe of a loving mother, if not grandmother. Banks are invariably honest, efficient, and economical. Automobiles presumably are selected for their smooth power, associated since the rise in energy costs with economy. One buys a home, no longer a house, because it provides the setting of a rocky moor, or because it is located on a brushy lane or has a lake view, not because it provides safe and comfortable shelter. The favored current words must be culled out of advertisements themselves, for like slang, the potent words of advertising soon wear out. Advertising language of a few years ago may now seem almost ludicrous.

Advertisers adjust their language by sensing the mood of the time, much as politicians do by polls. Advertisers' manipulation of language accordingly represents reactions to general users, not reasoned procedures to modify language itself. Procedures to modify language are generally initiated by idealists, as in attempts to reform language and to devise international languages.

11.8 Language Reform as Applied to English

Attempts to reform English have concentrated on its orthography. The English spelling system, as we noted in Chapter 10, was designed to reflect the pronunciation of Middle English when printing was introduced and has been retained ever since with little change. As a result the spelling of many words does not reflect current pronunciation. Reformers cite words with the same spelling but totally different pronunciation like: *though, through, tough, cough, hiccough, slough, hough, laugh.* George Bernard Shaw, who left a sizable sum to anyone proposing an improved orthographic system for English, delighted in citing *ghoti* as a possible spelling for 'fish.' The *gh* has the value of *gh* in *laugh, o* that of *o* in *women, ti* that of *ti* in *nation.* English-speaking schools are unique in staging spelling bees; in other language areas spelling so much resembles speech that such contests would be impossible. It is sometimes said that our elementary schooling is extended by two years because students need that time to acquire our cumbersome spelling system.

Past attempts to reform English spelling have had little success. Publishers object because their stock of books would become obsolete. Printers, stenographers, and many readers are little more receptive because they would be required to learn new patterns. Some reformers of the past have had slight success. Noah Webster succeeded in modifying the *-our* suffix to *-or,* in *favor* and the like, as well as in reversing the letters of the *-re* suffix to *-er,* as in *saber* and the like. Others have been quite unsuccessful, such as the Chicago *Tribune,* which long attempted to shift the spelling of *through* to *thru,* of *though* to *tho,* and to modify the spelling of a few more words. After some time the newspaper abandoned the effort.

Other languages have been more successful. For German, successive efforts have removed inconsistent spellings. Yet only in times of revolution, as in the Soviet Union after 1917, do efforts to bring about larger modifications achieve success. The growing use of English as an international language has led to renewed effort on behalf of reformed spelling; the spelling system of English is especially difficult for adult language learners, who have many responsibilities that interfere with learning a difficult system of orthography.

The remedy, however, must be carefully planned. Recommendations that the spelling be ''phonetic'' encounter the difficulty that a phonetic spelling for British English would differ from that for American English; both in turn would differ from a phonetic spelling for Australian English and other varieties. A purely phonetic system would bring about different spellings not only for many words in these languages but also for dialects within them.

Moreover, English spelling is for many words based on morphological criteria. The plural of *woman* has a different stem vowel from the singular: [wɪmən]; a phonetic spelling would not permit the sequence *wom-* in both. Nor could verb forms like *hear, heard* have the same spelling. Moreover, the relationships between forms like the following would be less transparent: *animate* (adjective), *animate* (verb), *animation; meter, metric, diameter;* and many more. A morphologically based system is by no means essential. Yet as these examples indicate, it has advantages. especially if consistent.

Revision of the English spelling system will only be successful if it enjoys the support of many influential speakers—businessmen, educators, publishers, international as well as national—and if the reforms are carried out on the basis of consistent principles. The failure of George Bernard Shaw's effort provides adequate warning to reformers who hope to modify the system, however idealistic they may be.

11.9 International Languages

Proponents of artificial languages have had little more success. Scholars have sought to devise one ever since Latin went out of use. A Polish physician, Ludwik Zamenhof, invented that with broadest following: Esperanto. It is based on the vocabulary and grammar of the Romance languages, regularized and simplified. In spite of devoted followers, there has been no dearth of others. The great Danish linguist Otto Jespersen devised Novial. Others support Interlingua. None has more than several million users, most far fewer. Even at international conferences, English is now preferred.[3]

[3] For further details on artificial languages see the account by Norman McQuown, *Encyclopaedia Britannica: Macropaedia,* 15th ed., Vol. 9 (Chicago: Encyclopaedia Britannica, Inc., 1978), pp. 741–744.

Among problems with artificial languages is the lack of attention to phonology. All include both /r/ and /l/. Yet Japanese has no /l/, Chinese no /r/; native speakers of these languages, a quarter of the world's population, would confuse words with these sounds. Further, the vocabulary is based on the Romance languages and accordingly would be simplest to acquire for those speakers who routinely master several languages and accordingly do not need an artificial language. Moreover, all international languages face the problem that infants first acquire a local language, and any subsequent language will be influenced by it. Cynics have stated that if an Esperanto speaker were to make a leisurely round-the-world trip, speaking Esperanto to colleagues in all stops, his Esperanto would not be intelligible to his associates at the conclusion of his trip. This is something of an exaggeration, but it illustrates the problem that proponents of artificial languages must surmount.

A language does not exist apart from a social group. Isolated social groups, whether of small countries, aboriginal tribes, or sophisticated intellectuals, can indeed communicate in their select language. But to have this language more widely adopted, they must also acquire broader social control, as did the Greeks under Alexander the Great, the Romans under their capable rulers, the Arabs with the expansion of Moslem faith, and others who have imposed their language on other peoples. Unless a language is associated with a society of prestige, whether with a military, literary, or scientific base, or all of these combined, it will not attract international followers. French achieved this role in the sixteenth century. English replaced it in the nineteenth, and today has a vastly greater attraction than has any language before it.

The earliest success of English may have been in the field of sports. Variants of the word *football,* only one of the many words so generalized, are used throughout the world for games involving a ball on the ground, whether soccer, rugby, or American football. Thereupon English words for technological advances, science, trade, and so on were established in many languages. And English is now the first choice of most speakers acquiring a second language for international communication. While native speakers of English rely on its widespread use, they encounter the problem of seeming unsympathetic to other nations, even of fostering imperialism, whether political, economic, or technological. It is highly embarrassing to be faced with hostile or proud inhabitants of other countries who may indeed be able to communicate in English but insist on using their own language to "ugly Americans." Native speakers of English are then faced with the paradox that their language is widely used, but they themselves must attempt to use the language of other countries to achieve genuine communication.

Language, as we have noted above, is intimately related to social and cultural attitudes and activities. Observers of language in use invariably find that speakers prefer to pray in their first language, to use it for mathematical purposes, and to turn back to it as they grow older. The dynamism of language has other roots besides efficiency of communication. Practically, the world would gain great advantages from adopting one language. Yet even small nations and individual tribes cling to their ancestral languages until their cultural and social conditions no longer support independence. As long as these conditions remain alive and dynamic, however, the language too will be vigorously maintained.

QUESTIONS FOR REVIEW

1. Sketch how a new technology illustrates the dynamism of language.

2. Describe the relationship of English to Celtic in the fifth century, to Scandinavian in the ninth and tenth, to Norman French in the eleventh and later, indicating also the results of the various relationships. Cite relationships between other languages that are similar to each of these and lead to similar results.

3. Contrast the attitude to dialects in the eighteenth century with that after the influence of romanticism in the nineteenth century.

4. What is the basis of the standard language of England? Of France? Of Germany? Of Italy?

5. Discuss the language situation in Norway from the time of the nineteenth century, comparing it with that in France and in Greece.

6. Why do modern nations seek to have one standard language? Review Chapter 2, noting the situation in contemporary China, and compare it with that in Switzerland. In what respects are the problems China faces to form one standard language more complex than they were in a country like France?

7. Compare the diglossic situation in medieval Europe with those in Russia, Arab countries, and India, citing for each of these the competing language of prestige.

8. Discuss some effects on English of the current recognition of sexist language.

9. Define *taboo*, indicating spheres in which it is applied in English and changes in attitude towards these spheres.

10. Discuss slang, including its possible permanent effects on language, its relationships to social groups, and its evidence for linguistic creativity.

11. Compare the use of language by politicians and advertisers, contrasting each with that of literary figures.

12. If English spelling is to be reformed, what principles would you advocate? Discuss differences between spelling systems based on phonological criteria and those based on morphological criteria.

13. Contrast the use of natural versus artificial languages for international use. Which in your view have a greater likelihood of success? What are some of the obstacles standing in the way of widespread use of artificial languages?

PROBLEMS FOR REVIEW

1. Japanese has borrowed many words from English, such as the following:

   badominton 'badminton' *pii-aaru-kaa* 'public relations car'
   buru-pen 'the bull pen' *shinema* 'cinema'
   hoomu-ran 'home-run' *shorudaa-paddo* 'shoulder pads'
   nikkaasu 'knickers' *sutoraiku* 'strike (in baseball)'
   pii-aaru 'PR = public relations' *wesuto-rain* 'waistline'

a. Which segment of Japanese, the phonological, syntactic, or lexical, was primarily influenced?
b. The Japanese phonological system contains fewer phonemes than does the English—only five vowels: /i e a o u/, which may be single or doubled; no /l/; and so on. Determine some of the substitutions that result from these differences between the two languages.
c. All Japanese syllables must end in a vowel or *n*. How does this requirement affect words borrowed?

2. In the diglossic situation that was found in England during its long use of Latin for learned purposes, the following words were incorporated into English:

edict	genus	hernia
juridical	molecule	lumbago
negotiate	nucleus	mucus
secede	sextant	placenta

On the basis of these examples, suggest spheres of communication in which Latin occupied a more prominent place than English.

3. When sketching the history of Black English, J. L. Dillard cites examples like the following for the Civil War period:[4]
Examples indicating lack of plural marker:

Ten dollar a month
We hab some valiant soldier here.

Examples indicating "non-differentiation according to sex":

I lub he. (he was a woman with seven children)
Ole woman one single frock he hab on.

Example indicating faulty use of subject-object form:

Him brought it on heself.

a. Compare these examples with Standard English, determining the Black English patterns.
b. Determine phonological differences from Standard English.

4. Among studies of university slang is that by Alan Dunden and Manuel R. Schonhorn.[5] In assembling their data, Dundes and Schonhorn gathered slang expressions for the following items. Note your own terms for these items and compare them with those of your friends, or with those of the students at Kansas University around 1960.
    1. To study extremely diligently for an examination
    2. An easy college course

[4] J. L. Dillard, *Black English* (New York: Vintage Books, 1973), pp. 106–107.
[5] Alan Dunden and Manuel R. Schonhorn, "Kansas University Slang: A New Generation," *American Speech* 38 (1963), 163–177.

   3. A difficult college course
   4. To fail to pass an examination
   5. To go alone to a dance or social function
   6. One who puts a damper on a party
   7. A particularly rough and noisy party
   8. A poor social evening, a wasted night
   9. What a person who has special influence is said to have
 10. Drunk

5. The following is an example of eighteenth-century gypsy slang:

> In a box[a] of the stone jug[b] I was born,
> Of a hempen widow[c] the kid forlorn,
>   Fake[d] away!
> and my father, as I've heard say,
>   Fake away!
> Was a merchant of capers gay,
> Who cut his last fling with great applause,
> Nix my doll pals,[e] fake away!
> To the tune of hearty choke with caper sauce.
>   Fake away!
> The knucks[f] in quod[g] did my schoolmen[h] play,
>   Fake away!
> And put me up to the time of day,[i]
> Until at last there was none so knowing,
>   No such sneakesman[j] or buzgloak[k] going.

[a] cell   [b] a prison   [c] woman whose husband has been hanged   [d] work   [e] Never mind, my friends   [f] thieves   [g] prison   [h] fellows of the gang   [i] taught me thieving   [j] shop-lifter   [k] pickpocket

  a. Which of the slang terms are still used? Which are obsolete?
  b. Identify the glossed terms that are extended forms of words.
  c. Identify others that appear to be neologisms.

6a. In Japanese, the numeral system was modified because the word taken over from Chinese, *shi* 'four,' was a homophone of *shi* 'to die.' In counting, the Japanese now commonly say *juuyon* rather than *juushi* for 'fourteen,' especially when counting human beings. The entity *yon* is a native Japanese word for 'four.' What linguistic process led to the substitution?

  b. The process of language change varies in its basis from period to period and from language to language. A British guide in the Lake District stated that in his youth the two counties Westmoreland and Cumberland were never given in this order because the abbreviation would have been WC, the commonly used euphemism for 'toilet' (from water closet). Would you expect this effect today? Would it be observed by a speaker of American English?

  c. Linguists generally hold that language is a system of arbitrary signs. How do you account for taboo if there is no inherent connection between the shapes of words and their meanings?

7a. It is often said that nonnative speakers of English would be assisted greatly in their attempts to learn the language if English spelling were more "phonetic." Discuss some of the problems involved in the devising of a "phonetic spelling." Whose pronunciation would you accept as standard: that of the Queen of England or the president of the United States or even some other figure? If you select the president, which one's pronunciation would you choose?

b. What consequences would a revision of English spelling entail? What effect would it have on extant books?

c. How long could a revised phonetic spelling be maintained? What would you suggest for American speakers who change *t* to *d* in such words as *butter, bottle, bottom?* How about the speakers in the South who make no distinction between the pronunciation of [ɪ] and [ɛ] in *pen, pin?* What device would you employ so that British English speakers who "drop their r's" would still be able to use the same spelling as Americans for words like *fare, far, for, fur, fire?*

FURTHER READING

Dillard, J. L. *Black English. Its History and Usage in the United States.* New York: Vintage Books, 1973.

Fishman, Joshua A., ed. *Advances in the Study of Societal Multilingualism.* The Hague: Mouton, 1973.

Jespersen, Otto. *Mankind, Nation and Individual from a Linguistic Point of View.* London: Allen & Unwin, 1946.

Key, Mary Ritchie. *Male/Female Language.* Metuchen, N.J.: Scarecrow Press, 1975.

Labov, William, *Sociolinguistic Patterns.* Philadelphia: University of Pennsylvania Press, 1972.

CHAPTER TWELVE

Language in Its Diversity

12.1 The Politician's Use of Language

According to Herodotus, when Croesus, King of Lydia, asked the oracle at Delphi whether he should attack the Persians, the oracle answered ambiguously, that if he did he would destroy a great empire. Croesus, as a confident ruler, misinterpreted the reply. The attack resulted in the destruction of his own empire rather than that of the Persians.

Political language is often highly ambiguous. Politicians flourish by devising expressions that their audiences interpret as favorable to themselves. Franklin Roosevelt was not at all beloved by the financial leaders of his day, but they could not take great offense when he referred to them as economic royalists. Even a stark put-down can be inoffensive because of its absurdity, such as Lyndon Johnson's alleged characterization of Gerald Ford: "He's so dumb that he can't walk and chew gum at the same time." Less elegant than Roosevelt's expression for his political opponents, this widely circulated comment scarcely ended Ford's political career, though his earlier criticism of Johnson now seemed somewhat pointless.

Political language may, however, be not at all gentle, especially on occasions of personal and general passion. Thus John Milton, although a strict follower of Cromwell, came under attack because after his wife's desertion he argued for divorce during a Puritan age. In reply he dismissed a critic as follows: "I mean not to dispute philosophy with this pork, who never read any." The pairing of 'philosophy' and 'pork' illustrates a device favored by Milton—the use of a simple word in conjunction with a learned one. Later in the essay he complains that he has been "put to this underwork of scouring and unrubbishing the low and sordid ignorance of such a presumptuous lozel" (one lost, worthless). Other pairings of his are: "unprincipled, unedified and laic rabble," "the pride of a metaphysical fume," "sapless dotages of old Paris and Salamanca." Secretary for Foreign Languages in the Cromwell government as well as a poet, Milton was not unacquainted with the rhetorical skills of politicians.

Other poets and religious leaders have been no less accomplished in invective, as a reading of Alexander Pope makes clear. His "Essay on Criticism" includes vigorous as well as gentle satire, often built on pairing of opposites, as in the following lines:

> What the weak head with strongest bias rules,
> Is pride, the never-failing vice of fools.

Ridicule against opponents or ideas is a weapon to overwhelm them with a well-chosen word, which Chesterton characterized as follows: "a stigma is a stick to beat a dogma with." Another period and a different language provide many examples of political invective. During the Reformation, Luther's opponents changed the spelling of his name to Luder 'carrion, carcass.' Not to be intimidated, Luther used devices like conflating the title and name of one of his opponents, Dr. Eck, to Dreck 'dirt, filth.' In our gentler and less gifted times, poets, religious leaders, and politicians devise less vigorous and less imaginative expressions. Sadly, we can only point to dull use of scatological terms, as exemplified in the Watergate tapes, which reflects a vacuous poverty of language, not even respectable for cheerless adolescents.

Like the politician, we all use language to persuade—when desperate to cajole or castigate. Effectiveness of such language varies in accordance with our own naivete and skill. Croesus, pleased with the ambiguous oracle and acknowledging it with costly gifts, has come down in history as an overconfident failure. Roosevelt is regarded as a masterful politician, as is Johnson, who used language like a whip to control Congress. As Abraham Lincoln's Gettysburg Address illustrates, the world responds to vigorous language, even more when it is accompanied by imaginative touches (see Figure 12.1).

12.2 The Poet's Use

While the politician seeks ambiguous language, the poet aims at precision. For Pope in his "Essay on Criticism":

> True wit is Nature to advantage dressed,
> What oft was thought, but ne'er so well expressed.

Fourscore and seven years ago our fathers brought forth on this continent a new nation conceived in liberty and dedicated to the proposition that all men are created equal. Now we are engaged in a great civil war testing whether that nation, or any nation so conceived and so dedicated can long endure. We are met on a great battlefield of that war. We have come to dedicate a portion of that field as a final resting-place for those who here gave their lives that that nation might live. It is altogether fitting and proper that we should do this. But, in a larger sense, we cannot dedicate, we cannot consecrate, we cannot hallow this ground. The brave men, living and dead, who struggled here have consecrated it far above our poor power to add or detract. The world will little note nor long remember what we say here, but it can never forget what they did here. It is for us the living rather to be dedicated here in the unfinished work which they who fought here have thus far so nobly advanced. It is rather for us to be here dedicated to the great task remaining before us—that from these honored dead we take increased devotion to that cause for which they gave the last full measure of devotion—that we here highly resolve that these dead shall not have died in vain, that this nation under God shall have a new birth of freedom, and that government of the people, by the people, for the people, shall not perish from the earth.

Figure 12.1   Diverse Strands in Lincoln's Gettysburg Address

Various uses of language, that of the politician, that of the poet, of the priest, and of the scientist—here a biologist—are illustrated in Abraham Lincoln's Gettysburg Address, which since its delivery has appealed greatly to the average speaker. Some characteristics of each use are indicated; others may be identified by readers.

Ambiguous and meaningless words are avoided. A poet has a specific concept; the poem is designed to have the reader understand this directly, as through images. Pope does not say: an actual insight corresponds to reality in the real world; rather, he directly confronts two concepts presented in concrete images: wit . . . nature.

Images so utilized are highlighted by poetic choice of words for their sounds. A masterful poet chooses language to underline his precise depiction of emotion. This skill requires long training as well as native gifts. Among outstanding poetic traditions of the past, one has produced the Homeric poems; another produced the Old Irish poetry that was the inspiration for great medieval verse, as in the Arthurian tradition. In ancient Ireland, as in many regions, composing poetry was a craft. The highest rank of poet underwent twenty-four years of training, mastering during this time highly demanding principles of versification. Besides end-rhyme, including rhymes of accented syllables with unaccented as in the following example, internal echoes highlight words central in the poem's imagery, for example, *storms . . . roar, slave . . . day, son . . . come*. Each line is limited in syllables, in this poem to seven. Such poetry had a powerful impact and attractiveness, so that it was transmitted orally for centuries.

The following stanza is from an Old Irish poem in which an old woman recalls the attractions of her youth, and her current loneliness in an active world as reflected by the vigorous sea and the winds.

> The waves of the great sea stir:
> storms rouse the roar of winter:
> no nobleman nor slave's son
> will come here today—no one.[1]

In spite of all the demands of his versification, the poet is still able to give us a concrete image, a picture of total loneliness.

Poetry, then, represents one of the sublime uses of language. Words are selected to sharpen images, yielding new concepts, new understanding of complex situations. We turn to poetry when we meet such situations—death, love, birth, awe of the unknown, visions of divinity. Forced by such events to recognize our separate existence, we seek out another individual's expression of past experiences in such situations, to clarify our own, to find companionship with another member in the long record of humans who have lived much as we do.

12.3 The Scientist's Use

Scientists also insist on precision in use of language. But they emphasize facts, not people and their feelings. Moreover, the facts must speak for themselves. Ideas are not to be conveyed through images or affected by human origins. Even living beings are stripped of their animation, including the scientists themselves. These aims lead to characteristic scientific styles of expression.

When writing English, scientists favor the passive, as we noted above. Use of the passive permits placing the inanimate fact in subject position, eliminating the agent entirely. Moreover, the content lodges in nouns and nominal expressions. In English these consist of nominal phrases built on nouns modified by adjectives and prepositional phrases; in German and Russian, the content is often lumped together in compounds: German *Sprechstundenhilfe* 'receptionist ⟨ office-hour-assistant,' Russian *bysokokvalifitsirovannyi* 'highly qualified.' The compactness achieved by such compounds in Germanic scientific writing is complemented by use of modifying adjectives or participles before nouns, rather than relative clauses after them, as in the following passage from Einstein's famous letter to the London *Times* of November 28, 1919:

[1] From "The Old Woman of Beare," in Ruth P. M. Lehmann, *Poems* (Austin: Westlake Press, 1977), p. 39.

Der Hauptreiz der Theorie liegt in ihrer logischen Geschlossenheit. Wenn eine einzige aus ihr geschlossene Konsequenz sich als unzutreffend erweist, muss sie verlassen werden; eine Modifikation erscheint ohne Zerstoerung des ganzen Gebaeudes unmoeglich.

"The chief attraction of the theory [of relativity] consists in its logical consistency. If a single result which is derived from it is demonstrated to be incorrect, it must be abandoned; a modification appears to be impossible without destroying the entire structure."

As in the adjectival preposed phrase *aus ihr geschlossene* 'which is derived from it,' German includes relative expressions of OV patterning, reducing in this way the number of subordinate clauses. Moreover, the complex nominal phrases lead to a structure more opaque to the nonspecialist than that of the poet or the politician.

Yet the scientist is precise in writing. To provide a pedagogical illustration of the preposed adjective construction, I once asked a capable German stylist to modify some passages of Einstein's. After some effort, he admitted failure, finding that Einstein's statements could not be expressed in any other way. The language was so close to the concepts conveyed that it could not be bent, even for the extraneous purpose of illustrating grammatical patterns. Scientists then compare with poets in closely fashioning language to express their views, but in the process the language is totally subordinated to compact expression of the ideas, even deformed in the eyes of many. Attention is directed to content with no interference from the author or the audience. Scientific writing contains few devices for pragmatic purposes.

12.4 The Priest's Use

The priest on the other hand employs many pragmatic devices, directing his message to a specific audience. This aim encourages patterns comparable to the poet's. Sequences are repeated, often exactly, as in Matthew 5:7–9:

> Blessed are the merciful: for they shall obtain mercy.
> Blessed are the pure in heart: for they shall see God.
> Blessed are the peacemakers: for they shall be called
>   the children of God. . . .

The repetitions engage the attention of the audience, as well as their participation, through established sequences, such as *amen; hallelujah; Glory, glory, hallelujah.* The priest raises emotions, though with somewhat different aims and devices from those of the poet.

For the priest seeks to have the emotions of the audience combined with awe, often drawing on archaic language to achieve the distance associated with it. A separate language, or separate sets of words, may be designated as divine language as opposed to that of humans. Germanic culture records such diverse languages in the Old Norse *Edda*. A dwarf, All-wise, informs Thor of the words used by gods and other supernatural beings for 'earth, heaven,' and so on. 'Fire,' for example, is *eldr* among humans, the word still in common use in the Scandinavian languages; compare Danish *ild,* Swedish *eld.* Among gods it is *funi,* an old Indo-European word related to our word *fire* (Alvissmal 25). Archaic language may be received as obscure, or when maintained by the mediocre as trite bombast. Yet when molded by a genius, the result is venerated as deeply as the poetic statements of a Shakespeare.

In Western culture the utterances of the Old Testament prophets still appeal to audiences of politicians as well as to priests and preachers; few politicians can resist promising to "beat their swords into ploughshares" (Isaiah 2.4). The Eastern world has maintained the utterances of Gautama Buddha, such as his Fire-Sermon:

> All things, o priests, are on fire. And what, o priests,
> are all these things which are on fire?
> The eye, o priests, is on fire; forms are on fire;
> eye-consciousness is on fire; impressions received
> by the eye are on fire; . . .
> And with what are these on fire?
> With the fire of passion, say I, with the fire of hatred,
> with the fire of infatuation; with birth, old age, death, sorrow,
> lamentation, misery, grief, and despair are they on fire.[2]

The language of the priest and of the prophet then includes devices of the poet and the politician, also drawing, like Isaiah and the Buddha, on concrete technological words to combine the numerous devices language provides for effective communication.

12.5 The Average Speaker's Use

Few of us use language as effectively as the consummate poet, politician, scientist, or priest; yet we employ the same devices as they, and we apply language in accordance with their various purposes.

Schoolchildren, like oral poets, play their games to the accompaniment of verses created centuries earlier. In studies devoted to nursery rhymes, the Opies found references to them long ago, after which they were transmitted through tradition, such as:

> Little Boy Blue,
> Come blow your horn,
> The sheep's in the meadow,
> The cow's in the corn:

---

[2] From Henry Clarke Warrren, *Buddhism in Translation,* Harvard Oriental Series III (Cambridge, Mass.: Harvard University Press, 1915), pp. 352–353.

> But where is the boy
>   Who looks after the sheep?
> He's under a haycock,
>   Fast asleep.[3]

As we have noted earlier, at a very young age infants practice language for persuasive purposes like those of the politician. Children, then, already use language like the poet and the politician; with improvement in our mastery, we apply such skills with greater effect. We come to be more articulate, to control in greater degree the features for bending others to our wills.

Control of the persuasive mechanisms of language is an accomplishment honed by anyone who needs to deal with children. Other adult experiences demand cultivation of further uses. Occupations—pursuit of business or management of a household—cultivate something of the precision of the scientist. And life's course introduces us to the traditional and consoling language of the priest. In applying these uses, we may also wonder about the mechanisms of language and of its roots.

But as with our other activities, we do not analyze this language, unless urged to do so by a specialist. As children we master language so thoroughly that we are unaware of its several components, even of the elements of these, such as individual phonemes. Speakers find it highly difficult to describe their stress and intonation patterns and to identify the meanings of these. Nor are we conscious of syntactic constructions like the clefts of the following example, let alone differences in meaning between them and the simple pattern: *We want action; What we want is action; It is action that we want.* Moreover, we are unaware of our shifts in style when we converse with a clerk, with someone in authority, when we answer the telephone. Language is simply an instrument for us; we normally analyze its structure as little as that of the fruit or bread we eat. However, when we seek explanations for particular patterns or aim at linguistic applications, we must proceed beyond naive mastery to informed analysis.

Such analysis is increasingly important as we concern ourselves with large and complex amounts of data. Chemists are faced with more than a million technical terms and medical specialists scarcely with fewer, like most technical experts today. Only by handling these in computer stores will they, or their assistants, control them. Advances are rapidly being made in using computers for the multiple applications of language, not merely the few signals required in securing airline reservations and the like. To the extent we understand language we will employ such possibilities skillfully.

Such understanding, in illuminating our means for expressing our thoughts and emotions, deepens our regard for capacities that we share with all human beings. All use vocal sounds, patterned in words, sentences, and texts. The sounds are comparable wherever in the present or past we find language, as are the sentence

---

[3] From Iona and Peter Opie, eds., *The Oxford Dictionary of Nursery Rhymes* (Oxford: Clarendon, 1951), pp. 98–99. Here a probable allusion to a rhyme in *King Lear*, Act 3, Scene 6, is pointed out.

patterns and other devices. Through the study of language in its diversity we come to appreciate its universal qualities, and also the oneness common to all humans.

QUESTIONS FOR REVIEW

1. Discuss reasons for the use of ambiguous language.
2. Find examples of political invective today, comparing it with that of Milton's and Luther's contemporaries.
3. Poetry is often said to be hard to understand, yet poets claim to use language with great precision. How do you account for the difficulty?
4. Cite devices that poets use to highlight words and images of importance in their verse.
5. Discuss characteristics of scientific language that make it ungraceful.
6. Compare the language of the priest with that of the poet, citing similarities and differences.
7. When literary references identify language of the gods, to what do they generally refer?
8. Why do average speakers remain unaware of the structure of language?
9. Cite reasons for seeking to understand the structure of language.

PROBLEMS FOR REVIEW

1. Antony's well-known funeral oration in William Shakespeare's *Julius Caesar,* Act 3, Scene 2, shifted the favor of the audience against Brutus and the other conspirators. Excerpts read as follows:

> Friends, Romans, countrymen, lend me your ears,
> I come to bury Caesar, not to praise him. . . .
> He was my friend, faithful and just to me;
> And Brutus says he was ambitious,
> And Brutus is an honorable man.
> He hath brought many captives home to Rome,
> Whose ransoms did the general coffers fill.
> Did this in Caesar seem ambitious?
> When that the poor have cried, Caesar hath wept,
> Ambition should be made of sterner stuff.
> Yet Brutus says he was ambitious;
> And Brutus is an honorable man.

Discuss Antony's statements, in view of line 2. Point out rhetorical devices employed in these lines.

2. These are the first nine lines of the fifth stanza of William Wordsworth's ode, "Intimations of Immortality":

> Our birth is but a sleep and a forgetting:
> The Soul that rises with us, our life's Star,
>   Hath had elsewhere its setting:
>   And cometh from afar:
>   Not in entire forgetfulness,
>   And not in utter nakedness,
> But trailing clouds of glory do we come,
>   From God who is our home;
> Heaven lies about us in our infancy.

Discuss the imagery, such as identification of birth with sleep, with forgetting; of God with home.

3. In his essay "The Awful German Language," Mark Twain lists characteristics he objects to, among them the following:

> Every noun has a gender, and there is no sense or system in the distribution; so the gender of each must be learned separately and by heart. There is no other way. To do this, one has to have a memory like a memorandum book. In German, a young lady has no sex, while a turnip has. Think what overwrought reverence that shows for the turnip, and what callous disrespect for the girl. See how it looks in print.—I translate this from a conversation in one of the best of the German Sunday-school books:

> GRETCHEN: Wilhelm, where is the turnip?
> WILHELM: She has gone to the kitchen.
> GRETCHEN: Where is the accomplished and beautiful
>   English maiden?
> WILHELM: It has gone to the opera.

What is the basis of his objections here? To what extent are they valid? Noting when he shifts from the use of "gender" to "sex" in this passage, can he have been serious? Can you cite contemporary examples of confusion between "gender" and "sex," whether purposeful or naive?

4. Among the essays in *Language and Learning,* Seymour Papert's deals with "The Role of Intelligence in Psychology." In his conclusion, Papert says:

> Grounds for optimism are to be found in the recent tendency to intermarriage between AI and styles of linguistic theory related to systemic and case grammars, and to much tighter interconnection between syntactic structures

and cognitive (some would say "semantic") structures. Since I can discuss only one example, I choose in the interests of simplicity the very general one that Chomsky calls "the structure-dependent property of linguistic rules." One possible answer to the question of how the child learns so easily to develop structure-dependent rules of language is that he has already come to do this outside of language.[4]

Point out differences between Papert's presentation and that of Mark Twain, citing from Papert characteristics of scientific language. Scientists are said to avoid use of "I." How do you explain Papert's use of it in the second sentence here, though not in the first?

5. The British journal *The Countryman* includes a column providing examples of the language of the average citizen. Examine those excerpts below for evidence of diplomatic, poetic, and other varieties of language.
   a. Cornishman discussing a neighbor: "I wouldn' call un a liar, but 'e d'andle the truth awk'ard."
   b. North Somerset villager after a tiff with a neighbor: "She don't be very tuneful today, do'er?"
   c. Welsh mother to small child: "Now don't you go from by here or I'll be taking you 'ome lost."
   d. Two Devonshire women discussing an absent third: "Er be that old, all the fluff be coming out of 'er woolies."
   e. Scottish islander commenting on a spell of fine sunny weather: "Aye, we had seven weeks of this in April."

6. Select from among the following suggestions any two types of text, and compare them for their linguistic characteristics: a recipe; a newspaper editorial; the lyrics to a rock song; a letter to a paper or magazine; advice to the lovelorn; answers to medical questions in the paper; your income tax form; a scientific essay; a quiz; your insurance policy; a passage from an Old Testament prophet; a literary description; a political speech; a class handout; an ode; a prophetical passage from the Book of Revelations, or one of the poetic books of the Old Testament.

7. In his book *The Tongues of Men*, J. R. Firth states:

The use of the English language is today the greatest social force in the whole world, and we in England should lead the way in training young people towards a critical understanding of language behavior of all kinds, and in the direction of developing any skill they may show in its use.[5]

What does Firth mean by calling "the use of English" a "social force"? How would you proceed to provide a "critical understanding of language behavior"?

[4] Seymour Papert, "The Role of Intelligence in Psychology," *Language and Learning*, ed. by Massimo Piattelli-Palmarini (Cambridge, Mass.: Harvard University Press, 1980).
[5] John R. Firth. *The Tongues of Men and Speech*, p. 137.

FURTHER READING

Bates, Elizabeth. *Language, Thought and Culture*. New York: Academic Press, 1976.

Casson, Ronald W., ed. *Language, Culture, and Cognition*. Anthropological Perspectives. London: Macmillan, 1981.

Firth, John R. *The Tongues of Men and Speech*. London: Oxford University Press, 1964. (Reprint of 1937 and 1930 editions.)

Jespersen, Otto. *Mankind, Nation and Individual. From a Linguistic Point of View*. London: Allen & Unwin, 1946.

Bibliography

Akmajian, Adrian, Richard A. Demers, Robert M. Harnish. *Linguistics: An Introduction to Language and Communication*. Cambridge, Mass. MIT Press, 1979.

Albert, M. L., and L. K. Obler. *The Bilingual Brain*. New York: Academic Press, 1978.

Austin, J. L. *How to do Things with Words*. Edited by J. O. Urmson. New York: Oxford University Press, 1965.

Bailey, Charles-James N., *Variation and Linguistic Theory*. Arlington, Va.: Center for Applied Linguistics, 1973.

Baker, Carl L. *Introduction to Generative Transformational Syntax*. Englewood Cliffs, N.J.: Prentice-Hall, 1978.

Bates, Elizabeth. *Language, Thought and Culture*. New York: Academic Press, 1976.

Bates, Elizabeth, and Brian MacWhinney. 'A Functionalist Approach to the Acquisition of Grammar,' pp. 167–211 of *Developmental Pragmatics*, Elinor Ochs and Bambi B. Schiefflin, eds. New York: Academic Press, 1979.

Bauman, Richard and Joel Sherzer, eds. *Explorations in the Ethnography of Speaking*. London: Cambridge University Press, 1974.

Benveniste, Emile. *Problems in General Linguistics*. Trans. by Mary E. Meek. Coral Gables, Fla.: University of Miami Press, 1971.

–––––––. *Indo-European Language and Society*. Trans. by Elizabeth Palmer. Coral Gables, Fla.: University of Miami Press, 1973.

Birdwhistle, Ray R. *Kinesics and Context*. Philadelphia: University of Pennsylvania Press, 1970.

Bloomfield, Leonard. *Language*. New York: Holt, 1933.

———. *Linguistic Aspects of Science*. Foundations of the Unity of Science 1.4. Chicago: University of Chicago Press, 1939.

Bolinger, Dwight. *Aspects of Language*. 2d ed. New York: Harcourt Brace Jovanovich, 1975.

Borden, Gloria J., and Katherine S. Harris. *Speech Science Primer. Physiology, Acoustics, and Perception of Speech*. Baltimore: Williams & Wilkins, 1980.

Bronstein, Arthur J. *The Pronunciation of American English*. New York: Appleton-Century-Crofts, 1960.

Brown, Roger William. *A First Language: The Early Stages*. Cambridge, Mass.: Harvard University Press, 1973.

Casson, Ronald W., ed. *Language, Culture, and Cognition*. Anthropological Perspectives. London: Macmillan, 1981.

Chambers, John K., and Peter Trudgill. *Dialectology*. Cambridge: Cambridge University Press, 1980.

Chomsky, Noam. *Syntactic Structures*. The Hague: Mouton, 1957.

———. *Aspects of the Theory of Syntax*. Cambridge, Mass.: MIT Press, 1965.

———. *Language and Mind*. New York: Harcourt Brace Jovanovich, 1972.

Chomsky, Noam, and Morris Halle. *The Sound Pattern of English*. New York: Harper & Row, 1968.

Clark, Herbert H., and Eve V. Clark. *Psychology and Language: An Introduction to Psycholinguistics*. New York: Harcourt Brace Jovanovich, 1977.

Clark, Virginia P., Paul A. Eschholz, Alfred F. Rosa, eds. *Language; Introductory readings*. 2d ed. New York: St. Martin's Press, 1977.

Curtiss, Susan. *Genie. A Psycholinguistic Study of a Modern-Day "Wild Child."* New York: Academic Press, 1977.

Dale, Philip S. *Language Development, Structure and Function*. New York: Holt, Rinehart & Winston, 1976.

Daniloff, Raymond, Gordon Schnuckers, and Lawrence Feth. *The Physiology of Speech and Hearing*. Englewood Cliffs, N.J.: Prentice-Hall, 1980.

Denes, Peter B., and Eliot N. Pinson. *The Speech Chain*. Garden City, N.Y.: Anchor Press, 1973.

Dillard, Joey L. *American Talk*. New York: Random House, 1976.

Dittmar, Norbert. *Sociolinguistics*. London: Arnold, 1976.

Dowty, David R., Robert E. Wall, and Stanley Peters. *Introduction to Montague Semantics*. Dordrecht: Reidel, 1981.

Dressler, Wolfgang U., ed. *Current Trends in Text Linguistics*. Berlin: de Gruyter, 1978.

Falk, Julia S. *Linguistics and Language: A Survey of Basic Concepts and Implications*. 2d ed. New York: John Wiley, 1978.

Firth, John R. *The Tongues of Men and Speech*. London: Oxford University Press, 1964.

Fishman, Joshua A., ed. *Advances in the Study of Societal Multilingualism*. The Hague: Mouton, 1978.

Fodor, J. A., T. G. Bever, and M. F. Garrett. *The Psychology of Language*. New York: McGraw-Hill, 1975.

Fromkin, Victoria, and Robert Rodman. *An Introduction to Language*. 2d ed. New York: Holt, Rinehart & Winston, 1978.

Gazdar, Gerald. *Pragmatics. Implicature, Presupposition, and Logical Form*. New York: Academic Press, 1979.

Gazzaniga, Michael S., and Joseph E. LeDoux. *The Integrated Mind*. New York: Plenum, 1978.

Gleason, Henry Allen, Jr. *An Introduction to Descriptive Linguistics*. New York: Holt, Rinehart & Winston, 1961.

Greenberg, Joseph H., ed. *Universals of Language*. Cambridge, Mass.: MIT Press, 1966.

Grimes, Joseph E. *The Thread of Discourse*. The Hague: Mouton, 1975.

Gumperz, John J. and Dell Hymes. *Directions in Sociolinguistics. The Ethnography of Communication*. New York: Holt, Rinehart & Winston, 1972.

Hall, Edward T. *The Silent Language*. Garden City, N.Y.: Anchor Press, 1973.

Heatherington, Madelon E. *How Language Works*. Cambridge, Mass.: Winthrop, 1980.

Heffner, Roe-Merrill S. *General Phonetics*. Madison: University of Wisconsin Press, 1949.

Hill, Archibald A. *Introduction to Linguistic Structures*. New York: Harcourt, Brace, 1958.

Hockett, Charles F. *A Course in Modern Linguistics*. New York: Macmillan, 1958.

Jakobson, Roman. *Child Language, Aphasia and Phonological Universals*. Trans. by A. R. Keiler. The Hague: Mouton, 1968.

Jakobson, Roman, and Linda Waugh. *The Sound Shape of Language*. Bloomington: Indiana University Press, 1979.

Jensen, Hans. *Sign, Symbol and Script*. 3d ed. Trans. by George Unwin. London: Allen & Unwin, 1970.

Jespersen, Otto. *Mankind, Nation and Individual. From a Linguistic Point of View*. London: Allen & Unwin, 1946.

———. *Growth and Structure of the English Language*. 9th ed. Oxford: Blackwell, 1946.

———. *Language*. Its Nature, Development and Origin. London: Allen & Unwin, 1922.

———. *The Philosophy of Grammar*. London: Allen & Unwin, 1924.

———. *Essentials of English Grammar*. University: University of Alabama Press, 1964.

Jolles, Andre. *Einfache Formen*. 2d ed. Darmstadt: Wissenschaftliche Buchgesellschaft, 1958.

Katz, Jerrold J. *Language and Other Abstract Objects*. Totowa, N.J.: Rowman and Littlefield, 1981.

Key, Mary Ritchie. *Male-Female Language*. Metuchen, N.J.: Scarecrow Press, 1975.

———. *The Relationship of Verbal and Nonverbal Communication*. The Hague: Mouton, 1980.

Kirshenblatt-Gimblet, Barbara, ed. *Speech Play*. Philadelphia: University of Pennsylvania Press, 1976.

Kurath, Hans. *Handbook of the Linguistic Geography of New England*. With the collaboration of Marcus L. Hansen, Julia Bloch, Bernard Bloch. Providence, R.I.: Brown University Press, 1939.

Labov, William. *Sociolinguistic Patterns*. Philadelphia: University of Pennsylvania Press, 1972.

Labov, William, and David Fanshel. *Therapeutic discourse: Psychotherapy as Conversation*. New York: Academic Press, 1977.

Ladefoged, Peter. *A Course in Phonetics*. New York: Harcourt Brace Jovanovich, 1975.

Leech, Geoffrey. *Semantics*. Harmondsworth: Penguin, 1974.

Lehmann, Winfred P. *Historical Linguistics: An Introduction*. New York: Holt, Rinehart & Winston, 1973.

———, ed. *Syntactic Typology*. Austin: University of Texas Press, 1978.

Lieberman, Philip C. *Intonation, Perception, and Language*. Cambridge, Mass.: MIT Press, 1967.

————. *On the Origins of Language; An Introduction to the Evolution of Human Speech.* New York: Macmillan, 1975.

Longacre, Robert E. *An Anatomy of Speech Notions.* Lisse: de Ridder, 1976.

Luria, Alexander R. *The Working Brain. An Introduction to Neuropsychology.* Trans. by Basil Haigh. New York: Basic Books, 1973.

Lyons, John. *Introduction to Theoretical Linguistics.* Cambridge: Cambridge University Press, 1968.

————. *Semantics,* vols. I and II. Cambridge: Cambridge University Press, 1977.

MacKay, Ian R. A. *Introducing Practical Phonetics.* Boston: Little, Brown, 1978.

Malkiel, Yakov. *Etymological Dictionaries. A Tentative Typology.* Chicago: University of Chicago Press, 1976.

Matthews, Peter H. *Inflectional Morphology.* Cambridge: At the University Press, 1972.

Mencken, H. L. *The American Language.* Edited by R. J. McDavid, Jr. New York: Knopf, 1963.

Miller, George A. *Language and Speech.* San Francisco: Freeman, 1981.

Moerk, E. *Pragmatic and Semantic Aspects of Early Language Development.* Baltimore: University Park Press, 1977.

Nida, Eugene A. *Towards a Science of Translating.* Leiden: Brill, 1964.

————. *Exploring Semantic Structures.* Munich: Fink, 1975.

Nilsen, Don L. F., and Alleen Pace Nilsen. *Language Play; An Introduction to Linguistics.* Rowley, Mass.: Newbury House, 1978.

Ochs, Elinor, and Bambi B. Schieffelin. *Developmental Pragmatics.* New York: Academic Press, 1979.

Pedersen, Holger. *Linguistic Science in the Nineteenth Century.* Trans. by J. W. Spargo. Cambridge, Mass.: Harvard University Press, 1931. Reprinted under the title: *The Discovery of Language,* Bloomington: Indiana University Press, 1962.

Perlmutter, David M., and Scott Soames. *Syntactic Argumentation and the Structure of English.* Berkeley: University of California Press, 1979.

Pfungst, O. *Clever Hans, The Horse of Mr. Van Osten.* New York: Holt, 1911.

Piattelli-Palmarini, Massimo, ed. *Language and Learning. The Debate between Jean Piaget and Noam Chomsky.* Cambridge, Mass.: Harvard University Press, 1980.

Pike, Kenneth L., and Evelyn G. Pike. *Grammatical Analysis.* Dallas: Summer Institute of Linguistics, 1977.

Potter, R. K., G. A. Kopp, and H. Green. *Visible Speech.* New York: Dover, 1947.

Premack, Ann J. *Why Chimps Can Read.* New York: Harper & Row, 1976.

Propp, V. *Morphology of the Folktale.* 2d ed. Trans. by Lawrence Scott. Austin: University of Texas Press, 1968.

Quirk, Randolph, Sidney Greenbaum, Geoffery Leech, and Jan Svartvik. *A Grammar of Contemporary English.* London: Longman, 1972.

Rumbaugh, D. M. *Language Learning by a Chimpanzee: The Lana Project.* New York: Academic Press, 1977.

Sapir, Edward. *Language: An Introduction to the Study of Speech.* New York: Harcourt, Brace, 1921.

Searle, John R. *Speech Acts.* Cambridge: At the University Press, 1969.

Sebeok, Thomas A., and Robert Rosenthal, eds. *The Clever Hans Phenomenon: Communication with Horses, Whales, Apes, and People.* New York: New York Academy of Sciences, 1981.

Shattuck, Roger. *The Story of the Wild Boy of Aveyron.* New York: Farrar, Straus & Giroux, 1980.

Shopen, Timothy, and Joseph M. Williams. *Standards and Dialects in English*. Cambridge, Mass.: Winthrop, 1980.

———. *Style and Variables in English*. Cambridge, Mass.: Winthrop, 1981.

Sonnenstein, Alan H. *Modern Phonology*. Baltimore: University Park Press, 1977.

Steinberg, Danny D., and Leon A. Jakobovits, eds. *Semantics: An Interdisciplinary Reader in Philosophy, Linguistics and Psychology*. Cambridge: At the University Press, 1971.

Terrace, H. S. *Nim*. New York: Knopf, 1979.

Thorpe, W. H. *Bird Song*. London: Cambridge University Press, 1961.

Trubetzkoy, Nikolay S. *Principles of Phonology*. Trans. Christiane A. M. Baltaxe. Berkeley and Los Angeles: University of California Press, 1969.

von Frisch, Karl. *The Dancing Bees*. London: Methuen, 1954.

Whorf, Benjamin Lee. *Language, Thought, and Reality*. Edited by John B. Carroll. New York: John Wiley, 1956.

Wolfram, Walt, and Ralph W. Fasold. *The Study of Social Dialects in American English*. Englewood Cliffs, N.J.: Prentice-Hall, 1974.

Index